'This is a must-read book! Those seeking to understand China and its role in the world economy are treated to a brilliant, deeply thoughtful, yet terrifically engaging story of how entrepreneurship in China has emerged, its unique characteristics and how it is pushing China towards the future. Highly recommended for anyone seeking to understand China and entrepreneurship!'

– *Assistant Professor Charles Eesley, Stanford University, Department of Management Science and Engineering, Stanford Technology Ventures Program*

'China's recent emergence as an economic power is a testament to the potential of entrepreneurship and new venture creation to help transform an economy. Since China's reforms of the late 1970s, both GDP and personal incomes have risen dramatically, and hundreds of millions have escaped poverty. Yet there is still much to do as many in China remain very poor and economic reforms still at times seem tenuous.

Thus, the timing of this fine new book by Professors Andrew Atherton and Alexander Newman could not be better. Much is known about Chinese entrepreneurs and Chinese entrepreneurship, and this information needs to be disseminated widely to students and managers, both inside and outside of China. *Entrepreneurship in China* provides a very thorough coverage of this important topic. In particular, it is very helpful in assisting readers in understanding the key philosophical and ideological underpinnings of Chinese culture, and how these and other cultural dimensions help to explain business practices in China and even among overseas Chinese. *Entrepreneurship in China* is a must-read for anyone seeking to understand business in China, and especially how China has built its vibrant private sector over the past several decades.'

– *Professor David Ahlstrom, Department of Management, Chinese University of Hong Kong*

'The emergence of the private sector, and of entrepreneurs, in China has been one of the key features of economic growth and reform. In this timely book, Andrew Atherton and Alex Newman examine the dynamics of this emergence, and propose that the vitality of the private sector is essential for China's future economic growth. This makes economic conditions inside China, and government policy, important, in that the right environment will enable entrepreneurship. In the early years of reform, entrepreneurs succeeded despite conditions that hampered their emergence. In the future, they can ensure China continues to grow, and will be more able to do this if they are promoted and recognised as a key driver of the economy. The authors make this case well, and succinctly, and frame their analysis within the context of China. They also look at how the private sector works, and how entrepreneurs in China do business within that country's distinctive cultural and social framework. This is a great book to understand the emergence of entrepreneurship in China, and essential reading for researchers, businesspeople and policymakers. If you read this, you will understand in more depth how today's China has emerged, and what it will look like in the future.'

– *Professor Justin Yifu Lin, Director of the Centre for New Structural Economics and Honorary Dean of the National School of Development, Peking University; Former Chief Economist at the World Bank*

ENTREPRENEURSHIP IN CHINA

The Chinese economy has grown faster for a longer period than any other economy in the world. It is now the second, and will soon become the largest, global economy. This is an astonishing transformation of a country that in the late 1970s was one of the poorest in Asia. Central to this economic miracle has been the emergence of a private sector of entrepreneurs who have started and grown businesses of all sizes and types. This book explores these wealth creators and builders of China's new economy, and offers guidance on the best ways to work with China's entrepreneurs and their growing businesses.

Entrepreneurship in China looks at the dynamic and changing nature of entrepreneurship, and the need for entrepreneurs to refine, adapt and evolve their approaches within an uncertain, fast-changing and volatile environment. This book examines the distinctive and particular context of China for entrepreneurs, and offers insights into how entrepreneurship has emerged as the driver of China's economy. This book will benefit business people, policy makers and researchers seeking to understand Chinese entrepreneurship and offers guidance to practitioners interested in working with private Chinese businesses.

Andrew Atherton is Professor of Entrepreneurship and Deputy Vice-Chancellor at Lancaster University in the UK. Previously, he was Senior Deputy Vice-Chancellor at the University of Lincoln, and before that worked at Durham University as Head of Department and Director of the Policy Research Unit within the Small Business Centre. He speaks Chinese, having studied at the School of Oriental and African Studies (SOAS), London University, and has been working on enterprise development and policy projects in China since 1997.

Alex Newman is Professor of Management and Associate Dean (International) for the Faculty of Business and Law, at Deakin University, Australia. Prior to joining Deakin he worked at Monash University, Australia for three years. From the period 2004 to 2012, he worked at the University of Nottingham, Ningbo China for eight years.

ENTREPRENEURSHIP IN CHINA

The Emergence of the Private Sector

Andrew Atherton and Alex Newman

LONDON AND NEW YORK

First published 2018
by Routledge
2 Park Square, Milton Park, Abingdon, Oxon OX14 4RN

and by Routledge
711 Third Avenue, New York, NY 10017

Routledge is an imprint of the Taylor & Francis Group, an informa business

© 2018 Andrew Atherton and Alex Newman

The right of Andrew Atherton and Alex Newman to be identified as authors of this work has been asserted by them in accordance with sections 77 and 78 of the Copyright, Designs and Patents Act 1988.

All rights reserved. No part of this book may be reprinted or reproduced or utilised in any form or by any electronic, mechanical, or other means, now known or hereafter invented, including photocopying and recording, or in any information storage or retrieval system, without permission in writing from the publishers.

Trademark notice: Product or corporate names may be trademarks or registered trademarks, and are used only for identification and explanation without intent to infringe.

British Library Cataloguing-in-Publication Data
A catalogue record for this book is available from the British Library

Library of Congress Cataloging-in-Publication Data
Names: Atherton, Andrew (Professor of Entrepreneurship), author.
Title: Entrepreneurship in China : the emergence of the private
sector / by Andrew Atherton and Alex Newman.
Description: First Edition. | New York : Routledge, 2017. | Includes bibliographical references and index.
Identifiers: LCCN 2017019513| ISBN 9781138650091 (hardback) | ISBN 9781138650121 (pbk.) | ISBN 9781315625126 (ebook)
Subjects: LCSH: Entrepreneurship--China. | China--Economic conditions--2000- | Business enterprises--China.
Classification: LCC HB615 .A87 2017 | DDC 338/.040951--dc23
LC record available at https://lccn.loc.gov/2017019513

ISBN: 978-1-138-65009-1 (hbk)
ISBN: 978-1-138-65012-1 (pbk)
ISBN: 978-1-315-62512-6 (ebk)

Typeset in Bembo
by Taylor & Francis Books

CONTENTS

List of figures   *viii*
Acknowledgements   *ix*
Funding   *x*

1. China's entrepreneurial transformation   1
2. China's entrepreneurs and private enterprises   9
3. The evolution and emergence of entrepreneurship in China   18
4. Models of entrepreneurship in China   36
5. China's market dynamics: Domestic competition and international expansion   56
6. Financing entrepreneurship in China   79
7. Chinese business culture and entrepreneurship   98
8. Dealing with the government   113
9. Doing business with Chinese entrepreneurs   130
10. The future of entrepreneurship in China   152

Index   *163*

FIGURES

2.1 Number of *getihu* and *getihu* employees 1995–2014   14
2.2 Numbers of *siying qiye* and *siying qiye* employees 1995–2014   14
2.3 The number of employees by industrial sector working for *getihu* and *siying qiye* enterprises 2005–2014   15

ACKNOWLEDGEMENTS

Andrew would like to thank his wife Helen for her support and the time she gave him to write this book, as well as his children Isaac and Lucas for the times they didn't see their father when he was away or upstairs writing. He would also like to thank Mark Smith and Lancaster University for allowing a mini-sabbatical to complete the book.

Alex would like to thank his wife Miyako and children Joe and Amelia for their support whilst writing this book. He would also like to thank Qing Miao at Zhejiang University for assisting him to obtain funding for this project and Jin Huang for her work as research assistant on several chapters of the book. He would also like to thank Mike Ewing and Amanda Pyman for providing him with time to research and write.

FUNDING

This research was supported by the Natural Science Foundation of China, grant number 71272166.

1

CHINA'S ENTREPRENEURIAL TRANSFORMATION

Introduction

China's recent emergence is the economic success story of the late 20th and early 21st centuries. Personal incomes soared and poverty fell as China grew at a faster rate than any other emerging economy between the late 1970s and mid-2000s. Over that period, China transformed itself from one of the poorest countries in Asia to one of the largest economies in the world. Its economic health and fortunes affect other economies – both developed and developing – and its own growth prospects are becoming a bellwether for global economic health.

There are many accounts of this emergence and celebrations of its success. The benefits of strong leadership, managed liberalisation and opening up of the economy, and the ability to attract huge amounts of foreign direct investment are all regularly cited. What is less reported is the emergence of private entrepreneurs as the primary driver of economic activity and growth in China itself. In 1978, at the beginning of China's current period of economic growth through reform, the economy was state-owned and controlled. There were, in practice, no private enterprises operating at that time. Nowadays, the private sector accounts for more than three-quarters of the economy, and is continuing to expand. Over the next two decades, it will generate almost all of China's economic activity, ensuring the country's transformation from planned to market economy.

This book is about the private sector that has emerged to dominate China's economy, and the entrepreneurs who have set up and run private businesses.

Entrepreneurship in the age of reform in China

Open the pages of a newspaper or surf your preferred business and news sites online and you will read about a Chinese company seeking to acquire a business in the United States (US), Europe or Japan. Walk through the streets of any city in China and you will see and experience bustling markets and a boom in retail and services. Travel through the Pearl River Delta; go to Shanghai's massive economic development zone of Pudong or any one of China's other growth 'hotspots', and you will come across privately owned firms owned and run by Chinese entrepreneurs alongside the factories of leading multinational corporations and global giants.

In Beijing, take a taxi to the Summer Palace, one of China's major tourist attractions, and you will pass by the high-technology zone of Zhongguancun, and its 'electronics street', in the University district of Haidian to the north-west of the city. China's own Silicon Valley, as it has been called, is home to businesses that trade nationally and internationally in software development and engineering, online media, electronics and other high-technology goods and services.

Go into the countryside and you will find thriving businesses that have been established in former paddy fields. These are now privately owned township and village enterprises (TVEs) that sprang up in the countryside in the 1980s, creating wealth and employment across rural China. Visit the 'rust belt' in the north-east of the country and see the emergence of a new economy, using state-of-the-art machinery, on the sites of formerly state-owned industrial enterprises that have closed down. These are the 'phoenix' firms that emerged after massive and highly inefficient state-owned enterprises (SOEs) shed tens of millions of employees in the second half of the 1990s.

Along the coast – from Dalian in the north to Ningbo and south of Shanghai, on to Xiamen and Fuzhou in Fujian province, and down the Guangdong coastline from Shantou to the Pearl River towards Macau – private entrepreneurs thrive in clusters, supplying foreign firms and increasingly the domestic Chinese market.

The same story of dynamic growth applies to consumers. Next to the French supermarket Carrefour in Fangzhuang in south-central Beijing are local stores selling everything imaginable to well-heeled local residents in their upmarket Hong Kong-style luxury apartment developments – and this is a moderately prosperous rather than exclusive neighbourhood. Go to the villas and millionaire's houses on the outskirts of Beijing near the airport and you will see Ferraris, Lamborghinis and Rolls Royce cars drive in and out of secure compounds owned by some of the more than 1.5 million Chinese millionaires. A recent fashion has been to build luxury housing in the style of a particular type of Western or other foreign architecture. In high-end developments across China, there are copies of the Arc de Triomphe and Champs Élysées at the heart of gated developments. Similarly, Big Ben, Times Square and other iconic sites lie at the centre of a London or New York development. The promise is of a luxurious and historical Western lifestyle.

After shopping in IKEA, shoppers are as likely to pop round the corner for Shanghainese Lion's Head or Beijing Duck as they are to top up on Coke and hot dogs within the superstore itself. Many will go to KFC or Starbucks instead of eating at local restaurants or drinking in a teahouse. Xintiandi in central Shanghai is a reconstructed village of 19th-century stone gate houses (*shikumen*), where the well-heeled shop, eat and drink in Chinese and Western outlets interchangeably. An interest in China's past is beginning to shape retail and leisure experiences across the country. In Chengdu, in central western China, Jinli Old (or Ancient) Street next to Wuhou Temple and the Wide and Narrow Alleys are modern reconstructions depicting China's past, and are among the city's most popular shopping and eating venues.

Rising consumption also extends into markets other than food and shopping. China is now the world's biggest market for cars. It has the largest number of mobile phone, particularly smartphone, users globally.[1] Online shopping and services are rapidly expanding and China will become the largest e-market in the world if the current pace of growth continues. International tourism is booming.[2] China, in other words, is already the largest market for consumer goods.

This consumer boom extends away from the large cities to most parts of China. In Sichuan Province's Leshan, home of one of the largest Buddha statues in the world, the whole of the west bank throngs with *xiba* beancurd restaurants, next to mobile phone stands and electronics stores selling the latest Xiaomi, Meizu, Oppo and Zopo smartphones. In remote Ningxia Province in north-western China, in cities near the Gobi Desert, residents crowd around a TV on the street to watch the latest soap opera or talent show after a day of shopping for *SeptWolves* designer menswear and *Bosideng* suits that you can also buy from any of the 100 former Greenwoods clothes stores in the United Kingdom, now owned by a Chinese company.[3]

Away from the cities, where farmers had built white-tiled multi-storey homes with blue-tinted windows as they first became wealthier in the 1980s and 1990s, new villas are now popping up next to their old single-storey brick buildings – three generations of farmer's housing sitting side by side. Spending money made on cash crops or new business ventures began on the farm or in nearby villages and towns, agricultural entrepreneurs are buying up the usual 'mod cons', starting with a mobile phone, television and motorbike and then moving on to white goods and four-wheeled vehicles. Repatriated earnings have come from sons and daughters working on the coast or in the Pearl River.

The scale and range of entrepreneurial activity across China – from metropolis to remote rural village – is huge and expanding. These landscapes of enterprise are a far cry from China in 1978, when the current period of reform began. At that time, the economy was dominated by huge state-owned enterprises (SOEs). Officially, the private sector did not exist, although in the countryside informal businesses grew produce and reared livestock, and communes were running their own commercial ventures. The state-owned collective sector 'filled in' around the state sector by offering a limited range of products for households.

Before the economic reform period that began in 1978, there was no real consumer economy, and almost all production was by quota according to a five-year plan. Clunky products such as *Flying Pigeon* bicycles – that would never defy gravity given the amount of metal used – were the mode of travel, rather than cars and trucks. City dwellers dressed in green and dark blue Mao suits and – in the bitter northern winters – long, quilted padded coats of the same two colours that dropped to well below the knee. In those more egalitarian times, government officials signalled their hierarchical position by the number and type of pens inserted in their jacket breast pocket. Food supplies were basic and rationed, with very small amounts of meat and the majority of food being vegetables and grains. Coupons (*Liangpiao*, literally grain tickets or notes) were the source of these staples, and also an informal currency used by households to trade for other goods.

In today's urban China, eating out is the norm, if not a national pastime. Diners eat in a vast range of outlets, from street restaurants with child-sized plastic seats huddled around a gas-fired mobile stove on a grimy pavement to invitation-only designer venues that would not be out of place in London or New York. In 1978, people ate standard fare in canteens within their own 'work units'. In large SOEs and government departments, these canteens were huge, with hundreds of dining chairs lined up in neat rows. In northern China, a common sight in November was delivery of a mountain of Chinese cabbage (*baicai*) covered by cardboard and quilts to keep it semi-frozen outside the industrial kitchens of the work units, as the only 'fresh' vegetable for diners until the thaws of early spring.

In Mao's China, foreign investment was extremely limited. The economy was insulated from world trade and investment, and was characterised by low levels of productivity, chronic under-employment of staff and poor returns on capital investment. Where equipment was purchased, it was typically second hand and years, if not decades, out of date. Rail transport used coal-powered steam rather than diesel or electric power. By the late 1970s, Mao's successor, Hua Guofeng, had been replaced by Deng Xiaoping, who wanted China to open up and develop economically. Deng proposed economic reform and liberalisation, albeit in careful words forged by the political rhetoric of the recent Maoist era. Deng was supported by a loose coalition of eight veterans of the Chinese Communist Party with a wide range of political views; most were nervous about, sceptical of, or openly resistant to excessive or too-rapid economic reform. At that time, the future pattern of development was far from clear and the inevitability of reform a fragile and distant possibility. The story of transition to a marketised economy has been one of ongoing debate and disagreement between proponents of reform, supported by a growing group of liberal intellectuals, westernised think tanks and government technocrats on the one hand, and 'hardline' conservatives on the other seeking to uphold – and latterly re-invent – the Maoist approach. This was particularly the case in the 1980s and early 1990s, when reform and retrenchment alternated depending on which part of the Communist Party had the upper hand.

Economic liberalisation, in other words, was not an inevitable outcome when Deng Xiaoping came to power in late 1978; its history over much of the reform period has been one of resistance and setback as well as progress and opening up. In the early years, reforms were much argued over, often tentative and incremental, relying on local initiatives and experiments that could be monitored centrally. There were, and have been, changes in policy since 1978, and at times a real prospect that a reformist path would not be maintained, most notably after June 1989, until late 2001. The anti-bourgeois liberalisation campaign of early 1987, followed by student demonstrations and marches on Tiananmen Square over New Year – in protest at the demotion of Hu Yaobang for pushing reform too hard and fast – reflected the ongoing conflict between reformers and conservatives that played out through the 1980s and early 1990s.

Overall, however, the trajectory has been one of 'opening up' through legislative and market liberalisation and reform. This has created the highest levels of economic growth of any country over a 30-year period since the industrial era began. Further, as China has become used to and increasingly reliant on sustained levels of world-beating Gross Domestic Product (GDP) growth, the logic of the market has become more strongly entrenched in social norms and personal values. For all the concerns about economic liberalisation, the hard facts of economic growth and rising prosperity won the battle at the increasingly pragmatic heart of the Chinese state. As the economy boomed, there was a general realisation that revolutionary ideology had destroyed lives, families, communities and the economic wellbeing of the country. As state officials benefitted from this growth, attempts to reinvigorate China's Maoist past became more and more infeasible.

The emergence of a large private sector populated by entrepreneurial owner–managers has been one of the most significant changes to the Chinese economy in recent years. The growth of the private sector has been a constant feature over the reform period, although its nature and characteristics have changed significantly. The private sector now accounts for 75 per cent or more of the economy in terms of output, and almost all of China's exports.[4] In 1998, the private sector accounted for only around 0.2 per cent of the Chinese economy. There are now more than 15 million private enterprises that have more than seven employees, and over 50 million private household enterprises in China. Private enterprises vastly outnumber the small and dwindling number of SOEs, and now account for almost all economic activity. This is China's entrepreneurial transformation, from state-owned and state-controlled to an economy dominated by private enterprises.

In part, these changes have been the result of a de facto privatisation that happened at a local level without fuss, by county and municipal government officials seeking to offload unprofitable and failing state-owned and collective enterprises. It is also the product of legislation that dates back to the 1980s encouraging smaller-scale and micro enterprise. It has been influenced by investors, entrepreneurs and managers from Hong Kong, Singapore, Taiwan and the overseas Chinese communities of East and Southeast Asia. Foreign direct investment from North America, Europe and the East Asian 'tiger' economies of Japan and South Korea has also fuelled growth across the country, especially in the major cities and along the east coast.

Throughout the reform period, the government has taken an active role in stimulating economic and enterprise development, in particular by encouraging exporting; promoting key industries; and kick starting growth when domestic or global macroeconomic conditions have been poor. This was seen in 2008 following the financial crisis, when the Chinese government intervened to prop up the economy. At its low point at the end of 2008, GDP growth was still close to 7 per cent, while other major economies were experiencing zero or negative growth. A massive stimulus package by the Chinese government helped the economy to post growth rates of over 8 per cent by summer 2009 and 9 per cent by the end of the year – close to the heady levels of more than 10 per cent growth seen in 2006 and 2007.

In response to the global downturn, there was a strong push to encourage more consumption, especially in rural areas, with farmers and the rural population receiving discounts on white goods and firms responding aggressively and rapidly to growing domestic market opportunities. This is in a country where consumption was concentrated in cities until recently, and where projections are that the urban population will rise from around 600 million to over one billion by 2030. Population and income growth in China's cities, and income growth in the countryside, will increase consumption, creating stronger domestic conditions for future economic growth, as well as some insulation against downturns in global economic conditions.

The entrepreneurial nature of China can be seen in response to the closure of tens of thousands of small businesses in the Pearl River Delta following on from the financial crash of 2008. These businesses were affected by a collapse in orders from their US and European customers. Since then, new businesses have started up and are being encouraged by a government that is pushing still-reluctant banks to invest in the private small business sector. The state recognises that in places like the Pearl River Delta, which is a major earner of export income, private businesses have driven much of the country's recent economic growth.

At the heart of this transformation of China's economy are the entrepreneurs themselves. Working in a challenging environment with cutthroat competition, unclear ownership rights and uncertainty over the role of the state, the owners and managers of private ventures often appear to be working against the odds. High rates of closure and failure of new businesses attest to the inherent volatility of markets in China. However, the increasingly dominant role of the private sector in the economy shows that entrepreneurship is China's driving force for growth and development – despite the many individual stories and experiences of unsuccessful entrepreneurship.

There will be losers as well as winners. Where you live and work will be important, with growing divergence between dynamic local economies, driven by entrepreneurs, and slower growing settlements in more remote areas. An imperfect and partial social welfare system, combined with variations in access to and affordability of healthcare, will make quality of life a lottery: good in some places, poor or non-existent in others. The wider environmental impacts of economic growth have still not been addressed sufficiently to clean up toxic rivers and brownfield sites, nor to prevent long-term health problems caused by polluters in places such as Wugang in Hunan Province or Baoji in Shaanxi, where local governments attracted lead and manganese smelting companies to boost the economy.[5] In Beijing, as well as other cities, cancers and respiratory illnesses because of air pollution are becoming major killers. Even with a shift to services and light rather than heavy industry, pollution and environmental degradation will be with China for many decades, undermining quality of life as incomes continue to rise. China's future economic development is likely to be strong, but will be characterised by growing disparities in health and quality of life, as well as wealth. As a result, inequalities will continue to grow and there will be a more noticeable divide between the 'haves' and the 'have nots'. This has already led to social tensions, and as inequality continues to rise, these are likely to become more prevalent.

Successful entrepreneurs are much more likely to be among the 'haves', but they also have a role to play in supporting the 'have nots'. The recent rise in social enterprises in China, and the growing role that some very successful business people have played in funding them, suggests that entrepreneurs could lead in delivering wider improvements to China's environment, health and quality of life. Some entrepreneurs, such as high-profile individuals like Jack Ma of Alibaba, have already begun to fund initiatives to improve China's civic and social conditions. However, there are still many entrepreneurs who do not take this wider view of philanthropy, and see their contribution in terms of how much they contribute to economic growth, and hence improved prosperity.

Outline of the book

This introduction summarises many of the key points that are explored in more detail throughout this book. Overall, the message is simple and hopefully both clear and compelling. That message is that the story of growth and reform in China is a story of entrepreneurs and entrepreneurship. Without individuals setting up and running their own enterprises, the economic growth of the last three decades would not have happened. These individuals have created businesses that have grown markets within the country. They have also taken over and restructured failing state-owned and collective enterprises, bringing them into profit. Private entrepreneurs generate the huge export earnings enjoyed by China, and they are expanding into markets overseas and building global businesses.

This book has ten chapters, including this introduction. In each chapter, we examine an aspect of Chinese entrepreneurship. In Chapter 2, we focus on who China's entrepreneurs are, what kinds of enterprises they operate, and regional differences in levels of entrepreneurship. Chapter 3 provides a brief history of entrepreneurship in China and its recent emergence as the dominant form of economic activity. Chapter 4 recognises the diversity of entrepreneurial activity across China, presenting different models of entrepreneurship. Chapter 5 examines domestic market dynamics, and the international expansion of private enterprises. Chapter 6 considers how Chinese entrepreneurs finance their businesses, and what challenges they face to raise funding. Chapter 7 examines the cultural foundations of Chinese society and assesses the implications for Chinese entrepreneurs. Chapter 8 recognises the key role that government plays in China's development, and how

8 Entrepreneurial transformation

state influences affect China's entrepreneurs and private businesses. Chapter 9 examines ways to do business with Chinese entrepreneurs and private enterprises, and offers recommendations on how to do this. Finally, Chapter 10 draws together key themes from this book and considers the future prospects for entrepreneurship in China.

Notes

1 Williams, R 2015, 'World's biggest smartphone market hits saturation as sales in China fall for first time', *The Telegraph*, 20 August 2016.
2 *Economist* 2016, 'China's consumers. Still kicking', *The Economist*, 30 April.
3 As reported by *Drapers*, the trade journal for fashion retail and design, in January 2009, Bosideng International acquired Greenwoods Menswear, a longstanding clothing retailer in the UK, when it filed notice of intent to appoint administrators, https://www.drapersonline.com/news/bosideng-snaps-up-menswear-retailer/5054032.article (viewed 3 June 2017).
4 Eckhart, J 2016, '8 things you need to know about China's economy', *World Economic Forum*, 23 June.
5 See reports from the BBC during August 2009 documenting these two cases: 14 August, 'Chinese children suffer lead poisoning', http://news.bbc.co.uk/1/hi/world/asia-pacific/8202429.stm (viewed 3 June 2017); 16 August, 'China "smelter poisoned children"', http://news.bbc.co.uk/1/hi/world/asia-pacific/8204275.stm (viewed 3 June 2017); and, 17 August, 'China villagers storm lead plant', http://news.bbc.co.uk/1/hi/world/asia-pacific/8204689.stm (viewed 3 June 2017).

2
CHINA'S ENTREPRENEURS AND PRIVATE ENTERPRISES

Introduction

In order to better understand the distinguishing features of entrepreneurship in China, it is useful to gain a clear understanding of who are China's entrepreneurs, what kinds of enterprises they operate, and in which parts of the country entrepreneurial activity is concentrated. This chapter examines the demographic profile of entrepreneurs in China, and identifies the main generational cohorts of Chinese entrepreneurs. It also compares entrepreneurs and non-entrepreneurs, and examines the key industries in which private enterprises operate. In doing so, this chapter scrutinises the contribution made by private enterprises to creating employment in different industrial sectors. Finally, this chapter examines regional disparities in entrepreneurial activity across China.

Demographic characteristics of Chinese entrepreneurs

Previous research has established that Chinese entrepreneurs tend to be relatively young and well educated, compared to entrepreneurs in other countries.[1] According to the Global Entrepreneurship Monitor 2012 report, China has a significant proportion of young entrepreneurs, with around 57 per cent aged between 18 and 34, and less than one-quarter aged between 45 and 64.[2] The Chinese Panel Study of Entrepreneurial Dynamics (CPSED) found that the average age of nascent entrepreneurs in China is around 31 years. They also found that around 70 per cent of the nascent entrepreneurs sampled were aged between 18 and 34, and only 12 per cent were aged over 45.[3]

Although the Global Entrepreneurship Monitor and CPSED did not distinguish between entrepreneurs who had experience in overseas markets and entrepreneurs who only had domestic experience, growing research has highlighted the importance of returnee entrepreneurs for the development of innovation-based sectors of the Chinese economy.[4] Li and colleagues found that returnee entrepreneurs working in new high-tech ventures in Beijing's Zhongguancun science park had higher levels of education and associated human capital than did local entrepreneurs. For example, 40 per cent of returnee entrepreneurs had a doctor of philosophy, compared to six per cent of locals, while 39.8 per cent of returnees had a master's degree, compared to 22 per cent of locals.

The findings from previous research also indicate that Chinese entrepreneurs are relatively well educated. For example, the CPSED found that 4.5 per cent of those entrepreneurs surveyed held postgraduate degrees, 33 per cent held undergraduate degrees, and 28 per cent were college graduates. Of the entrepreneurs with a university education, around 44 per cent majored in science, technology, agriculture and medical science, while around 26 per cent majored in economics and management.[5] In regard to the demographic breakdown of entrepreneurs in China by gender, the CPSED found that more than two-thirds of the entrepreneurs surveyed were male.

Research has also examined the work experience of entrepreneurs before they established their first business. The CPSED found that around 46 per cent of nascent entrepreneurs were company employees before starting their business, and around 17 per cent were students.[6] The CPSED also found that around 78 per cent of entrepreneurs had work experience prior to starting their own business. Of those entrepreneurs with work experience, around 55 per cent had fewer than five years of work experience and 45 per cent had more than five years of work experience. Around 57 per cent of the entrepreneurs surveyed had work experience in the same industry, while around 78 per cent had prior management experience.

Generational cohorts of Chinese entrepreneurs

Chinese entrepreneurs can be classified into three main groups according to the generational cohort from which they originated.[7] The first generation of entrepreneurs are those who seized the opportunity to start businesses during the 1980s, in the early years of economic opening-up and reform. These individuals had typically gained technical and managerial experience from working in state-owned or township and village enterprises. This generation of entrepreneurs identified opportunities that arose from market liberalisation and successfully transitioned their organisations towards the market. Entrepreneurs falling into this cohort include Zhang Ruimin (Haier Group), who transformed a run-down state-owned refrigerator manufacturer into the world's largest appliance maker, and Lu Guanqiu (Wanxiang Group), who converted a small township and village enterprise producing agricultural machinery into one of the world's largest manufacturers of automobile components. Other prominent entrepreneurs, such as Ren Zhengfei (Huawei), were former military personnel. Ren gained experience working for the Chinese military as a technologist in the People's Liberation Army's information technology research unit. He employed this experience to establish an enterprise focusing on the manufacture and supply of telecommunications equipment. This first generation of entrepreneurs typically focused on the manufacturing sector.

The second generation of entrepreneurs started their businesses in the early to mid-1990s as the Chinese government actively began to encourage entrepreneurship through regulations that allowed individuals to establish private enterprises. In 1992, Deng Xiaoping's six-week tour to the south of the country – during which he called on policymakers to open up Chinese markets to the world – led many individuals to take the plunge into entrepreneurship. In addition, the *Zhuada Fangxiao* ('Keep the Big, Let Go of the Small') policy – under which the government sold off small and medium-sized enterprises to their former managers and employees – allowed many individuals to become entrepreneurs overnight. A growing number of government bureaucrats and academics also left their jobs to become entrepreneurs.[8] Unlike the first generation of entrepreneurs, these entrepreneurs are generally better educated and have more experience in market economics. They also began to diversify into industrial sectors other than manufacturing, as the government began to allow private enterprises to establish service-oriented businesses. Entrepreneurs falling into this cohort include Li Shufu (Geely Group) and Chen Dongsheng (Taikang Life) who established automobile manufacturing and insurance businesses respectively.

The third generation of entrepreneurs began their businesses after the start of the internet boom in the late 1990s to early 2000s.[9] They typically have high levels of education and experience working and studying overseas. They are more open to copying business models from developed countries and adapting them to suit local conditions, and are more adept at obtaining capital from equity markets than are their predecessors. They typically focus on the service sector, rather than manufacturing, and make use of new and emerging technologies.[10] Prominent entrepreneurs in this cohort include Robin Li (Baidu), who founded China's largest internet search engine, and Ma Huateng (Tencent), who established an internet business offering a wide range of services, including instant messaging and online gaming.

Case study: Wanxiang Group

Wanxiang Group is a large multinational automobile components manufacturer based in Hangzhou, Zhejiang Province. In addition, it has subsidiaries operating in the agriculture, real estate and aquaculture industries. It began as a township and village enterprise producing agricultural machinery in the late 1960s. Under the leadership of entrepreneur Lu Guanqiu, who signed a contract with the local government to operate and later purchase the enterprise, it refocused its business on manufacturing automobile components to meet the growing needs of automobile manufacturers.

After establishing itself in the national market during the 1980s, it began to expand internationally in the 1990s by buying up failing components manufacturers in the United States. As a private enterprise, Lu realised that international expansion was critical in allowing Wanxiang Group to grow its business because, during this stage of opening-up and reform, it was restricted from entering many product categories in China due to government regulations that protected state-owned enterprises. Wanxiang Group now has close to 30 manufacturing operations in the US.[11] In recent years, it has acquired American manufacturing companies, such as Rockford Powertrain; lithium-ion battery developer, A123 System; and Fisker Automotive – a plug-in hybrid sports car manufacturer.

Comparing entrepreneurs and non-entrepreneurs

Using data from the Chinese Household Income Project Survey in 2000, researchers have compared the characteristics of entrepreneurs and non-entrepreneurs.[12] Although entrepreneurs were found to earn approximately 20 per cent more than non-entrepreneurs, they were similar in regard to socioeconomic status, marital status, educational attainment and age. The survey also established that entrepreneurs had less work experience than non-entrepreneurs, yet were more likely to have experienced being made redundant. In regard to political background, the survey revealed that non-entrepreneurs were more likely to be Communist Party members than were entrepreneurs.[13] However, entrepreneurs were found to have larger social networks than non-entrepreneurs, highlighting the importance of social capital to entrepreneurial activity. Finally, the survey also examined attitudinal differences between entrepreneurs and non-entrepreneurs.[14] Although both groups were found to value wages, social security, learning and working conditions equally, entrepreneurs were less concerned about job stability and job dignity than were non-entrepreneurs. Entrepreneurs were also found to be less inclined to have their own children become entrepreneurs than were non-entrepreneurs.

Similarly, Djankov and his team compared differences between entrepreneurs and non-entrepreneurs.[15] They found no differences between them in terms of cognitive scores or educational background, yet established that the entrepreneurs were wealthier, more mobile and more willing to take risks. They also found that the entrepreneurs were more likely to be the children of wealthier parents who had been managers or entrepreneurs themselves. Compared to the non-entrepreneurs, they also found that the entrepreneurs were more likely to have close friends from childhood and adolescence and family members who were also entrepreneurs. These findings suggest that social networks are important in determining the propensity of individuals to engage in entrepreneurship.

Djankov and his team also examined differences between entrepreneurs and non-entrepreneurs in motivation, values and beliefs.[16] They found that, although the entrepreneurs did not perceive themselves as happier than the non-entrepreneurs, they were more motivated to make money, more likely to consider themselves successful in life, and more willing to take risks. Although few differences were found between the entrepreneurs and non-entrepreneurs across many values and beliefs, the entrepreneurs valued work and political freedom higher than the non-entrepreneurs, and were more trusting of other businesspeople. They were also more likely to consider bribery as justifiable. Finally, the entrepreneurs had more positive perceptions of the institutional environment than did the non-entrepreneurs. Fewer entrepreneurs than non-entrepreneurs considered tax rules, inflation, macroeconomic stability, inefficient courts, corruption and crime to be problems. In addition, non-entrepreneurs viewed public infrastructure and public goods provision more negatively than entrepreneurs. While the entrepreneurs had more positive perceptions of the local government's attitudes towards business than the non-entrepreneurs, the opposite was the case in relation to the central government.

Classification of private enterprises by legal form

Chinese private enterprises can be classified according to the legal form they adopt. In China, there are two main types of legal form adopted by small and medium-sized private enterprises: the *getihu* (individual household or sole-trading enterprises with no more than seven employees) and the *siying qiye* (private limited enterprises with more than seven employees). As indicated in Figures 2.1 and 2.2, as of 2014, there were close to 50 million *getihu* enterprises and more than 15 million *siying qiye* enterprises in China.[17]

The last two decades have witnessed a huge increase in the number of private enterprises. As presented in the figures below, while the number of registered *getihu* doubled from 25 million in 1995 to 50 million in 2014, the number of *siying qiye* rose more than 23-fold from less than 700,000 in 1995 to 15 million in 2014.[18] The explosion in numbers of *siying qiye* can be attributed to the economic reforms adopted during China's opening-up and reform period, which gradually allowed the establishment of private limited enterprises in an increasing number of economic sectors.

The last two decades have also witnessed an explosion in the numbers of people employed by private enterprises. As demonstrated in Figures 2.1 and 2.2, while the number of people employed by *getihu* enterprises increased from 46 million in 1995 to around 106 million in 2014, the number of people employed by *siying qiye* enterprises increased from just under 10 million in 1995 to around 144 million in 2014.[19] Together, both forms of enterprise accounted for around 250 million employees in 2014.

Industrial breakdown of private enterprises

As highlighted earlier, the early generation of entrepreneurs in the opening-up and reform period predominantly established businesses in the manufacturing sector. However, later generations of entrepreneurs have begun to recognise the potential of the service sector as a result of growing consumer demand for services in China and the loosening of government regulations on the service sector. Recent research revealed that a high proportion of new private enterprises are established in the service sector.[20] As evidenced in Figure 2.3, the service sector – especially retail and wholesale trade – accounts for a growing percentage of employment in private enterprises.[21] In the decade from 2005 to 2014, employment across key service

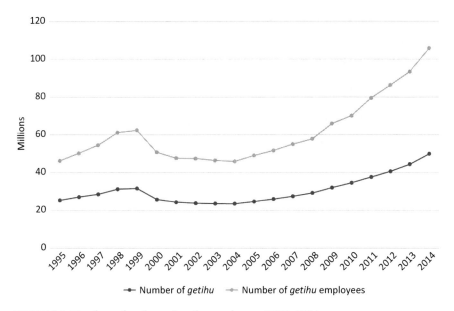

FIGURE 2.1 Number of *getihu* and *getihu* employees 1995–2014

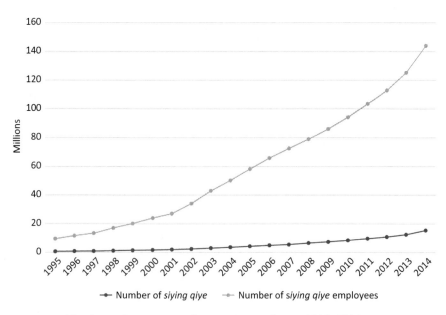

FIGURE 2.2 Numbers of *siying qiye* and *siying qiye* employees 1995–2014

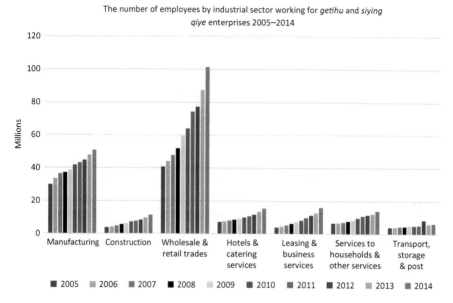

FIGURE 2.3 The number of employees by industrial sector working for *getihu* and *siying qiye* enterprises 2005–2014

industries more than doubled. Significant growth in employee numbers has also been witnessed in the construction sector. Employment has also grown in the manufacturing sector, albeit at a slower pace.

Regional disparities in entrepreneurial activity

A large proportion of the growth in the private sector has occurred in urban areas of the country, as migrants from rural areas migrate to the cities in search of job opportunities. While the number of people employed in *getihu* enterprises in rural areas has hardly grown in recent years – from around 30 million in 1995 to around 35 million today – the number employed in *getihu* enterprises in urban areas has grown significantly – from around 16 million in 1995 to around 70 million today. In contrast, the number of people employed in *siying qiye* enterprises has grown significantly in both urban and rural areas, albeit at a faster pace in urban areas. From 1995 to 2014, the number of people employed in urban *siying qiye* enterprises increased from around 5 million to 99 million, and in rural *siying qiye* enterprises increased from around 5 million to 45 million. Overall, these figures suggest that entrepreneurship in urban areas is growing at a faster pace than in rural areas.

As well as disparities between the levels of entrepreneurship in rural and urban areas, significant regional disparities can be noted in the rates of entrepreneurship across different regions of China. Entrepreneurial activity tends to be higher in more developed provinces and cities on the east coast of China, and lower in less developed provinces across the rest of the country. For example, researchers from

Tsinghua University found significant regional disparities in private enterprise start-up rates across China.[22] Their work revealed that start-up rates in developed provinces and cities on the east coast of the country (Shanghai, Tianjin, Beijing, Jiangsu, Zhejiang and Guangdong) were significantly higher than in less developed regions of the country due to differences in income growth. They found that such disparities could be explained by differences in levels of technological development, human capital, unemployment, private wealth, establishment size and entrepreneurial culture. Further analysis also revealed that such disparities increased from 1996 to 2006, during the period of rapid economic growth in China. In order to deal with such disparities and encourage private entrepreneurship in the underdeveloped western regions of the country, the Chinese government introduced the 'Go West' policy in 1999.[23] However, while this policy led to an increase in Gross Domestic Product (GDP) in western provinces, it did not close the economic gap between the east and west, and rates of indigenous entrepreneurship did not significantly increase.[24]

Notes

1 Ahlstrom, D & Ding, Z 2014, 'Entrepreneurship in China: an overview', *International Small Business Journal*, vol. 32, no. 6, pp. 610–618.
2 Xavier, SR, Kelley, D, Kew, J, Herrington, M & Vorderwulbecke, A 2013, *Global Entrepreneurship Monitor, 2012 Global Report*, Global Entrepreneurship Research Association, London.
3 Long, D, Yang, J & Gao, J 2010, 'Anatomy of nascent entrepreneurship in China', *Journal of Chinese Entrepreneurship*, vol. 2, no. 2, pp. 129–147.
4 Li, H, Zhang, Y, Li, Y, Zhou, LA & Zhang, W 2012, 'Returnees versus locals: who perform better in China's technology entrepreneurship?', *Strategic Entrepreneurship Journal*, vol. 6, no. 3, pp. 257–272.
5 Long, D, Yang, J & Gao, J 2010.
6 Long, D, Yang, J, & Gao, J 2010.
7 Teng, BS & Xiang, B 2007, 'Three generations of Chinese entrepreneurs: will the third generation be as successful?', *Ivey Business Journal*, November/December.
8 Tse, E 2015, *China's disruptors*, Penguin, London.
9 Tse, E 2015.
10 Liu, W 2015, 'Young entrepreneurs share ideals but can't ignore business principals', *China Daily*, 8 May.
11 Chiang, L 2014, 'Wanxiang finds success in US', *China Daily*, 28 July.
12 Yueh, L 2007, 'China's entrepreneurs', Department of Economics, University of Oxford Discussion Paper, Oxford.
13 Yueh, L 2007.
14 Yueh, L 2007.
15 Djankov, S, Qian, Y, Roland, G & Zhuravskaya, E 2006, 'Who are China's entrepreneurs?' *American Economic Review Paper and Proceedings*, vol. 96, no. 2, pp. 348–352.
16 Djankov, S, Qian, Y, Roland, G & Zhuravskaya, E 2006.
17 National Bureau of Statistics of China 1995–2014, *China statistical yearbooks*, China Statistics Press, Beijing.
18 National Bureau of Statistics of China 1995–2014.
19 National Bureau of Statistics of China 1995–2014.
20 Long, D, Yang, J & Gao, J 2010.
21 National Bureau of Statistics of China 2005–2014.

22 Gao, J & Shude, S 2013, 'Regional disparities in new firm formation in China', in T Zhang & RR Stough (eds) *Entrepreneurship and economic growth in China*, World Scientific, Singapore.
23 Goodman, DSG 2004, 'The campaign to "Open Up the West": national, provincial-level and local perspectives', *The China Quarterly*, vol. 178, pp. 317–334.
24 Richburg, KB 2010, 'China's push to develop its west hasn't closed income gap with east, critics say', *Washington Post*, 9 June.

3

THE EVOLUTION AND EMERGENCE OF ENTREPRENEURSHIP IN CHINA

Introduction

Chinese communities worldwide have been highly entrepreneurial, creating businesses and trading networks that have driven the economic development of many countries, particularly those in Southeast Asia. More recently, mainland Chinese entrepreneurs have stimulated economic growth along the west coasts of the US and Canada, and increasingly in sub-Saharan Africa.[1] In China itself, entrepreneurs have emerged as drivers of the economy since the start of economic reforms in the late 1970s.

This has led some commentators to propose that China has an entrepreneurial culture that is intrinsic to the country and its people, which was suppressed during the Maoist period from 1949 to the mid-1970s, when communism and the planned economy dominated. As the economy opened up and state control over markets relaxed, the latent entrepreneurial capabilities of Chinese people re-emerged.

In this chapter the evolution of entrepreneurship in China is explored, first during imperial and pre-communist times, and then since 1949. There is little evidence of a pre-communist culture or tradition of entrepreneurship, indicating that the recent emergence of private entrepreneurs is a feature of economic reform and liberalisation over the last three decades. During the current reform period there have been multiple factors that have stimulated entrepreneurship, although there are some aspects of government action that constrain entrepreneurs. Overall, however, there has been a fundamental shift in the economy, away from the state to private ownership. Finally, this chapter assesses the prospects for future development of private enterprise in China's 'new normal' of lower economic growth and rebalancing of the economy.

Dynasties, order and the emperor

Imperial China was an ordered and autocratic society, in which strict social hierarchies and norms dictated people's lives and behaviours.[2] At the pinnacle was the emperor, surrounded by his household and associated families, and supported by a court and socioeconomic system that considered the assets and resources of China to be at his disposal. Advancement came from recognition within this imperial system, reinforcing pressures to conform, rather than to challenge or create one's own future outside the established social system.

This world of order, focused on the emperor and his wishes and decisions, was punctuated periodically by dynastic changes, following on from invasion or domestic turmoil. Three dynasties ruled China from 1271 to 1911, two of which arose from invasions by non-Chinese nationalities. The Yuan (or Mongol) Dynasty spanned from 1271 to 1368, and absorbed various states, creating a national geography that suggested a unified China. The Ming Dynasty was established in 1368 and collapsed in 1644, in large part due to restrictions in the supply of silver to China.

The Qing (or Manchu) Dynasty lasted from 1644 to 1911. For much of the Qing era China's economy grew, especially during the 1700s. Agricultural productivity increased as land was redistributed and taxes reduced. Domestic and foreign trade was encouraged and exports of tea and silk expanded. The result of this growing prosperity, accompanied by more than 200 years of dynastic stability, was a rapid increase in China's population, from somewhere between 50 and 150 million in 1644 to almost 500 million by 1911.[3]

Both the Ming and Qing dynasties adopted and reinforced neo-Confucian values, and deployed these values as the basis of government and social order. These values privileged scholars and farmers over merchants and craftspeople. Neo-Confucianism, as developed during the Tang and Ming dynasties, considered the generation of profits an unethical act, so creating social values that did not recognise or reward entrepreneurs. Through both the Ming and Qing dynasties, there was resistance from Confucian scholars to commercial decisions, such as the adoption of silver as the basis for China's currency and the encouragement of trade in the 18th century. These values – adopted and endorsed by the emperor – created social views of entrepreneurship as an inferior and less acceptable activity.[4]

During the Ming Dynasty, and particularly during the reign of the Yongle Emperor, the imperial examinations system was reinvigorated and became the basis for social advancement. This continued into the Qing Dynasty.[5] Success in the imperial examination system required expertise in philosophy and legal knowledge. Commercial and economic knowledge was not included in the examinations, even though magistrates who passed them became the emperor's local tax collectors, and hence economic agents. In other words, magistrates were educated and tested on subjects that were underpinned by philosophies of social order, and hence a logic of government and control, and were not exposed to notions of trade, commerce and enterprise. It was inevitable that their formative education in governance and control, rather than enterprise and commerce, meant that magistrates and government officials had little understanding of entrepreneurial activities.[6]

Throughout both dynasties, the basis of the state, and subsequently the economy, was under the control of the emperor. Through his court, ministers and magistrates, the emperor directed the allocation of resources and decided upon the nature of economic activity and development. In other words, imperial rule was directive, in the sense that economic development was dictated by the emperor and his advisors. Major development projects were undertaken by the imperial state, especially those that were lucrative. For example, salt extraction generated major revenues for the emperor. Large-scale infrastructure projects – in particular the Grand Canal – were conceived and developed by fiat of the emperor.[7]

As well as being directive, imperial control over the economy was extractive – designed to generate sufficient revenues to fund the emperor and his support system, both nationally and locally. The economic system of local tax collection by magistrates was created in order to provide the emperor with sufficient revenues to run his household and court, and to raise and fund armies during times of war and unrest.

Even when the emperor was disposed to encourage economic growth, the approach could not be considered conducive to or encouraging of entrepreneurship. Imperial China during the Qing Dynasty experienced waves of commercial and economic growth, although there were also restrictions imposed by the emperor on international trade. The confinement of foreign traders to Guangzhou arose from the emperor's concerns over the revenues generated from trade with other countries – in particular Europe – and a desire to control these activities. 'Cantonment' (literally the closure of all ports except Canton to international trade) allowed the emperor to control foreign trade, and therefore ensure that tax revenues could be generated and channelled to him. Cantonment occurred because of concerns that other cities, such as Ningbo, were attracting foreign merchants keen to avoid the costs and restrictions of trading with China through Guangzhou. The emperor prevented these cities from continuing to trade because there were no means in place to ensure that sufficient shares of the income from international commerce were paid to the emperor.[8] China's opening-up to foreign trade during the Qing Dynasty highlights the anti-entrepreneurial nature of economic organisation in China, in that the single port decision of Cantonment restricted trade and channelled profits to imperial coffers, rather than enabling open international commerce.

During the Qing Dynasty, there is some evidence of an emerging economic system underpinned by entrepreneurship. Within China, domestic trade grew as the prosperous Yangzi River valley and parts of the coast became wealthier than poorer areas of inland China. A textiles industry emerged, mainly serving China, but also exporting. More prosperous regions of China around the Yangzi River Delta sold textiles and other manufactured or processed products domestically, including to less prosperous areas that did not have their own productive capacity.[9] In addition, some financial institutions were established in order to facilitate internal trade – most notably the pawnshops of Shanxi and the finance houses of

Shanghai.[10] Each of these components of a growing Chinese economy demonstrated a degree of entrepreneurial activity, and the emergence of an ecosystem of entrepreneurship and commerce focused on the most economically developed cities in eastern China.

However, the extent of entrepreneurship was constrained for several reasons, each of which indicates that entrepreneurial activity was limited to certain areas of Imperial China. First, the majority of manufactured products were sold in less prosperous areas of China, thereby making this a lower income market. Although there was some exporting and trade along the more developed coast, much of the trade was of lower value and priced products sold in inland China, which was largely agrarian. Second, the finance institutions that emerged were very much focused on social networks and communities, based around trading networks emerging from particular cities and towns. Although this enabled trade within China, these funding sources were limited to tightknit networks of merchants, rather than offering wider access to finance. This would have constrained access to finance for entrepreneurs outside these small, close-knit networks. Third, China did not develop the institutions of technical specialisation that characterised pre-industrial Europe. In particular, craft peoples' guilds were less evident in China.[11] In Europe, the development of guilds and trade associations created economic structures that enabled open trade, based on the application of increasingly specialised skills and techniques that allowed for more sophisticated production and processing. In Europe, finance to fund trade became transnational, allowing for increasing flows of goods without personal relationships mediating these exchanges. In contrast, in Ming and Qing China, production and trading – like finance – were undertaken mainly through family and community networks and relations, and were subsequently constrained by the extent and reach of these personalised interactions.

China's trade with Europe and other parts of the world increased significantly in the 18th and 19th centuries. This funded rapid increases in imports of silver from South America, which was used as China's currency through most of the Ming and Qing periods. Although textiles and other manufactured products were exported, tea accounted for most of China's exports during this period.[12] In cases such as china products, which were manufactured in China and sold in Europe, exports led to import substitutions by domestic European companies, such as Wedgewood in Britain and manufacturers in places such as Delft in the Netherlands. Pottery produced in the United Kingdom and other parts of Europe underwent significant process innovation, thereby improving design, quality and finish. China's pottery did not keep up with many of these advances, even though china from places like Jingdezhen remained popular in Europe. China's export growth depended heavily upon tea – a simple processed product – and there was some substitution of manufactured goods by importing nations.

Overall, we can conclude that there is no strong evidence that Chinese entrepreneurs flourished in Imperial China. Although the first 150 years of the Qing Dynasty brought rapid economic growth to China, there is no evidence of a Chinese industrial revolution to parallel the developments in Europe that led to the emergence of an entrepreneurial 'class' of capitalists.[13] Instead, the economy was dominated by agriculture, with some processing industries emerging, and trade occurred mainly within agrarian China. The imperial system controlled the economy and developed it for its own ends and benefits rather than to create an entrepreneurial economy.

Stasis and failed reform in late Imperial China

By the second half of the 1800s, China's economic growth had slowed in comparison with Europe, where industrialisation had generated rapid increases in household incomes and stimulated technological innovations. The military power and industrial sophistication of the European powers became increasingly evident to China through a series of wars and confrontations that China lost. However, the challenges to Imperial China did not only come from overseas. Domestic unrest and rebellions – in part against the monopolisation of key posts by Manchu families and the imposition of Manchu cultural mandates – destabilised the state. The Taiping rebellion in particular created instability and economic damage that would be long lasting.

Towards the end of the 19th century, a group of advocates of reform and Westernisation made the case for acquiring European technologies and developing Western-style institutions. This was partially successful, in the sense that there was some adoption of non-Chinese practices and institutions – such as a national postal system and the creation of coastal defences and military arsenals to store weapons and ammunition. Ultimately, however, the push for wide-ranging and fundamental reform failed in the face of strong opposition from conservatives, who extolled the virtues of Confucianism over the adoption of Western practices. This is in clear contrast to Japan, which underwent the Meiji restoration during the late 19th century, during which many institutions were adopted from the US and Europe, building a platform for economic growth in the 20th century.

In late Imperial China, the market institutions that stimulated entrepreneurship did not emerge as an outcome from institutional transformation. For example, a transparent and open financing system was not developed. Further, extensive communication and transport infrastructure was not created across China, thereby failing to establish an efficient and integrated domestic market. This is in contrast to the US in the 19th century, when roads and railways were built, connecting markets, producers and customers across the country. These improvements to transport and mobility integrated the US economically, creating a strong domestic market that continues to drive the country's prosperity to this day. In contrast, Imperial China did not create modern economic systems and structures. Instead, there were attempts to revive traditional Confucian values – principally to bolster an imperial dynasty that was becoming less credible and legitimate.[14] As noted earlier in this chapter, these representations of Confucian values were antagonistic to the notion of entrepreneurship and its practice in China.

Turbulence and war in early 20th-century China

In 1911, the Republic of China was announced through the instatement of Sun YatSen (Sun Zhongshan) as president, and, in 1912, Emperor Puyi abdicated. Sun did not remain President long, being replaced by Yuan Shikai that year. China then began to disintegrate as a unified country, with the emergence of warlords and local rulers during the 1910s and 1920s. During this period, areas of China were ruled locally as the nation splintered. China had no functioning national state between the late 1910s and late 1940s, with successive governments unable to reunify the country, resolve local disputes and prevent national war.

Japan invaded Manchuria in 1931 – three years after the Guomindang (which went on to rule Taiwan) declared a republic. China remained fragmented until reunification in 1949 by the Chinese Communist Party. During that period, the Guomindang and Communist Party fought against Japanese invasion, and then fought each other over who would rule China. Thus, overall, the post-imperial period can be characterised as turbulent, rather than stable. The emphasis was on mobilisation for war and territorial control, rather than on creating the right conditions for economic growth and prosperity. During this period, China could be considered an imploded and failed state, made up of small, local entities ruled by warlords and rival groups during the late 1910s and 1920s, and subject to invasion and civil war during the 1930s and 1940s.

Under these circumstances, a unified Chinese market no longer existed, and there were major barriers for Chinese businesses seeking to expand beyond their particular political geography. Even in parts of China where there was some growth in entrepreneurship – specifically, the Yangzi River and Shanghai – this was short lived as war affected the whole country. The economic data for China in the 1920s and 1930s show that there were small annual increases in per capita GDP, and that this growth was concentrated in specific locations within China, rather than being evenly spread. China's growth was largely due to some industrialisation in the Yangzi River basin and in north-eastern China, where the Japanese established heavy industry to support their war efforts. This period of marginal growth was short and should be contrasted with falling GDP after the mid-1930s and economic stasis during the 1910s.[15] Following the political stasis and periodic instabilities of late Qing rule, when entrepreneurs were viewed with disdain, the period from 1911 to 1949 was too turbulent and chaotic for entrepreneurship to thrive.

We can conclude that there was only limited emergence of entrepreneurship during imperial rule and before the communists took power in the 20th century. Between 1911 and 1949, civil war and social turbulence were the norm, creating conditions unconducive to entrepreneurship. The period after the 1850s saw China's decline and the emergence of conditions and state policies that did not enable entrepreneurship. The likelihood that entrepreneurship thrived during most of China's imperial past appears unlikely, given the nature of imperial rule and the antipathy of state-sponsored Confucian values towards entrepreneurs. If entrepreneurship emerged, it was most likely during the relatively brief period of rapid population and economic growth of the early Qing, which lasted for around 150 years between 1700 and the mid-1800s. However, the period preceding that was dominated by conservative neo-Confucian values that viewed entrepreneurship as an inferior and undesirable pursuit, and privileged the national examination system and strict social hierarchies created by this system, as well as highly centralised imperial rule. Therefore, we can conclude that the recent emergence of entrepreneurship did not arise from the renaissance of a pre-revolutionary tradition of dynamic entrepreneurship that can be traced back to Imperial China.

The revolution arrives – Mao's China emerges

As the Red Army marched into Beijing in 1949 to announce the creation of communist China, many Chinese people were relieved that there would be an end to civil war, unrest and national fragmentation. Those who supported the communists viewed this as the start of a different China, and were optimistic about the future. They saw the rejection of feudal values and traditional society as a means of liberation from the roles and social positions that had constrained them and their predecessors. However, some were apprehensive about the policies of this new government – particularly in regard to asset-holding landowners and entrepreneurs. This so-called 'capitalist class' stood to lose its assets if the Communist Party upheld its pledges to redistribute wealth in order to create a more equal society.

In its very early years, the Communist Party was relatively tolerant of entrepreneurs. Individuals running their own businesses received reassurance from the government that they would be tolerated. This was a pragmatic decision, based on a need to continue to generate economic activity in a country that had seen its enterprises depleted and industry wane during the previous two decades of domestic conflict and unrest. To close these businesses in 1949 would have significantly raised unemployment, reduced tax revenues and pushed China into major economic recession.

Attitudes towards entrepreneurs began to deteriorate as the redistribution of land held by private landowners occurred between 1950 and 1953. Land transfers were a politicised activity, with local groups of untenanted and poor peasants encouraged to denounce landowners and take their property. Although not directly targeted at entrepreneurs, this redistribution meant that a key source of asset funding of business – namely, land – was taken away from propertied families, some of whom were also entrepreneurs. It also strengthened a broad commitment to public ownership and an antipathy towards private control of assets. By 1953, with land redistributed, the state's tolerance of private ownership and enterprise ceased. All private enterprises were nationalised and the notion of private ownership was rejected. The public pronouncement indicated that the state controlled and ran the economy, and that private entrepreneurs were no longer required. Expropriation of private assets transferred valuable resources and revenues to the state in the short term. However, management of these enterprises by state officials tended not to maintain performance at historical levels, reducing the economic contribution of nationalised enterprises over time.[16]

Maoist China was a planned public economy where there was no space for private entrepreneurs. The state determined the nature of economic development, and then managed the enterprises and assets it controlled. Hence, there is no evidence of the emergence of private entrepreneurs during this period. On the contrary, private entrepreneurship was written out of the logic of economic organisation in Maoist China. Entrepreneurship in its formal sense disappeared in the early 1950s in China.

However, the central role of the state in economic development during the Maoist era created a positive legacy that was exploited during the initial stages of reform after 1978. In Mao's China, the state (rather than the market) determined the allocation of resources for economic production and development. This created a belief inside government that the state could determine the direction and nature of national and local economic development. Before the introduction of reforms that liberalised markets, state interventions to develop the economy were largely disastrous, as exemplified by the Great Leap Forward, which was China's attempt to not only industrialise but also reach a level of industrial development comparable with that of the West and Russia. When reforms were introduced after 1978, public investment combined with market liberalisation produced successful localised models of economic growth. In many parts of China, economic development was actively stimulated as well as supported by local government officials. The developmental role of the state – which can be traced back to Mao's time in power – therefore became a central feature of reform era China, especially in the 1980s and 1990s.[17]

Two further aspects of Mao's China also contributed to the economic growth that followed the introduction of market reforms in the late 1970s. The first was investment in human capital, which improved not only education but also health levels, given the positive correlation between primary and secondary education and rapid falls in child mortality.[18] In the 1950s and 1960s, the Chinese state introduced basic healthcare in rural areas by training 'barefoot doctors' to offer primary care, which drastically reduced illness and mortality rates.[19] Primary and secondary schooling were also introduced universally, thereby improving levels of literacy and numeracy, and universities were established and merged in order to create a science base in China. As a result, health improved and overall levels of education attainment increased. These improvements to the human capital of China would be felt two and three decades later, when rapid economic growth was fuelled by the migration of low-cost, yet healthy and educated workers from the rural areas to the development zones of China's coastline.

There was some indication of tentative, and small-scale, experimentation with economic liberalisation in the early to mid-1970s. After the radical politics and mass mobilisations of the early stages of the Cultural Revolution threatened party control and led to sharp drops in economic output, the Red Guards were reined in and party committees at district and county level were encouraged to make their own economic decisions based on local conditions. Greater local discretion allowed officials to make decisions on agricultural and industrial production that were of benefit to and appropriate for their own cities, towns and districts. The introduction of work points created an environment where farmers were rewarded for their efforts, thereby incentivising harder work by households that increased yields. At national level, some steps were taken to move away from self-sufficiency by importing industrial machinery and opening up dialogue with the US and other countries. Deng Xiaoping's period as lead Vice-Premier from 1974–1976 presaged some of the early reforms of the late 1970s and early 1980s.

Although Mao's China removed the private sector and entrepreneurs from economic planning and political recognition, improvements in China's human capital and tentative efforts to engage internationally in the 1970s provided some foundation for the economic liberalisation and opening-up of the reform period. However, these contributions were far outweighed by the anti-capitalist political economy of Maoist China, where the narrative of the party and state was actively disposed against entrepreneurs. By 1978, less than 0.1 per cent of economic activity was generated by private enterprises.[20] Thus, at the start of the reform period, China's economy was state owned, with entrepreneurs generating almost no economic growth.

China's reform period – hyper-growth and economic transformation

In December 1978, the Third Plenum of the Chinese Communist Party formally endorsed the proposals for reform put forward by Deng Xiaoping under the banner of 'reform and opening-up' (*gaige kaifang*). Although these reforms were formally approved, different factions within the party held contrasting and often opposing views about economic development and the role of the state in shaping the economy. Maoists remained powerful within the government and party, and on many occasions won out against the proposals and policies of reformers. These differences continued throughout the 1980s and into the 1990s, as indicated by the responses to key events and crises, such as Tiananmen in 1989 and the crackdown after student protests in late 1986 and early 1987. The 'anti-bourgeois liberalisation' campaign of early 1987 was a victory for the Maoists seeking to slow down if not reverse reforms. Hu Yaobang, the reforming premier, was the primary victim of this public outbreak of internal party politics; however, the immediate aftermath also saw a slowdown in reform. The reforms that were introduced in the 1980s and early 1990s were contested and fought over within the party, rather than being unanimously supported. Differences between leftist supporters of a planned economy on the one hand and economic liberalisers on the other have affected government policy during much of the reform era.

Early liberalisation: late 1970s to mid-1990s

Opening up China to investment by foreign businesses was a key strategy in the early years of reform, and has continued to be a core dimension of China's growth strategy. Currently, China (including Hong Kong) receives more foreign investment than any other country, and almost all of the world's largest companies are active in China, either manufacturing or offering products and services to a growing consumer market. Initially constrained to Special Economic Zones that were closed off from the rest of China to prevent ideological and intellectual 'contamination', the encouragement of foreign direct investment (FDI) extended in the 1980s to 15 coastal cities and then to most of China – often in the form of trade and development zones established in tier one and two cities. Over time, this spilling out of foreign businesses from the protected zones and cities of the coast to other parts of China introduced international business practices to their local partners and suppliers. This exposure is most evident in the Pearl River Delta, which has become highly integrated into the global economy, and has developed supply chains and clusters outside the original Special Economic Zone of Shenzhen. In a growing number of places in China, Chinese entrepreneurs operate next to global corporate giants, large state-owned and controlled domestic enterprises, and increasingly entrepreneurs from overseas.

The other major focus of early reform was agriculture. The household responsibility system was introduced in the early 1980s, allowing farmers to sell surplus produce above quota through markets, rather than through the plan. Local initiatives in rural areas, particularly Anhui and Sichuan, contracted out production, and later land, to households, creating stronger incentives to maximise yields and be more enterprising. Contracting production and land to households led to widespread diversification of farming, away from staples of grain and rice to cash crops, such as fruit and fish, which captured premium prices from a population with rising incomes. In only a few years, almost all farmland shifted from being within collectives to household production. Yields and productivity quickly rose as a result. Household incomes in most rural areas also increased, reducing poverty considerably across most of China's countryside. Between 1978 and 2000, around 220 million Chinese people emerged out of poverty (as defined by the Millennium Development Goals), which is the largest instance of poverty reduction globally.[21] When China's poverty reduction figures over the last thirty years are included in global figures, poverty falls worldwide. However, without China, global poverty rises over that period.

Price liberalisation was especially important in incentivising farmers. During the 1980s, prices of agricultural produce were liberalised, initially by allowing produce above quota to be sold on open markets, and then over time by removing state controls over prices. The 'grain coupons' (*liangpiao*) provided to all individuals to purchase a wide range of goods were scaled back, until they only provided for grain and rice (their original focus in the 1950s), before being removed completely in the mid-1990s. There was a shift from coupon-driven rationing of key foodstuffs to consumption through markets at prices increasingly determined by demand–supply dynamics.

A third focus was diversification of economic activity, both in the countryside and in cities. In the countryside, township and village enterprises (TVEs) were permitted in order to encourage new forms of economic activity. These enterprises were owned by local government, but run independently – typically by entrepreneurs on agreed contracts with local officials that involved profit sharing, payment of a fixed management fee, or performance pay. TVEs became a highly successful development model in China, driving rapid growth in rural areas between the early 1980s and mid-1990s. They were one of the most significant instances of 'hybrid capitalism', satisfying the party's requirement that the means of production be owned by the state, while allowing for entrepreneurial management to generate rapid, and for a period sustained, growth. Thus, they represented a transition in the governance of economic activity from the state towards private creation of wealth, albeit with the assets still being publicly owned.

In both cities and rural areas, 'household enterprises' were allowed. These were self-employed individuals or small family-run and operated businesses of up to seven staff that were typically established with low levels of capitalisation, based on the skills held or developed by family members. Most were low value-added services, such as bicycle repairs, food stalls, laundries, retail booths and stands, and so on. The rationale for encouraging household enterprises was twofold. First, they were considered a means of reducing unemployment. With many young adults returning to their home cities after being 'sent down' to the countryside during the Cultural Revolution, there was an increase in urban unemployment. Also, as state-owned enterprises restructured in the 1980s and particularly 1990s, many laid off workers continued to be paid a small monthly stipend but were economically inactive. Over time these 'laid off workers' (*xia gang*) lost these rights and had to find employment. They also provided a source of work for migrant workers, moving into the cities from the countryside. Household enterprises, such as family restaurants and food stalls, were seen as a means of absorbing unemployed labour. Second, household enterprises created new forms of economic activity – in particular a consumer and service economy that was virtually non-existent before reforms began. Household enterprises were considered 'sideline' businesses that 'filled out' parts of the economy in which state-owned enterprises (SOEs) did not operate. As well as having the benefit of not creating competition for SOEs, sideline household enterprises rapidly developed a rudimentary service sector that families and individuals could purchase from, as economic growth quickly increased incomes.

The combination of liberalisation of agriculture, encouragement of TVEs in order to industrialise the countryside, encouragement of micro-enterprises, and attraction of FDI – mainly to enjoy very low labour costs – created strong conditions for rapid economic growth in the 1980s. These four aspects of reform were particularly strong drivers of growth because they were highly localised, in the sense that they could emerge in any part of China (apart from FDI, which was limited to certain coastal cities). As such, they could not easily be coordinated, and hence controlled, by Beijing. Instead, local government and their lead officials could contribute to the localised growth effects if they wished. The ability of local governments to stimulate growth increased in the 1980s when fiscal reforms gave these administrations greater power over the collection and allocation of taxes.[22] In most parts of China, and particularly in the east and along the coast, where significant national investment was concentrated, local governments saw tangible benefits in supporting growth. As a result, most local governments became proponents and drivers of economic development within their administrative boundaries.[23] The developmental state at local level was instrumental in guiding economic growth in the first two decades of the reform period.

Scaling back the state: mid-1990s to early 2000s

By the mid-1990s, many of China's drivers of economic growth were fading away. During the 1980s, freeing up prices and handing over agricultural production to households had produced rapid improvements in production and productivity; however, by the early 1990s, these were beginning to plateau. Many TVEs experienced falling profits from the late 1980s and, by the mid-1990s, many were loss-making or barely profitable. Many SOEs were also loss-making, either because they had lost their competitive position in an increasingly marketised economy, or because they had been persistently in deficit during the period of early reform. Central government experienced significant reductions in its revenues in comparison with economic growth, and was increasingly burdened with the debt of many large SOEs that were loss-making and becoming increasingly indebted. In addition, the state-owned banks had become dangerously exposed to high levels of non-performing loans, many to loss-making SOEs. At the same time, local governments had become highly indebted, both through supporting loss-making TVEs and through issuing bonds to finance expenditure.[24]

The response was to reduce the size of government and transfer losses out of the state. The primary policy for this was 'releasing' smaller SOEs to private ownership. There was also extensive re-structuring of large SOEs in an attempt to address their indebtedness and make them profitable. Locally, governments took their own initiative and transferred ownership of loss-making TVEs to private ownership. At the same time, the total size of the government reduced significantly by around 40 per cent in the late 1990s and early 2000s. As a result of these structural changes to the Chinese economy, public employment and state-controlled enterprise output fell sharply after the late 1990s. And, as a result of wholesale privatisation – through national policy and local design – the size and importance of the private sector grew rapidly.

Over around six years between the late 1990s and early 2000s, there was a rapid switch from an economy that was mainly state-owned to one where a growing proportion was private. This economic restructuring coincided with China's accession to the World Trade Organization (WTO). WTO accession integrated China more into international trade networks and flows, accelerating the shift to the private sector. In little over half a decade, China shifted fundamentally from a state economy to a mixed economy with private entrepreneurs driving economic activity and growth.

The emergence of the private sector as the driver of growth: 2000s

The sudden increase in the private sector in the early 2000s was because of wholesale transfer of ownership from the collective and state sectors to entrepreneurs, rather than as a result of a significant rise in new ventures. The private sector that emerged in China in the early 2000s was made up of formerly state-owned enterprises or collective firms that underwent changes in ownership. Former SOEs and TVEs had been taken over by entrepreneurs, whose first task was to make these under-performing businesses profitable. The entrepreneurs now managing these businesses cut their labour force, reducing under-employment, renegotiated contracts to remove perks and inefficient ways of working, and in doing so further reinforced the pervasive unemployment that was a feature of urban China in the late 1990s and early 2000s.

Over this period of structural change in the Chinese economy, FDI continued to rise, at rates higher than earlier in the reform period. By the late 1990s, China received more FDI than any other emerging economy, and, overall, only the US received more foreign investment than China worldwide. As investment into China soared, its manufacturing base became highly integrated into global supply chains. This dependence upon manufacturers and markets overseas – in the developing world, as well as the post-industrial rich nations of the West – brought economic growth, yet at the price of interdependent reliance on the economic fortunes of the countries to which China exported increasingly huge volumes of its outputs.

Growing interdependence and integration into the global economy, based on soaring exports, were reinforced by China's entry into the WTO. WTO entry had a positive impact on private sector development because it partly helped rebalance the 'playing field' between SOEs and other enterprises inside China. During the reform period, SOEs have been consistently supported and privileged by the state. This continued after the wholesale transfer of smaller SOEs and many TVEs into private hands, through a state policy promoting national champions in key industries, such as oil and gas. However, entry to the WTO brought requirements that China open its markets to overseas businesses in ways that allowed them to compete more fairly with Chinese enterprises, both state owned and private. This was a positive development for private Chinese businesses because it created a legislative environment and policies within China that privileged SOEs somewhat less.

More broadly, the re-structuring of the state and transfers to the private sector of many enterprises heralded a renegotiation of the state's relationship with these enterprises and markets. Before this re-structuring of the Chinese economy, the state controlled the economy through ownership of state and collective enterprises, which accounted for the majority of businesses at that time. Reducing public spending on local government and the transfer of many enterprises to the private sector meant that the state had significantly less control over the economy. Its role shifted from managing production to creating the conditions to stimulate the growth of an economy that was increasingly reliant on private entrepreneurs.

This led to successive proclamations and legislation that officially recognised the private sector, and more recently has sought to protect it. This contrasts with earlier policy, which was reactive to the emergence of different forms of entrepreneurship.[25] In 2000, the State Council formally recognised the importance of private enterprises to employment, as well as the particular contribution made by high-tech small and medium enterprises (SMEs) to innovation. In 2001, entrepreneurs were allowed to join the Communist Party and, in 2003, all municipalities were required to establish SME support systems locally.[26] However, implementation of the 2003 legislation requiring local governments to better support private enterprises has been poor, with most local governments not creating effective SME 'support systems'.[27] In 2007, the Property Law was passed, which formally protected private ownership of assets for the first time. Even though compliance has been limited, this legislation is the first legal and formal recognition of private ownership in China, and so is symbolically important as well as legally significant.

During the 2000s, private enterprises became increasingly important in the Chinese economy, accounting for more than half of employment and around three-quarters of economic activity. The rate of transformation of China's economy from state owned and controlled to private has been rapid and profound. In 1990, private enterprises accounted for a small proportion of industrial employment. By 2010, they accounted for well over half of industrial employment. Over this period, the importance of SOEs to employment and economic activity fell drastically. By the late 2000s, China had become an entrepreneurial economy, with the majority of wealth and jobs generated by private enterprises. Although the remaining SOEs were individually huge and influential and still enjoyed preferential treatment from the state, the total population of private enterprises combined was much larger and, by the end of the first decade of the 21st century, drove China's economic growth.

Economic slowdown – China's 'new normal' in a less-than-normal global economy

China's private sector was hard hit by the 2008 global financial crisis. In the Pearl River Delta in 2008, around 60,000 private SMEs closed down due to a reduction in the value of orders of around two-thirds from overseas customers. Many of the cities at the heart of this region's export economy posted negative growth after having enjoyed double-digit growth for two decades. The effects of the 2008 financial crisis were felt more widely across China because its growth had become increasingly dependent upon global economic conditions, especially since WTO entry. The export-driven part of China's economy had driven GDP growth during the reform period, and demand for manufactured and consumer products made in China collapsed after 2008. Moreover, FDI into China also fell considerably after 2008, as credit dried up for many global corporations and businesses seeking to invest in China. This had a major effect on China's economic growth, highlighting the increased level of dependence on other countries and the global economy.

The Chinese government responded with a massive stimulus and deflationary programme that generated some short-term growth and helped stabilise the currency. However, underlying weak conditions in the global economy lasted beyond this stimulus programme and, in 2012, China recorded significantly reduced growth, which has since continued to decline to less than seven per cent. In that same year, many Chinese businesses posted losses or much reduced profits as demand weakened both domestically and internationally. Some of this fall in GDP growth is due to underlying weaknesses in China's own economy, including in particular the high level of indebtedness of local government and state-owned banks, as well as low levels of return on investment and public expenditure.

The figure of seven per cent annual growth is highly symbolic within China because it has been perceived as the minimum annual growth rate needed to generate sufficient increases in household incomes to satisfy rising expectations of quality of life. The party view of the seven per cent threshold was that this was the minimum growth rate that needed to be delivered by the state for it to maintain its credibility. Even though this growth rate was historical, in the sense that inflation has fallen in China since this threshold was proposed, the wider social resonance of falling below seven per cent annual growth is profound. Xi Jinping, the Party General Secretary, has described this as China's 'new normal', and characterised it as a new phase in the country's development, during which a slower but still healthy growth rate, combined with a rebalancing of the economy, will create a more sustainable basis for future growth. This builds on the state's focus on rebalancing the economy away from over-reliance on capital-intensive production and investment that has been a concern in public policy statements since the mid-2000s.

Since 2012, China's growth rate has continued to fall to below seven per cent and, based on current trends, is likely to continue to fall in coming years, most likely to between five and six per cent. Although this still represents the highest growth rate of any large economy globally, these levels of growth are causing concern in China itself. Some commentators have suggested that, if GDP growth falls to these levels and continues to decline gradually, then China may become caught in a middle-income 'equilibrium trap', not unlike the 'high level equilibrium trap' China experienced in late imperial times.[28] In this scenario, China will not grow beyond its current middle-income status and its growth will flatten out. As a result, the country could become 'trapped' in a development phase that does not allow it to reach the levels of prosperity of higher income nations.

Although this is a possibility, it appears implausible for several reasons. First, China's dependence upon the global economy means that, when this economy improves, there will be a positive impact on China's rates of economic growth. Second, China has the largest domestic market in the world and so has the capacity to stimulate demand through internal growth. The private sector has an important role to play in stimulating domestic growth as well as international trade. Although private enterprises have been adversely affected by global economic conditions, there are indications that entrepreneurship in China is growing and new start-ups are becoming increasingly common.

In 2014, the Chinese government simplified the regulations and requirements for registering a new business – a key step in starting a new venture. Steps to simplify registration have led to an increase in new business registrations of almost 50 per cent in 2014 compared with 2013.[29] This is a significant increase in the number of new businesses in China. Rapid growth in new firm registrations suggests a shift to a more typical profile of the private sector, as seen in developed economies in the West, where new ventures start up to increase competition and challenge incumbents. In this Schumpeterian world of entrepreneurial new venture creation, while a minority of new ventures grow quickly to become large and successful, the majority of new ventures remain small, and there is churn in the economy, with businesses closing as well as opening. The proportions of high-growth versus small-scale ventures, and firm start-ups versus firm closures is as yet unclear, but will determine the extent to which entrepreneurs will generate significant future growth in China.

A growing number of entrepreneurs in China are creating innovative, high-tech and large businesses that can compete domestically, and to an extent internationally, with established domestic and global giants. Examples of start-ups that now compete against well-established enterprises include Xiaomi, the third-largest manufacturer of smartphones, which was only started in 2011; Alibaba, the world's largest online trading platform; and Tencent, China's largest internet service provider and increasingly a partner and investor in digital technology worldwide.

Although some of these businesses have faced challenges moving beyond their initial phase of hyper-growth, most notably Xiaomi, they are disrupting their own markets and introducing new products and forms of competition. A growing number of private enterprises have a strong market share in China, and are expanding internationally. These businesses have developed effective strategies for competitive success in China, and are adapting their approaches to enter new markets worldwide. They are able to compete within China against giant SOEs and internationally against market leaders in other countries.[30]

However, the future growth potential of these entrepreneurial ventures is not unconstrained, particularly within the parameters of the 'new normal'. Although there are efforts to rebalance the economy, and in particular to stimulate greater consumer spending and growth in services, these parts of the Chinese economy are still relatively underdeveloped. The rebalancing of China's economy towards services and a consumer economy should encourage more entrepreneurship, and so the current stage of development of this part of the economy represents an opportunity for entrepreneurs.

The ways in which markets are governed in China, and in particular how the interests and rights of private enterprises are actually promoted and upheld by the state, will determine the extent to which entrepreneurs will be able to drive future economic growth. Until recently, growth could be managed by the state by injecting huge amounts of capital into SOEs and collectives through direct funding, bonds and state banks. Recent crackdowns on local government financing, by restricting bonds issues and the sale of land, in order to reduce unsustainable levels of public debt have reduced the ability of municipal and district officials to provide soft money to their own SOEs and collective enterprises. Nationally, restrictions on lending on favourable terms by banks to SOEs have meant that growth through relatively inefficient investment in these enterprises has become more difficult and costly. Recent stimulus packages represent an alternative model, but infrastructure investment is slowing as China's main railway and road routes are expanded. The ability of the state to directly drive economic growth is becoming more limited as these varied interventions are producing lower returns or are drying up.

With these restrictions in place as part of a national policy to reduce government debt and deficits, China will need to introduce and uphold more market-based drivers of growth if entrepreneurs are to continue to expand the economy. This will entail the promotion and protection of institutions that enable markets to operate transparently and efficiently. However, China's market institutions are still underdeveloped, and protection of the assets, rights, and operating autonomy of private enterprises is weak and inconsistent. In China's 'new normal', entrepreneurs are the primary source of future growth; however, to enable this, the state will need to develop policies and institutions that actively support entrepreneurship, and ensure that private enterprises operate on a 'level playing field' with SOEs and state entities.[31]

Notes

1 Weidenbaum, M & Hughes, S 1996, *The bamboo network: how expatriate Chinese entrepreneurs are creating a new superpower in Asia*, Free Press, New York.
2 Windrow, H 2006, 'A short history of law, norms, and social control in Imperial China', *Asian-Pacific Law & Policy Journal*, vol. 2, no. 1, pp. 244–301.
3 Deng, K 2015, 'China's population expansion and its causes during the Qing period, 1644–1911', LSE Economic History Working Papers No. 219/2015, http://www.lse.ac.uk/economicHistory/workingPapers/2015/WP219.pdf (viewed 3 June 2017).
4 Atherton, A & Newman, A 2016, 'The emergence of the private entrepreneur in reform era China: re-birth of an earlier tradition, or a more recent product of development and change?' *Business History*, vol. 58, no. 3, pp. 319–344.
5 Elman, B 2000, *A cultural history of civil examinations in late Imperial China*, University of California Press, Berkeley.
6 Wagner, R 2009, 'Alternatives to magistrate justice: merchant guild resolution and the foreign trader driven litigation and arbitration reforms of late imperial and early republican China', *Journal of Comparative Law*, vol. 4, no. 2, pp. 257–290.
7 Pomeranz, K 2000, *The great divergence: China, Europe, and the making of the modern world economy*, Princeton University Press, Princeton.
8 Hung, H 2001, 'Imperial China and capitalist Europe in the eighteenth-century global economy', *Review (Fernand Braudel Center)*, vol. 24, no. 4, pp. 473–513.
9 Hamilton, G & Chang, W 2003, 'The importance of commerce in the organization of China's late imperial economy', in G Arrighi, T Hamashita & M Selden (eds), *The resurgence of East Asia: 500, 150 and 50 year perspectives*, Routledge, London, pp. 173–213.
10 Wilson, C & Yang, F 2016, 'Shanxi Piaohao and Shanghai Qianzhuang: a comparison of the two main banking systems of nineteenth-century China', *Business History*, vol. 58, no. 3, pp.433–452; Zein, M 2013, 'Chinese business practices in the late imperial period', *Enterprise & Society*, vol. 14, no. 4, pp. 769–793.

11 Liu, K 1988, 'Chinese merchant guilds: an historical inquiry', *Pacific Historical Review*, vol. 57, no. 1, pp. 1–23.
12 Deng, K 2015.
13 Elvin, M 1973, *The pattern of the Chinese past*, Stanford University Press, Stanford; Lin, J 2008, 'The Needham puzzle, the Weber question, and China's miracle: long-term performance since the Sung dynasty', *China Economic Journal*, vol. 1, no. 1, pp. 63–95.
14 Wang, H 2009, *The end of the revolution: China and the limits of modernity*, Verso, London.
15 Brandt, L & Rawski, T 2008, *China's great economic transformation*, Cambridge University Press, New York; Brandt, L 1989, *Commercialization and agricultural development: Central and Eastern China 1870–1937*, Cambridge University Press, Cambridge; Rawski, T 1989, *Economic growth in prewar China*, California University Press, Berkeley.
16 Dikotter, F 2013, *The tragedy of liberation: A history of the Chinese Revolution 1945–1957*, Bloomsbury Books, London.
17 Oi, J. 1995, 'The role of the local state in China's transitional economy', *The China Quarterly*, vol. 144, pp. 1132–1149.
18 For an example of how this correlation holds in China, see: Chen, J, Xie, Z & Liu, H 2007, 'Son preference, use of maternal health case, and infant mortality in rural China, 1989–2000', *Population Studies*, vol. 61, no. 2, pp. 161–183.
19 World Health Organization 2008, 'China's village doctors take great strides', *Bulletin of the World Health Organization*, vol. 86, no. 12, pp. 909–988; http://www.who.int/bulletin/volumes/86/12/08-021208/en/ (viewed 3 June 2017).
20 Naughton, B 1995, *Growing out of the plan: Chinese economic reform 1978–1993*, Cambridge University Press, Cambridge, p. 14.
21 Fan, S, Zhang, L & Zhang, X 2004, 'Reforms, investment, and poverty in rural China', *Economic Development and Cultural Change*, vol. 52, no. 2, pp. 395–421.
22 Oi, J 1992, 'Fiscal reform and the economic foundations of local state corporatism in China', *World Politics*, vol. 45, no. 1, pp. 99–126.
23 Oi, J 1995, 'China's transitional economy', *The China Quarterly*, vol. 144, pp. 1132–1149.
24 Ong, L 2006, 'The political economy of township government debt, township enterprises and rural financial institutions in China', *The China Quarterly*, vol. 186, pp. 377–400; Wong, CPW 1991, 'Central–local relations in an era of fiscal decline: the paradox of fiscal decentralization in post-Mao China', *The China Quarterly*, vol. 128, pp. 691–715.
25 Atherton, A 2008, 'From "fat pigs" and "red hats" to a "new social stratum": the changing face of enterprise development policy in China', *Journal of Small Business and Enterprise Development*, vol. 15, no. 4, pp. 640–655.
26 Atherton, A & Smallbone, D 2013, 'Promoting private sector development in China: the challenge of building institutional capacity at local level', *Environment and Planning C*, vol. 31, no. 1, pp. 5–23.
27 Atherton, A & Fairbanks, A 2006, 'Stimulating private sector development in China: the emergence of enterprise development centres in Liaoning and Sichuan provinces', *Asia Pacific Business Review*, vol. 12, no. 3, pp. 333–354.
28 Elvin, M 1973, *The pattern of the Chinese past*, Stanford University Press, Stanford.
29 Atherton, A 2015, 'Six things China can do to become the World's most entrepreneurial economy', *The Conversation*, 17 February; https://theconversation.com/six-things-china-can-do-to-become-the-worlds-most-entrepreneurial-economy-37191 (viewed 3 June 2017).
30 Atherton, A, Zhan, G & Huang, Q 2014, *China's next 100 global giants*, ACCA Accountancy Futures Academy, London; http://www.accaglobal.com/content/dam/acca/global/PDF-technical/futures/pol-afa-cngg-chinas-next.pdf (viewed 3 June 2017).
31 Atherton, A 2015, 'China's move to entrepreneurship – will the private sector continue to grow?', China Policy Research Institute, Nottingham University; http://blogs.nottingham.ac.uk/chinapolicyinstitute/2015/02/06/chinas-move-to-entrepreneurship-will-the-private-sector-continue-to-grow-in-the-future/ (viewed 3 June 2017).

4
MODELS OF ENTREPRENEURSHIP IN CHINA

Introduction

This chapter will examine the main models of entrepreneurship in China. The focus will be on particular patterns in how private enterprises are configured and have emerged. The first models to be examined are the network-based models of entrepreneurship that developed in the coastal provinces of Zhejiang, Jiangsu and Guangdong in the early period of opening up and reform.

The focus will then move to innovation-based models of entrepreneurship that have developed in recent years as the Chinese government has supported a shift away from low-cost manufacturing, construction and mining. As well as looking at the key high-technology zones in which innovation-based entrepreneurship is thriving, this section will focus on how innovation-based entrepreneurship has been supported in such zones. The channels of financial support for innovation-based entrepreneurship will also be examined, and challenges facing this model of entrepreneurship analysed.

Finally, more socially oriented models of entrepreneurship that have developed in China will be examined. More specifically, this section will focus on new models of social entrepreneurship that have sprung up to deal with social issues resulting from China's uneven economic growth which has resulted in growing inequality between rich and poor.

In examining these models of entrepreneurship in China, it must be kept in mind that such models account for less than half of all private sector activity in China. As in all countries, sole trading enterprises (known as *getihu* in China), with no or a small number of employees, account for a significant proportion of Gross Domestic Product (GDP) and the lion's share of employment.

Network-based entrepreneurship

In the early 1980s, the Chinese market was filled with opportunities for entrepreneurs due to the inefficiencies of a centrally planned economy that was unable to meet pent-up demand in the market. Early economic reforms in the post-Mao era, such as the removal of price controls, stimulated industrial output in rural areas as collectively owned enterprises and households sold off excess production on sideline markets. However, it was extremely difficult for those who had identified entrepreneurial opportunities to exploit them, due to a lack of institutional support for entrepreneurship, and a lack of financing mechanisms for businesses and individuals. Entrepreneurs had virtually no access to resources such as capital, skilled labour, market information, and land or distribution/sales channels.[1] For all intents and purposes the Chinese economy was still a planned economy and lacked most core features of a market economy. For example, enterprises were prevented from employing people, unable to rent land and excluded from the state's distribution networks. To deal with a lack of institutional support, network-based forms of entrepreneurship sprang up in the late 1980s and 1990s across provinces in South-east China where there was less state involvement in the economy than in the north and west of the country, and local governments colluded with entrepreneurs to support private sector development. In the following sections each of these models will be examined.

The Wenzhou (Zhejiang) model

Wenzhou is viewed by many as the birthplace of network-based entrepreneurship in China as it was the first place in which private enterprise developed on a large scale during the opening up and reform period. This model of network-based entrepreneurship is characterised by large numbers of family businesses working together in network clusters (groups of small-scale enterprises in the same geographical location) to manufacture labour-intensive, low-cost products such as garments, apparel, toys and other consumer goods.[2] Entrepreneurs in Wenzhou tended to focus on labour-intensive manufacturing because barriers to entry in this industry were relatively weak and they had limited access to adequate sources of financing needed to invest in more technology-intensive manufacturing. For example, network clusters in Wenzhou were among the world leaders in the manufacturing of plastics, buttons, shoes and cigarette lighters.

A number of factors supported the growth of entrepreneurship in Wenzhou. First, its mountainous terrain meant the central government neither interfered nor invested significant resources in its development. Its remoteness and inaccessibility meant that Wenzhou – distant from Beijing and seldom visited by officials – was relatively free to experiment and develop its own models of local economic development and growth. In China, places such as Wenzhou and other coastal cities were 'distant from the emperor and lay behind tall mountains' (*tiangao diyuan*), and so were largely left to their own devices rather than controlled by the state economic system. This meant that the people of Wenzhou were able to govern themselves in an autonomous way and introduce reforms without too much interference from Beijing.[3] Second, Wenzhou lacked natural resources but had historical domestic and international commercial links, including to Taiwan – offering a strong basis for the emergence of entrepreneurship as the primary economic activity. Entrepreneurship tends to emerge in places where natural resources are scarce because individuals need to rely on their own skills and capabilities to create wealth that does not arise from the use of natural resources. Wenzhou's long history of engaging in commerce with the outside world meant its people had a strong commercial instinct and contacts in other parts of China and across the world. Such networks have proved extremely useful in helping to distribute and market their products in China and globally.[4] In both Imperial China and in the early years of opening up and reform, the people of Wenzhou exhibited a willingness to travel to other parts of China and across the world to do business. In the late 1980s it was estimated by the Wenzhou government authorities that around 1.6 million sales agents from Wenzhou were operating across the Chinese mainland, and around 0.5 million outside China.[5]

Although private enterprise was denounced during the political campaigns of the Mao era, small-scale rural entrepreneurship at the household level survived in Wenzhou, albeit being driven underground. This provided a basis for the rapid re-emergence of the private sector as soon as the opening up and reform policies were introduced by the Chinese government in the late 1970s. At that time, private enterprises continued to face restrictions in accessing credit and hiring employees; however, entrepreneurs used their personal networks (*guanxi*) with family members, relatives and friends to gain access to support from government officials and obtain orders from managers in state-owned enterprises as subcontractors. In many cases they were supported by local government officials who turned a blind eye to, and in some cases openly supported, their development.[6] For example, before 1988 entrepreneurs were not permitted to employ more than seven employees because they were only allowed to operate as an individual household business (*getihu*). To get around such restrictions and expand their businesses, many entrepreneurs adopted the popular 'red hat' strategy whereby they concealed their private ownership by registering as a collective enterprise or subsidiary/department of a state-owned enterprise in collusion with local government.[7] In return for government assistance in hiding their true status, entrepreneurs typically agreed to pay a percentage of their profits to local government. To overcome the lack of state funding for entrepreneurs, informal and 'shadow' banks, lending circles and credit associations were also established.[8] Households pooled their money and formed lending syndicates and money houses to fund entrepreneurial activity across the city.[9] These underground funders of entrepreneurship operated outside the formal system, offering capital to businesspeople through the early reform period. This strategy supported the widespread emergence of entrepreneurship during the early years of opening up and reform, and provided a basis for the growth of the private sector until the mid-1980s, when the central government introduced legislation that allowed the establishment of private enterprises (*siying qiye*) that were allowed to employ eight or more individuals. Introduction of this legislation formally recognised the scale of private sector activity in places like Wenzhou, where new businesses grew rapidly and quickly became much larger than the small-scale 'household' enterprise that had been permitted, and legislated for, in the early 1980s.

Research has highlighted the importance of *guanxi* with government officials to entrepreneurial success in the earlier years of opening up and reform. *Guanxi* for entrepreneurs allowed the development of ongoing relationships with government officials, state-owned enterprises and other entities that could offer commercial opportunities to these new enterprises. They were important both in acquiring the resources and raw materials entrepreneurs needed to manufacture goods, and also to sell to the state in China and allow for exports at a time when there were restrictions on international trade for many Chinese businesses. Researchers have found that *guanxi* assists entrepreneurs to accumulate the social capital that allows them to build legitimacy and compensate for a lack of formal institutional support.[10]

Although private entrepreneurship originated in Wenzhou, variants of the Wenzhou model – family businesses concentrated in clusters of economic activity – sprang up in other parts of Zhejiang Province and throughout Southeast China during the 1980s. The Wenzhou model is therefore sometimes known as the Zhejiang model.[11] Like Wenzhou, other cities in Zhejiang Province such as Ningbo witnessed the growth of private sector development during the 1980s and became home to network clusters focusing on the development of different products. For example, Ningbo is famous for the production of textiles, electrical products and chemicals. The key feature of these models of entrepreneurship was specialisation in specific products by entrepreneurs within a city or town, leading to high levels of competition, generating cost and process efficiencies. The key indicator for the Wenzhou model, which can still be seen in many prosperous settlements along the coast in eastern China are streets and neighbourhoods dominated by private enterprises all producing the same types of products. This level of intense specialisation produced skills and capabilities that spread between businesses, creating superior local knowledge and expertise in their specialised product categories.

Weaknesses of the Wenzhou (Zhejiang) model

In recent years the Wenzhou (Zhejiang) model of network-based entrepreneurship focusing on labour-intensive, low-cost production has come under pressure as a result of increasing labour costs.[12] There is a shrinking pool of labour from which to recruit as workers are unwilling to toil in factories for wages that had been acceptable a few years ago. Industries that were once profitable are facing increased global competition from lower-cost manufacturing locations. As a result, many small and medium-sized enterprises (SMEs) have gone out of business due to lower profit margins. For example, the Wenzhou cigarette lighter industry has been affected by global competition from cheaper markets such as Vietnam and India.[13] The industry has contracted from around 3,000 manufacturers at its peak to fewer than 100 manufacturers today.[14] Although some entrepreneurs in Wenzhou have moved into higher value-added sectors of the economy as labour costs have increased, others have begun to invest in labour-intensive manufacturing overseas, and others have exited completely. This has led some commentators to herald the end of the Wenzhou model.[15]

Case study – Metersbonwe

Zhou Chengjian is one of Wenzhou's most famous entrepreneurs. He established the Metersbonwe Group in 1995 with 200,000 RMB and developed it into one of the largest fashion brands in China. The success of Metersbonwe can be put down to the innovative network-based business model adopted by Zhou when he set up his business. Instead of seeking to undertake manufacturing and sales in-house like his main competitors, he decided to outsource these lower value-added functions of the business to a network of suppliers and franchisees, and concentrate on higher value-added activities such as research and development, marketing and logistics. By keeping the entry costs for franchisees relatively low and assisting them through providing training and consultation he was able to build up a large retail network across China in a very short time. In addition, through establishing a global design team that works with leading designers in many countries including France, Italy and Hong Kong, and using the latest information technology to link its design team with its procurement and logistics departments, Metersbonwe is able to bring the latest fashion to market very quickly.[16] However, in recent times the bricks and mortar business model has faced significant pressure from online retailers. In response to this, Metersbonwe has also begun to adapt its network-based business model to technological developments. For example, it has recently developed apps to involve customers in the process of design and marketing. It has begun to realise that it needs to continue to innovate to survive.[17]

The Southern Jiangsu (Sunan) model

The Sunan model was another network-based model of entrepreneurship that facilitated the development of private enterprise in rural areas of the country. As this approach to development of the non-state sector was originally trialled in the south of Jiangsu Province, it is known as the Southern Jiangsu or Sunan model. The Sunan area encompasses the cities of Suzhou, Wuxi and Changzhou. Unlike the Wenzhou model, this model focused on the development of township and village enterprises (TVEs), which were rural non-state-owned enterprises subordinate to the township or village governments where they were based, and run on a collective basis.[18] Although the managers of TVEs did not own the enterprises they worked for under this model, they shared much in common with private entrepreneurs under the Wenzhou model, in that they relied on alliances with local government to deal with the institutional uncertainties their enterprises faced and had *de facto* operational responsibility for the business without day-to-day interference from local government; meaning they were effectively operating as independent managers of the enterprise. Through building personal networks (*guanxi*) with local government, managers were able to gain access to distribution and marketing channels, hire adequate labour and obtain financial resources. The management of TVEs acted in a similar way to more traditional enterprises in that they sought to adapt to the needs of the market and obtain a profit. The profits obtained by TVEs were typically shared between management and local government.

Ultimately, as a result of globalisation and increasing competition from private enterprises, TVEs lost competitiveness and a movement away from collective ownership was witnessed in the 1990s as their profitability reduced. The worsening finances of many TVEs resulted in them going out of business and led the government to encourage TVEs to collaborate with foreign investors or go private. For example, during the 1990s the government in Jiangsu Province encouraged TVEs to seek foreign direct investment. It introduced a raft of preferential policies to attract foreign investors, including low tax rates and tax holidays. As a result, foreign direct investment flowed into Jiangsu, particularly into Suzhou – which had established the Singapore Industrial Park – and many TVEs established joint ventures with foreign investors. From the middle of the 1990s, local governments began to transfer loss-making TVEs to their managers, or sold them to entrepreneurs who took on the business' losses. This led to mass privatisation of the vast majority of TVEs in most parts of China, and thus the rapid emergence of a much larger private sector. Almost overnight, China's collective enterprises became private businesses, removing this hybrid form of enterprise from the country's economic organisation. Under this policy, managers and former employees of many TVEs were able to purchase their shares at a reduced cost and convert the enterprises for which they were buying these shares into individually owned private enterprises. By the end of 2000, over 90 per cent of TVEs in Sunan had transferred from collectively owned to private enterprises.[19]

The Guangdong (Pearl River Delta) model

The Guangdong or Pearl River Delta model is an alternative network-based model of entrepreneurship that sprang up in the south of China. In a similar way to the Sunan model, it initially focused on the development of TVEs under the direction of local government. However, after Shenzhen, Zhuhai and Shantou were designated as Special Economic Zones in the 1980s, TVEs attracted significant investment from overseas in the form of capital from overseas diaspora, notably from Taiwan and Hong Kong.[20] The involvement of foreign ownership facilitated access to technology, management know-how and distribution channels in overseas markets. Over time, the shift from collective TVEs and the influx of private enterprises from overseas, particularly from Hong Kong and Taiwan, created a very large and highly dynamic private sector engaged in low-cost manufacturing and assembly within global supply chains for industrial, business and consumer goods. In more recent years, and particularly since China entered the World Trade Organization – further opening up international supply opportunities – an indigenous private sector has grown from new businesses starting up in existing clusters of economic activity and exporting across the Pearl River Delta.

Over the last decade or so, from the mid-2000s to the 'new normal' of lower economic growth since 2012, Guangdong has embarked on a further phase of economic re-structuring, which has led to new forms of economic activity and organisation. As labour costs have risen, Guangdong has encouraged a shift inland of labour-intensive, low-cost manufacturing, and has encouraged those businesses staying in the Pearl River Delta to become more innovative, and to move up the value chain. It has also encouraged investment in new industries, to stimulate greater technological intensity among its private enterprises.

Innovation-based entrepreneurship

At the beginning of the 21st century the Chinese government realised it could no longer rely on low-cost, labour-intensive manufacturing and construction for continued economic growth, and needed to take steps to support the development of high-technology enterprises and internet start-ups. It began to look to a new generation of entrepreneurs to develop innovation-based business models to drive economic growth and provide jobs into the future.

To support innovation-based entrepreneurship, the government established high-technology zones across the country and introduced financial reforms to support the development of venture capital and equity markets. Recent research suggests that enterprises located in these zones have higher levels of new product development than enterprises located outside these zones.[21] The government also introduced policies such as the *Thousand Talents Scheme* to attract Chinese scholars educated overseas to work in high-technology and internet industries,[22] and has supported the establishment of business incubators across the country to support university graduates, especially those coming back from overseas to establish businesses.[23]

The following sections will highlight the key high-technology zones across China in which innovation-based entrepreneurship is thriving, and examine how entrepreneurship has been supported in those zones. Following this, the channels of financial support for innovation-based entrepreneurship will be examined and constraints on this model of entrepreneurship analysed.

Beijing

Zhongguancun Science & Technology Zone (or simply Zhongguancun) is China's largest technology hub. Affectionately known as China's Silicon Valley, it is located in north-west Beijing close to key universities such as Peking and Tsinghua, and the Chinese Academy of Sciences. It was established in 1988 and has seven parks. A number of famous local companies grew up in Zhongguancun, including Lenovo Group and Stone Group, and it is home to many of the top global technology companies such as Google, Intel and Microsoft. The government provides various benefits for enterprises located in Zhongguancun. As well as lower rates of corporation tax, new entrants to the zone are given a tax holiday for three years.[24]

As of 2015, there were around 20,000 enterprises operating across the seven parks in Zhongguancun, with over 1.5 million employees. It is considered one of the main locations for internet start-ups outside of Silicon Valley in the United States of America. A significant proportion of Chinese entrepreneurs who have established start-ups in Zhongguancun are returnees from overseas. Many of them come with foreign PhDs, work experience overseas and new technologies that they hope to exploit in the Chinese market.[25] For example, Baidu (a leading search engine), Sina (a leading web portal), Sohu (a leading web portal) and Dangdang (a leading e-commerce company) are internet start-ups established by returnees from overseas.

However, the majority of start-ups have been established by local entrepreneurs who gained their experience and generated their business ideas while working in China – typically Beijing. Many of these local entrepreneurs have established successful companies focused on the domestic market over the last few decades, in particular since the early 2000s. More recently, a growing number of these indigenous businesses have secured dominant market share and high profile not only in China, but also internationally as investors have targeted them. These include Didi Chuxing (a taxi-hailing app now linked with Uber), Ayibang (a household services app) and Helijia (a beauty service app).

In 2014, the authorities of Zhongguancun established InnoWay, a 200-metre long street dedicated to start-ups. InnoWay contains start-up cafes, co-working spaces, accelerator programmes that assist start-ups to launch their businesses, and other start-up ecosystem players such as venture capitalists. In cafes such as Garage and 3W, entrepreneurs can use high-speed network connections for videoconferencing, hire meeting rooms and network with similar-minded individuals. These cafes also hold events at which successful entrepreneurs share their experience of running start-ups with budding entrepreneurs. InnoWay is a strong indication of the continued efforts by the local district government to create an environment that is conducive for starting new businesses. Facilities such as this, as well as proximity to the capital's universities – clustered in the Haidian district in north-west Beijing – create the conditions for some of China's brightest citizens to begin new ventures.

Case study – Didi Chuxing

Didi Chuxing – a taxi-hailing app-based enterprise – is China's answer to Uber, and was created through the 2015 merger of two large start-ups: Didi Dache and Kuaidi Dache. These start-ups were established in 2012 by Cheng Wei and Lu Chuanwei respectively, and have been supported by early-stage, ongoing investment by Alibaba and by Tencent. At present, Didi Chuxing controls over 80 per cent of the app-based taxi market in China. It has tweaked its business model to build legitimacy with government authorities and meet the needs of local consumers. For example, it has developed good relationships with local governments in cities across China by working to fulfil legal requirements, and works closely with local taxi companies to deliver its services, as well as subcontracting its work to private drivers like Uber. In addition, it provides a number of flexible payment options in a country where credit card use is not widespread, allowing its users to pay through AliPay or WePay apps. Didi Chuxing's recent contest with Uber led to the latter selling its Chinese operation to Didi Chuxing, conceding control of the Chinese market to the local start-up. This followed a period of intense competition between the two companies to secure dominance in China. Securing its domestic market may serve as the basis for future expansion into other markets.

Shanghai

Zhangjiang Hi-Technology Park is located in the Pudong district of Shanghai. It is home to leading multinationals in pharmaceuticals and biotechnology (e.g. GSK, Novartis and Astra Zeneca), technology (e.g. Lenovo, eBay, Infosys and Intel) and semiconductors, and a growing number of innovative SMEs. In 1988, the Shanghai government established the Shanghai Technology Innovation Center, which acts as a technology incubator. This incubator assists high-technology enterprises to commercialise the technologies they develop.

To compete with Beijing, the Shanghai government has taken steps to attract new start-ups to the city. Entrepreneurs are able to lease offices in high-technology parks at half the cost of those in Beijing, and the government has made it easier to hire foreign talent. Although Shanghai is a global finance centre, the ecosystem supporting start-ups is underdeveloped compared to other finance centres and to Beijing. In particular, Shanghai lacks venture capitalists and angel investors, and so has less capacity to offer risk capital to new technology start-ups that require high levels of cash flow in their early period of operation.

Zhejiang and Jiangsu provinces

Zhejiang and Jiangsu provinces have well-established and thriving private sectors that have been supported by local governments, especially in more prosperous cities such as Hangzhou and Suzhou. Suzhou Industrial Park (SIP) was established in the mid-1990s with investment from and adoption of approaches developed in Singapore. SIP has since grown to be a major concentration of businesses in China. As it has grown, SIP has sought to attract high-tech businesses, and is focused on advanced materials such as graphene, establishing research institutes to enhance the park's capacity to enable innovation.

To upgrade traditional industries and foster innovation-based entrepreneurship, Zhejiang Province established a number of high-technology towns in 2015, including 'internet Town', a campus-like facility in Hangzhou that has space for 2,000 technology start-ups. The Zhejiang government intends to turn Hangzhou into a technology hub to compete with those in Beijing and Shanghai, and build on the success of the Alibaba Group and its subsidiary enterprises (Taobao, TMall and Alipay), which are based in the city and provide a foundation for supporting new digital businesses. Alibaba invests in new and particularly cloud technologies; through investment subsidiaries such as AntFinancial, it funds micro-enterprises as well as high-tech new ventures in Hangzhou and nationally in China's high-tech 'hotspots'. Leading tech companies such as Alibaba and Tencent increasingly are becoming national funders of high-tech businesses, at the start-up stage and as they grow, helping to create more innovative businesses that can compete with global technology companies. They are recognising they must take on responsibility to foster the development of the nascent technology sector in China rather than expecting government authorities to take the initiative.

To support entrepreneurs in the start-up phase, government authorities in Hangzhou have provided a whole host of incentives including free office space, information technology infrastructure and tax concessions. In addition, a government office on campus assists start-ups to register their businesses in less than one week, and patent the technology that they develop. Working with the Bank of Hangzhou and Hangzhou United Bank, the Zhejiang government has also established a start-up fund to assist university graduates to establish their own businesses. Under this scheme the provincial government provides seed funding and the banks subsidise loans ranging from 20,000–50,000 RMB. If the money is repaid on time the government provides a 50 per cent subsidy on the interest.[26] Significant and ongoing investment by municipal authorities in the major cities, and also in other cities in Zhejiang and Jiangsu provinces such as Wuxi, Changzhou, Ningbo and Shaoxing, is encouraging high-tech businesses to locate themselves there.

Shenzhen

Shenzhen in Guangdong Province is also home to a thriving start-up scene. As well as being home to Tencent, it is also the centre of the world's electronics industry. This makes it an attractive place for start-ups focusing on hardware to establish their businesses. They are able to come to Shenzhen with an idea for a new piece of hardware (whether it be a consumer device, gadget, toy or appliance), run their idea through an incubator, develop a prototype, crowdfund their idea, and meet manufacturers and suppliers within the space of a few months. The start-up scene in Shenzhen has spawned a number of successful enterprises including DJI Technology, one of the world's largest manufacturers of personal drones, and Makeblock, a robot kit manufacturer.[27] Incubators such as HAX run accelerator programmes that provide start-ups with seed funding, mentorship, office and lab space, and assistance in design and sourcing.[28] Foxconn, one of the largest electronics manufacturers in China, whose clients include Apple, Nokia and Xiaomi, has also launched its own incubator, Innoconn, to help hardware start-ups from overseas design and launch their products.[29] By providing an extensive infrastructure for companies to launch innovative new products, Shenzhen is seeking to be a centre for hardware start-ups.

The government in Shenzhen has introduced a number of policies aimed at fostering innovation-based entrepreneurship. In 2015 it established a 200 million RMB fund to support hardware start-ups, and aims to support more than 50,000 of these over a four-year period. The government has also made it easy for entrepreneurs to register a business, and has the most developed support system for small businesses and start-ups, with business advice agencies, funding and credit guarantee schemes, and a focus in their local plan on entrepreneurship.

Other areas of the country

In other regions of the country, provincial and local governments have looked to foster innovation-based forms of entrepreneurship on a smaller scale. For example, governments in larger cities such as Nanjing, Chengdu, Chongqing and Xian have all looked to support start-ups in high-technology zones through sponsoring incubators and providing financial support for start-ups.

Channels of financial support for innovation-based entrepreneurship

Unable to obtain sufficient debt financing to fund the early stages of start-up growth due to a lack of collateral and credit history, entrepreneurs are increasingly seeking private equity financing from venture capitalists and angel investors to ensure they scale up quickly to reach a size where it is easier to prevent competitors from copying their business models. In a dynamic market like China, competition is intense, so growing rapidly to become more established is a key driver for seeking finance by most entrepreneurs.

Some of the world's largest private equity and venture capital firms including Sequoia Capital and Tiger Global have established offices in key high-technology zones such as Zhongguancun, and invested heavily in internet start-ups. Indigenous private equity firms such as Innovation Works and Trustbridge Partners have also begun to invest significant amounts in new ventures. Innovation Works is a Beijing-based private equity firm established by the former head of Google China, Lee Kai-Fu, in 2009. It has the backing of numerous investors from the technology sector including the founder of YouTube, Steve Chen. Examples of the start-ups in which Innovation Works has invested are DianDian (a blogging platform) and PaPa (a photo sharing network). Trustbridge Partners, based in Shanghai, has made significant first and second stage investments in start-ups such as Meican (a food ordering platform), Renren (a social networking site), Changing Edu (an education app) and Douban (a social networking site for college students).

Increasingly, China's leading high-technology companies, such as Alibaba, Tencent and Baidu, have become leading funders of start-ups, in much the same way as private equity firms. They believe strategic partnerships with start-ups will allow them to provide added value to their customers in the form of content delivered through their internet platforms. Alibaba, for example, has invested in numerous start-ups including ByeCity (an online travel provider), Wasu Media (a digital media provider) and Youku (a video portal). Similarly, Tencent has invested in a growing number of start-ups such as Renren, Didi Kuadi and Linktech Navi (a mapping service provider), JD (an e-commerce portal), Edaixi (a laundry pick-up app), Leju (an online real estate portal), Ly.com (an online travel provider) and Dianping (a group coupon provider). Many services provided by these start-ups are now provided through Tencent's WeChat and QQ platforms. These partnerships appear to be growing in China, and serve both the existing tech company and the new venture well. For established businesses, new digital businesses use their online products and so expand their business while also becoming ambassadors for China's 'new economy' and the lead tech companies in it. Start-ups also offer opportunities for new ways of working, improved business models and enhanced technological solutions that large, established players such as Alibaba, Baidu and Tencent can tap into. They also offer a form of 'social responsibility' for these large companies that creates wider societal and political goodwill, and as a result improve public profiles and serve as insurance against negative actions by the state, should this arise.

Challenges faced by innovation-based start-ups

Growing criticism has been aimed at many Chinese innovation-based start-ups with regard to their innovativeness compared to start-ups based in North America or Europe. Some commentators argue that entrepreneurs in the Chinese high-tech sector are more risk averse than those overseas, and tend to mimic successful business models of start-ups from overseas, rather than develop innovative business models of their own.[30] A number of reasons have been highlighted for the proposition that the Chinese are unwilling to think out of the box and develop innovative new business models. The first relates to the fact that Chinese culture is significantly influenced by Confucian values such as deference to hierarchy, emotional control and obedience, values that are not naturally compatible with entrepreneurship. Confucianism values knowledge as something that should be shared (a social good), rather than something than could be commoditised and protected under the law.[31] This acts as a disincentive for individuals to engage in innovation and constrains entrepreneurial activity.

The second factor that constrains innovation-based entrepreneurship is the Chinese education system, a product of Confucian values that emphasises rote learning and memorisation over creativity. At present, entrepreneurial education remains a fairly new concept in the Chinese education sector. There is general agreement that more entrepreneurship education is necessary at all levels from elementary school to university to foster entrepreneurship. The university sector in particular should consider following the model used in the US and the United Kingdom by constructing comprehensive entrepreneurship education programmes, hosting entrepreneurs-in-residence and encouraging student entrepreneurship through start-up labs.[32]

The third factor constraining innovation-based entrepreneurship relates to the *One Child Policy* adopted by government authorities in the late 1970s. Recent research suggests this has resulted in a generation of people who do not have the entrepreneurial drive and risk-taking attitude of their predecessors.[33]

However, copying business models already developed in other countries could also be considered a sensible and effective strategy for many entrepreneurs. China is still in the process of transition from a planned to a market economy, and demonstrates aspects of each economic system that can generate contradictions and ambiguities in how markets work. Some industries are still protected and heavily regulated by the state, and state-owned enterprises receive favours and resources that enable them to become huge and thus dominant in certain sectors, such as oil and gas. In addition, despite passing of a property law in 2007 that recognises private ownership, private entrepreneurs cannot always be confident that this legislation will be upheld and that government will recognise their rights. Expropriation of assets and businesses by the state continues. In addition, the consumer market, although growing quickly, is relatively immature. Under these circumstances, taking a proven business model that works in another country and applying it to China makes a lot of sense. It reduces the risk that the venture will fail, even when the model needs to be adapted to local conditions. It also allows new venture founders to assess the viability of a model borrowed from elsewhere in China itself. Moreover, borrowing a model from elsewhere does not mean that the model is exactly the same. All business models need adaptation to different markets, and this is particularly so in China, which is a distinctive and unique case of economic development. Examples of successful businesses that took models from elsewhere and made them work in China abound. One of the most successful is ctrip.com, which took its original business model from the US travel website Priceline. Although Ctrip essentially began with the same model as Priceline, it has since developed and adapted that model for success in China. For example, Ctrip has developed a much wider after-sales support presence in key cities and travel nodes, which is essential to business success, and it has also upgraded its website considerably to offer wider and better functionality to users. As it has done this, it has developed its own business model for the Chinese market. Budget hotels such as HomeInns have a similar story, initially modelled on budget hotel and motel chains in the US, but over time adapting these models to China, which has its own patterns of business and internal travel.

Another challenge facing the sector, which has resulted from overinvestment by venture capitalists and angel investors looking to buy into the latest hot industry, is intense competition between innovation-based start-ups for the same consumers. This has led to unhealthy competition between start-ups in the form of price cuts as they seek to build up market share, and has ultimately resulted in bankruptcy for a growing number of enterprises. Intense competition has also led to a recent wave of mergers between start-ups within sectors such as Didi Dache and Kuaidi Dache (taxi-hailing apps) and across sectors such as Meituan and Dianping (food delivery and group buying apps) as these businesses seek to build economies of scale.[34] In these cases, forced collaboration can be of benefit to emerging tech companies, because they create larger businesses that are better able to take market share and attract investment. Although the funding sources for technology-based start-ups have improved in places like Zhongguancun, start-ups outside the main technology zones continue to face challenges in accessing adequate sources of finance.

Social entrepreneurship

As a result of the transition from a centrally planned to a market economy, China has experienced rapid economic growth. However, this has been accompanied by a whole host of environmental and social problems. In addition, the shrinking welfare state has meant than there is much less social protection than in the past, when these services were offered to individuals by their own work unit (*danwei*). Greater prosperity has generated growing pressure on public services as people live longer, diet and obesity are a greater problem and the effects of pollution have taken hold. To address such problems, foreign organisations such as the British Council, non-government organisations (NGOs) in China such as Non-profit Incubator (NPI), YouChange and the Foundation for Youth Social Entrepreneurship, and academic institutions such as the Social Enterprise Research Centre Beijing, have begun to highlight the importance of fostering social entrepreneurship, and provide training for social entrepreneurs.

Globally, social entrepreneurship has emerged as an important cultural and economic phenomenon over the last decade.[35] Social enterprises are those that engage in business to address social problems while maintaining a focus on meeting commercial objectives.[36] In the Chinese context, most social enterprises achieve social impact through employing individuals from marginalised groups such as disabled people, migrant workers, retired farmers and victims of domestic violence.

In China, the British Council was one of the first organisations to introduce the idea of social entrepreneurship through its *Skills for Social Entrepreneurs Programme*.[37] Under this programme, the British Council supports social entrepreneurs by providing professional mentoring and access to funding opportunities through their global partners. Similarly, the NPI has fostered social entrepreneurship by providing office space and capacity building training to social entrepreneurs in sectors of the economy including healthcare, education, environmental protection, and employment and disability services. It has over 200 employees working across China and partners with local governments and business consultants such as JP Morgan to provide social enterprises with access to capital. Since 2007 it has amassed funds from large corporate partners and supported more than 300 social enterprises. In 2010 it developed the Shanghai Social Innovation Park, and its success led NPI to establish the Nest at Shanghai Gongyi Xiantiandi in conjunction with the local government. The Nest acts as an incubator for social entrepreneurship, bringing together around 50 social enterprises in one physical space and supporting them to scale up their operations. As well as providing management training, the Nest encourages social enterprises to collaborate and share ideas.

Youchange is another organisation that supports social entrepreneurship in China. It was established in 2008 and is funded by private donations from entrepreneurs in mainland China, Hong Kong and Taiwan. As well as providing grants for social enterprises in their early stages of development, it established the Centre for Social Innovation, which provides skills-based training for social entrepreneurs, works with universities to deliver classes on social entrepreneurship and organises the Social Innovation Carnival in Shanghai together with NPI to raise awareness of social entrepreneurship among the general population.

The Foundation for Youth Social Entrepreneurship also does a great deal to support social entrepreneurship in China. Established in 2008, it seeks to develop and implement innovative programmes that assist social entrepreneurs to grow their businesses while tackling pressing social and environmental issues. For example, from 2010 to 2012 it developed an incubator programme called the *Paragon Fellowship* through which young entrepreneurs in China and other Asian countries were provided with the training and tools to expand their businesses through scaling their social innovations. In recent years it has developed similar programmes to help female social entrepreneurs. This programme assists women to identify entrepreneurial opportunities and supports them in the start-up phase of their businesses.

Even though we have witnessed a growth in the number of social enterprises, China is home to very few mature social enterprises. According to the 2012 China Social Enterprise Report, more than half of the surveyed social enterprises in China were less than three years of age.[38] In addition, most social enterprises are located in urban areas, with two-thirds situated in Beijing and Shanghai, and the remaining third largely located in other large cities. The introduction of a new law that imposes security controls on foreign NGOs has also affected the nascent social enterprise sector, as foreign NGOs that support social enterprise development become increasingly reluctant to expand their operations in China.

Models of social enterprise

Although some countries have begun to develop legal frameworks for social enterprises, China has yet to introduce specific legislation to govern their operation.[39] As a result, social enterprises in China are typically registered as non-profit organisations or commercial enterprises.[40] This makes it difficult to determine the size of the social enterprise sector in China. In the early stages of its development, the sector primarily consisted of non-profit organisations looking to develop sustainable business models that were commercially viable. If a social enterprise chooses to register as a non-profit – referred to in Chinese as a social organisation (*shehui zuzhi*) – it is able to choose between three legal forms: social organisations (*shehui tuanti*); civil non-enterprise institutions (*minban fei qiye danwei*) or foundations (*jijinhui*). However, social enterprises are increasingly choosing not to register as social organisations because of legal and regulatory barriers imposed by the government to limit their numbers. Instead, many registered as commercial enterprises when starting up their operations.[41] This provides them with a greater degree of legitimacy, but prevents them from accessing government support and utilising donations to fund their operations.

Case study – Canyou Group

Shenzhen Canyou Group is a group-based organisation that is made up of 32 social enterprises operating in the software, cartoon and e-commerce industries. It also has overseas operations in 11 countries. It was established by Zheng Weining in 1999 to provide employment for disabled people who found it difficult to access mainstream employment. It has grown from an organisation with five employees to one employing more than 3,700 employees across the world, of which 95 per cent have disabilities. Although Canyou Group began by providing an internet service to disabled people across China, through the recruitment of talented employees over time it was able to establish a number of high-tech subsidiaries. Although its subsidiaries are registered as commercial enterprises, the Zheng Weining Charitable Foundation owns 90 per cent of their shares. Canyou provides dividends to the foundation that are then used to invest in charitable projects and in the establishment of additional subsidiaries.

Financing of social enterprises

One of the key challenges faced by social enterprises is acquiring adequate access to financing for their business. For example, the Foundation for Youth Social Entrepreneurship found that in 2012, only 43 per cent of businesses achieved financial sustainability and many relied on handouts from friends and family to maintain their business.[42]

In recent years there has been a growth in the number of philanthropic foundations that invest in social impact initiatives by providing early-stage financing to social enterprises. In 2012, there were over 2,700 foundations in China, of which more than half were established by private individuals. Foreign foundations such as the Ford Foundation and Ashoka have also actively funded social enterprises in China.

As well as providing direct funding, a number of organisations have set up specific programmes to provide seed funding to social entrepreneurs. For example, in 2013, the British Council and its partners in China set up the *Social Investment Platform* to facilitate social impact investment and provide support for promising social enterprises in China identified through a multi-stage competition. Under this framework, social investment partners assist social enterprises to scale up their businesses through the provision of angel financing and hands-on consultancy. In the first two years, nine partners provided over 19 million RMB in debt and equity investments and incubation support to 33 social enterprises through the platform, and by 2015 the platform had expanded to 12 partners. For example, Innovate 99 Impact Investment Consulting invested in Lang Dyslexic School in Beijing and in Golden Home Care Services in Fuzhou City. These services meet growing social needs but operate on a commercial model where users pay for services. Innovate 99 was founded by Steve Koon, a graduate in social entrepreneurship from Harvard Kennedy School. Yu Venture Philanthropy has also invested in a number of projects with the British Council including Golden Wings – a social enterprise that uses art therapy to improve the lives of disabled children and sells their artwork to fund its operations – and Xixiang Women's Development Association, which provides microfinance and training to underprivileged women in Shaanxi Province. The latter was founded by Robin Zhang, a former consultant with the Boston Consulting Group.

Similarly, the NPI supports social entrepreneurship through its venture philanthropy fund. It provides grants to start-up social enterprises and has funded projects such as China Dolls, a social enterprise that sells postcards through retail outlets and e-commerce platforms to support the families of children with rare diseases; and 1 Kilogram, a travel agency that encourages voluntourism by arranging for its clients to visit rural schools and make donations to local schoolchildren.

Challenges faced by social enterprises

As highlighted earlier, one of the key challenges faced by the social enterprise sector is obtaining adequate access to finances for their operations. This influences their ability to scale up their business and expand into new areas of the country. At present, most social enterprises are located in the large metropolitan areas of the country, such as Beijing and Shanghai, and operate only at the city or village level.[43] Few have been able to scale up and operate at the national level, and make a contribution to the economies of lesser developed areas of the country where they can have the largest impact. The social enterprise sector is relatively small in the west of the country, where social entrepreneurs have limited access to education, mentorship, advice networks and philanthropic support.[44]

In addition, the lack of legal recognition for social enterprises means many of them are unable to benefit from tax exemptions when run as commercial enterprises. In a 2015 survey of social entrepreneurs by SEFORÏS (Social Entrepreneurship as a Force for more Inclusive and Innovative Societies), 47 per cent of respondents highlighted government policy or the lack of such policy as a severe or momentous challenge to their operation.[45] The lack of a supportive policy framework for social enterprises means that many of them are unable to achieve financial sustainability, with less than half of social enterprises being profitable.

Another challenge faced by social enterprises is in attracting and retaining human capital with adequate skills and knowledge.[46] This challenge results from the fact that social enterprises are unable to match the salaries of commercial enterprises when competing for staff with the right mix of skills and experience. According to a recent survey, around 52 per cent of social enterprises viewed this as a severe challenge and 21 per cent, a significant challenge. This challenge leads many social enterprises to rely on volunteers to do a significant proportion of their work, and means they are unable to build up a team of experienced and committed full-time employees to support the growth of the enterprise.

Future of social enterprise in China

The social enterprise sector is likely to grow over the next decade as local and national governments look to support innovative ways of addressing social problems that result from growing inequality in Chinese society, especially in rural areas of the country where levels of poverty are higher. The legitimacy of social enterprise in the eyes of the people and its popularity as a business model are being enhanced, as the media and academia devote increased attention to social enterprise. A growing number of universities have developed education programmes for social entrepreneurs, and research institutes focusing on social enterprises.[47] These developments will continue to lead many non-profits to become social enterprises and focus more on being commercially minded and market oriented.

However, there are also concerns that government authorities in China may not support the growth of the social enterprise sector, if it means allowing private organisations – which influence the social welfare of individuals and communities – to operate autonomously outside the state system. Recent political developments, including the crackdown on foreign NGOs, many of which are actively involved in China's social enterprise sector, suggest that Chinese government authorities see independent social forces within civil society as a threat to their authority. These developments suggest that the social enterprise sector is likely to grow, but only under high levels of government supervision.

To fully reap the benefits of social enterprise, the sector needs to consider innovative models such as social franchising or open source replication, which allow social entrepreneurs to scale up quickly and ensure their business models have the greatest impact.[48] Social enterprises will also benefit from the provision of support and training to enable them to measure the social impact of their business activities. This may be done through the establishment of social enterprise incubators by government authorities. Local and provincial governments can also help the social enterprise sector to grow by providing contracts to social enterprises and ensuring they are paid market rates for their services. They can also reduce the red tape faced by social enterprises and make it easier for them to expand outside their city of registration.[49]

According to commentators, sectors of the economy that hold the most promise for social enterprises include education, medical care and elderly care, as these have the greatest potential to be scaled up.

Other models of entrepreneurship

Although we have introduced three important models of entrepreneurship in this chapter, we must keep in mind that such models account for less than half of all private sector activity in China. As highlighted in Chapter 2 sole trading enterprises (*getihu*) with fewer than seven employees count for less than half of all employment in China. As in all countries, these individually run enterprises account for a significant proportion of GDP and their importance is often overlooked by scholars examining the phenomenon of entrepreneurship in China.

Notes

1 Li, H 2013, 'History and development of entrepreneurship in China', in T Zhang & RR Stough (eds), *Entrepreneurship and economic growth in China*, World Scientific, Singapore.
2 Walcott, SM 2007, 'Wenzhou and the third Italy: entrepreneurial model regions', *Journal of Asia-Pacific Business*, vol. 8, no. 3, pp. 23–35.
3 Parris, K 1993, 'Local initiative and national reform: the Wenzhou model of development', *The China Quarterly*, vol. 134, pp. 242–263.
4 Liu, APL 1992, 'The "Wenzhou model" of development and China's modernization', *Asian Survey*, vol. 32, no. 8, pp. 696–711.
5 Yang, Q 2012, *The development of entrepreneurship in China*, Lambert, Berlin.
6 Yang, Q 2012.
7 Chen, W 2007, 'Does the colour of the cat matter? The red hat strategy in China's private enterprises', *Management & Organization Review*, vol. 3, no. 1, pp. 55–80; Xin, KR & Pearce, JL 1996, '*Guanxi*: connections as substitutes for formal institutional support', *Academy of Management Journal*, vol. 39, no. 6, pp. 1641–1658.
8 Tsai, K 2002, *Back-alley banking: private entrepreneurs in China*, Cornell University Press, Ithaca, NY.
9 Liu, YL 1992, 'Reform from below: the private economy and local politics in the rural industrialization of Wenzhou', *The China Quarterly*, vol. 130, pp. 293–316.
10 Carlisle, E & Flynn, D 2005, 'Small business survival in China: *guanxi*, legitimacy, and social capital', *Journal of Developmental Entrepreneurship*, vol. 10, no. 1, pp. 79–96.
11 Wang, Z 2006, 'The growth of China's private sector: a case study of Zhejiang Province', *China & World Economy*, vol. 14, no. 3, pp. 109–120.
12 Anderlini, J 2011, 'A workshop on the wane', *Financial Times*, 16 October; Tsai, KS 2016, 'Cosmopolitan capitalism: local state–society relations in China and India', *The Journal of Asian Studies*, vol. 74, no. 2, pp. 335–361.
13 Rabinovitch, S 2011, 'Wenzhou factories adapt to the times', *Financial Times*, 10 July.
14 'Flame flickering out for Wenzhou's lighter industry', 2012, *Want China Times*, 22 January.
15 Li, J 2011, 'When Wenzhou sneezes', *New China*, December.
16 Yang, Q 2012.
17 Zuo, M 2015, 'How China's young entrepreneurs are "overthrowing tradition" to revitalise business through technology', *South China Morning Post*, 30 April.
18 Wei, YHD 2010, 'Beyond new regionalism, beyond global production networks: remaking the Sunan model, China', *Environment & Planning C: Government & Policy*, vol. 28, pp. 72–96.
19 Yang, Q 2012.
20 Walcott, SM 2007.
21 Deng, Z, Hofman, O & Newman, A 2013, 'Ownership concentration and product innovation in Chinese private SMEs', *Asia-Pacific Journal of Management*, vol. 30, no. 3, pp. 717–734.
22 Ho, T & Qi, M 2013, *The EY G20 Entrepreneurship Barometer 2013: China*. Ernst and Young, Beijing.
23 Ho, T & Qi, M 2013.
24 Eesley, CE 2009, 'Entrepreneurship and China: history of policy reforms and institutional development', Stanford University Working Paper, Stanford, CA.
25 Li, H, Zhang, Y, Li, Y, Zhou, LA & Zhang, W 2012, 'Returnees versus locals: who perform better in China's technology entrepreneurship?' *Strategic Entrepreneurship Journal*, vol. 6, pp. 257–272.
26 Ho, T & Qi, M 2013.
27 Chaney, J 2015, 'Shenzhen: China's start-up city defies skeptics', *CNN*, 24 June.
28 Whitwell, T 2014, 'Inside Shenzhen: China's Silicon Valley', *The Guardian*, 13 June.
29 Bea, F 2014, 'Inside Innoconn: Foxconn's new hardware startup incubator', *CNET*, 27 May.

30 Abrami, RM, Kirby, WC & McFarlan, FW 2014, 'Why China can't innovate', *Harvard Business Review*, vol. 92, no. 3, pp. 107–111; Thompson, C 2015, 'How a nation of tech copycats transformed into a hub for innovation' *Wired*, 29 December.
31 Lehman, JA 2006, 'Intellectual property rights and Chinese tradition section: philosophical foundations', *Journal of Business Ethics*, vol. 69, pp. 1–9.
32 Bastin, M 2014, 'Entrepreneurship education needed in China' *Financial Times*, 31 January.
33 Cameron, L, Erkal, N, Gangadharan, L & Meng, X 2013, 'Little emperors: behavioral impact of China's One Child Policy', *Science*, vol. 339, 22 February, pp. 953–957.
34 Tan, V 2016, 'China's tech startups poised for a tough 2016', *Channel News Asia*, 25 January.
35 Dacin, PA, Dacin, MT & Matear, M 2010, 'Social entrepreneurship: why we don't need a new theory and how we move forward from here', *Academy of Management Perspectives*, vol. 24, no. 3, pp. 37–57.
36 Weerawardena, J & Mort, GS 2006, 'Investigating social entrepreneurship: a multi-dimensional model', *Journal of World Business*, vol. 41, pp. 21–35.
37 Zhao, M 2012, 'The social enterprise emerges in China', *Stanford Social Innovation Review*, Spring 2012, pp. 30–35.
38 Zhao, Z 2014, *The state of social entrepreneurship in China: SEFORÏS country report*, The European Union.
39 Yu, X 2011, 'Social enterprise in China: driving forces, development patterns and legal framework', *Social Enterprise Journal*, vol. 7, no. 1, pp. 9–32; Zhao, Z 2014.
40 *China social enterprise and impact investment report*, 2013, Social Enterprise Resource Centre, Beijing.
41 Shieh, S & Deng, G 2011, 'An emerging civil society: the impact of the 2008 Sichuan earthquake on the grass-roots associations in China', *The China Journal*, vol. 65, pp. 181–194.
42 Elliott, D 2013, 'The rise of social entrepreneurship in China', *The New Global Citizen*, 2 May.
43 Zhao, Z 2014.
44 Lane, A 2012, *China social enterprise report 2012*, Foundation for Youth Social Entrepreneurship, Beijing.
45 Zhao, Z 2014.
46 Zhao, Z 2014.
47 Lane, A 2012.
48 Hubbard-Miles, N & Yang, L 2015, 'Social enterprise in China: an interview with Michael Norton', *The Guardian*, 18 February; Brubaker, R & Li, F 2014, *Scaling social entrepreneurship in China*, International Centre for Social Franchising, Shanghai.
49 Brubaker, R & Li, F 2014. 'The shape of social enterprise in China', 2015, *The Guardian*, 7 May.

5

CHINA'S MARKET DYNAMICS

Domestic competition and international expansion

Introduction

This chapter explores the competitive behaviours and growth strategies of emerging Chinese businesses, examining both domestic competition in China and international expansion. China's domestic competition is intense, and has several aspects that are particular to China. Some of these give an advantage to indigenous businesses, partly because of their local knowledge and partly because of their cultural understanding of China. State protection and support of some sectors, as well as management of information and certain technologies, also give local businesses advantages that have enabled successful entrepreneurial endeavours in China. Competition has driven improvements in performance and placed greater emphasis on innovation. The chapter also examines the process by which Chinese businesses have moved from a model of low-cost exporting to building brands and market presences in a wide range of international markets, including high-, middle- and low-income countries.

China's markets are highly competitive, with most major global businesses active, alongside entrepreneurial private Chinese businesses, government-supported state-owned enterprises (SOEs), and smaller enterprising businesses from the West and other Asian countries. Some of these businesses are aggressive price discounters who can absorb low margins or losses for sustained periods. Although demand is high, competition is intense and increasing.

The rise in the number of private ventures operating in China, alongside the market influence of SOEs, means that indigenous competition is strong. Foreign entrants intensify this competition as they seek market share and niches. As discussed later in this chapter, local private enterprises are becoming more sophisticated, better managed and able to deploy a combination of technical skills and local knowledge to develop business models and products that are highly competitive in

China. Success in Chinese markets is hard won and does not come easily to local businesses or new entrants from overseas.

Domestic economic growth and the rise of the consumer economy

China is growing at lower rates than during its earlier years of economic reform. This has been reported as the country's economic slowdown and the start of a shift to a much slower pace of development. However, this representation exaggerates the pace of the slowdown, and does not reflect the continued dynamism and strength of the Chinese economy. Even in this 'new normal' of annual growth rates of six to seven per cent, China is one of the most rapidly expanding economies in the world, outpacing the West by some margin. Growth at rates above other large economies is likely to persist for some time, even though over time there will be convergence with a slower overall global growth rate.[1] Convergence will be gradual and so is likely to occur over several decades, rather than in the next few years. In the near future, and indeed over the next two decades or so, China will continue to be one of the most successful economies in the world, growing at rates higher than the global average and most likely higher than all of the world's mature economies. Suggestions that China is cooling quickly and has moved beyond its period of economic growth are exaggerated and appear unlikely to reflect actual development patterns for some time into the future.

This continued growth is having a significant and positive impact on consumer incomes and consumption. Official inflation rates have been consistently lower than wage rises for much of the recent period of economic growth, and, since 2008, inflation has oscillated around two per cent per annum, with some yearly rises to close to three per cent. Over the same period, wage rises have slowed – from around 15 per cent per year between the late 1990s and late 2000s, to around 10 to 12 per cent in recent years. In other words, over the last 20 years or so, real wage growth has been high and sustained, transforming the personal and household incomes of many Chinese people and families. This has led to a marked increase in gross domestic product (GDP) per capita since the mid-1990s, reflecting rising personal incomes. This has been most notable since 2007 to 2008, when GDP per capita was around $2,000 US dollars (USD). Since then, it has quadrupled to $8,000 USD in 2016.[2]

The effects on personal consumption, and hence on growth in the service sector, have been significant and are still relatively new. With personal incomes increasing at these rates, both consumer and business demand will drive future economic growth. Over time, continued increases in household and personal incomes will produce greater balance between business-to-business growth and personal consumption, creating a more diversified and hence more stable base for economic development. The Chinese government is supporting the shift to a more consumer-focused economy, with a larger and more competitive service sector; however, the overall trend outlined above indicates that this will happen regardless of state intervention and policy.

Continued growth at rates above most other economies means that domestic markets are still dynamic and highly competitive, with established businesses competing against new ventures, new entrants and existing competitors. Indeed, as growth has slowed and new start-ups have developed innovative business models, competition has increased in most sectors in China. In many industries, successful businesses have been forced to develop strategies to overcome aggressive price-cutting from rivals that has reduced corporate profitability. These three dynamics – tighter economic growth, an explosion of new businesses, and incremental improvement of business strategies in successful companies – have combined to create conducive conditions for continued market development and growth.

This looks set to continue, as China becomes more entrepreneurial and the private sector continues to expand. Rates of business start up have rapidly increased since simplification of registration procedures in 2014, creating more new ventures and more 'churn' in the economy as these businesses either grow or fold.[3] The private sector – and in particular new firms – now generate more than eight out of ten new jobs and account for an increasingly dominant proportion of economic activity and output. The private sector's continued expansion is the most likely source of future GDP growth as other parts of the economy slow.[4] Should current trends continue, China will become a private enterprise economy, apart from a small number of huge state-owned and sponsored enterprises, concentrated in strategic industries and markets where economies of scale bring benefits to the largest corporations.

The continued role of state-owned and controlled enterprises

This economic structure – of very large state-owned and controlled enterprises (SOCEs), sitting alongside an entrepreneurial and dynamic private sector – will be somewhat similar to Japan and South Korea, although the state will play a much greater role in the control and development of SOCEs in China. In Japan, cross-ownership created large *keiretsu* (literally 'headless combined network')[5] business associations, made up of inter-dependent companies, and led to the emergence of the *kigyo shudan* (literally 'horizontally diversified business groups') corporations, which became major global corporations with significant market shares in industries such as heavy engineering and automotive production.[6] These corporations were private, yet supported through industrial development strategies and economic policy by the Japanese government – most notably through the Ministry of International Trade and Industry, which promoted specific industrial sectors and supported emerging corporations within them. In Korea, the government sponsored the emergence of a small number of large corporations in manufacturing and engineering that have since become dominant in their domestic markets and have secured global market share. Typically family owned, these *chaebol* (literally 'wealth or property faction or clan', but generally translated as conglomerate) account for a larger proportion of the domestic Korean economy than do China's SOCEs. Both corporate structures have produced corruption and ambiguities in relations between government officials and managers that cause public and governance problems.

In many ways, the current and likely future economic structure of China faces comparable problems arising from the existence of huge corporations that dominate their industries. Corruption and governance ambiguities are commonplace in all three systems as a result of this structure. However, China's economic structure may have some advantages over Japan's and Korea's that mean that domestic competition will become more regulated by markets than the state over time. For example, in Japan, the large corporations influence a much larger proportion of the domestic economy through both the cross-ownership structures of the *keiretsu* system and the development of mature and long-standing supply chains that tie many smaller manufacturing and engineering businesses to the *kigyo shudan* corporations. In Korea, the 10 largest *chaebol* – in particular Samsung and Hyundai – accounted for 80 per cent of the economy in 2011, up from just over 50 per cent in 2002.[7] This level of extreme concentration of economic activity in a very small number of huge corporations has squeezed out many smaller and medium-sized enterprises, presenting a risk of over-reliance on the performance of these corporate entities. Moreover, an economy dominated by huge, typically bureaucratic corporations is less likely to be adaptable and innovative than an economy with a dynamic private sector of growing and new enterprises that are developing new business models, products and services.

In China, SOCEs are increasingly limited to a small number of sectors – in particular energy, extraction, heavy industry, aerospace – where their global market shares and competitiveness are notably weaker than their Japanese and Korean equivalents. The political economy of these SOCEs dominating strategic industries reinforces this, as the Chinese government seeks to secure resources and key industrial inputs in response to its concerns about whether these commodities and products could be procured from other countries should political relationships change or deteriorate. In other words, the driver for the emergence of SOCEs in China is more about ensuring access to and availability of essential energy and materials, as well as basic industrial products, than it is about creating dominant corporations that control specific sectors.

The emergence of the private sector as the dominant economic driver

The private sector has come to dominate most markets and sectors in China, and now accounts for three-quarters or more of the economy. This emergence has been rapid – in 1990, private enterprises accounted for only a small proportion of economic activity, and there were no large private businesses. By 2010, the private sector dominated, and large to very large private companies had emerged as market leaders. This is a strong trend that is continuing at pace, strengthened by recent government policy to ease business registration and ongoing efforts to improve the supply of finance to private entrepreneurs. Based on the recent and ongoing trajectory, private enterprises will account for almost all of the Chinese economy in the next few years because of their growth and expansion as a population, even though many SOCEs also continue to grow and dominate their particular sectors of the economy. Thus, China's future domestic economy will be increasingly characterised by healthy competition by more entrepreneurial private businesses that will generate and exploit economic opportunities that do not place them in direct competition or conflict with the country's huge SOCEs. The scale of China – as a market and in terms of population – enables this situation, creating a large domestic market with many sectors and opportunities for business start up and growth.

As well as a surge in domestic new firm registrations and private sector expansion overall, there is also growing competition from overseas businesses investing and setting up in China. Most large international businesses now have a presence in China and, in recent years, there have been increases in the number of small and medium-sized businesses that have established a presence in China – either to sell products and services or to manufacture or source products. In particular, there has been a shift from considering China a low-cost manufacturing hub to one of the largest and fastest-growing domestic markets in the world. Although most manufacturers continue to produce goods in China for export to other markets, an increasing number of these and other businesses see China as their target market, in both business-to-business and consumer markets. The Chinese government continues to gradually open up the domestic market to businesses from other countries by relaxing registration and reporting requirements. This is now extending into sectors that were previously carefully controlled and monitored, such as e-commerce and digital business.[8] We can expect a growing number of non-Chinese businesses to enter China, and for these and existing ventures to seek to secure greater sales and market share. The shift towards seeing China as the world's most attractive domestic market (which is underway, but not yet attained) will continue, making domestic competition greater, but also introducing new practices and best practice into China. Domestic businesses will learn from these practices and become more competitive as a result.

Overall there is strong competition in China's domestic markets, and this will continue to intensify as Chinese entrepreneurs and managers and overseas businesses enhance their business models and competitive practices. Many of the most successful businesses face daily under-cutting on price by competitors who are ready to discount their prices aggressively in order to secure market share, attack incumbent businesses or generate sales. For many of these businesses, price-cutting is not a sustainable strategy, and those who persist will encounter bankruptcy or business closure. For businesses to be successful in this context – where there will always be competitors who will compete on price – sustainability depends on developing strategies that do not lead to price reductions, but instead focus on other aspects of business strategy. Inevitably, this type of competition will lead to higher levels of 'churn', as companies go out of business. However, for those that survive and develop business models and strategies that can overcome competition through discounting, China offers opportunities for hyper-fast growth of successful firms – often at annual growth rates of well over 20 to 30 per cent for sustained periods of at least five years, and frequently longer.[9] The businesses that not only survive, but also thrive, in this hyper-competitive environment will be highly capable and subsequently serious competitors for companies seeking to enter their markets in China.

The spatial nature of China's domestic markets

China is a huge market, with the largest population of consumers in the world, a large and expanding business-to-business market, and one of the world's fastest growth rates, ahead of those in other major economies. These prospects have attracted international businesses and investors over the last four decades, drawn by continually rising demand for products and services, and by the opportunity to secure market share in the world's most dynamic economy. These forays into the China market have not always been as successful as hoped or intended, especially during the early years of economic reform. Many businesses that established substantial presences in China in the 1980s and 1990s found that it took much longer than expected to generate the hoped for profit levels. The rules for foreign businesses kept changing, competition was intense, and building in-country capacity and networks took longer and was costlier than expected. Over time, many of these ventures became profitable and grew; however, the time, cost and effort required to secure market advantage in China tended to be much greater than initially anticipated. Thus, there were considerable up-front costs to enter China and establish a successful market presence for much of the reform period and, although it is less challenging and costly now, successful entry remains a significant undertaking for most international businesses.

This continues to be the case when international businesses seek to establish capacity or networks outside areas where there has been a lot of foreign direct investment in the past, which has created localised infrastructures and support mechanisms that make market entry easier. For example, it is easier for a non-Chinese business to establish a China presence in Pudong, Shanghai, or the Pearl River Delta, where international trade flows are high, than it is in the less developed inland cities and areas of western China. Local knowledge is an essential component of a successful China entry strategy, as is an understanding of the Chinese state and customers. China is a country where it is essential to have contextual understanding of the unique 'national situation' (*guo qing*). However, China is also a large economy made up of local markets and economic areas that are developing at different rates. Local knowledge is as important as an understanding of China's specific national situation. Understanding these differences *within* China, as well as understanding why China is different to other emerging markets globally, is an important factor in ensuring successful market entry.

In addition, China cannot yet be viewed as a single integrated market, even though there has been intense investment in upgrading domestic air, rail and road networks. The patterns of early economic reform – when the coast and in particular the south-eastern provinces were opened up to foreign investment and exporting – have shaped development within China. This has led to inequalities in economic development and wealth across China. The prosperous coastal provinces and major cities (Beijing, Shanghai and Tianjin) have much higher personal incomes and GDP per capita than other parts of China, and in general wealth decreases the further west one travels.

However, spatial inequalities in China are more complex than this east–west transition from greater to lesser prosperity suggests. There is also a strong urban–rural divide, with larger cities being much more developed and prosperous than rural areas. State policy has tended to allocate more resources and privileges to the cities, in particular the largest metropolises, reinforcing this urban–rural divide. In addition, there are high levels of inequality within developed parts of eastern China, generated by wealth creation being concentrated in 'hot spots' of economic and entrepreneurial activity. For example, in Guangdong province, parts of the Pearl River Delta have among the most competitive economies and levels of GDP, whereas parts of western Guangdong province approach the levels of income and economic development seen in some of China's poorest provinces.[10] Even in provinces such as Jiangsu and Zhejiang, which have well-developed and distributed economies, there are surprisingly wide variations in local economic development and prosperity.

Overall, spatial inequalities have intensified in recent years, as GDP per capita has risen, making China much less equal in terms of wealth and income. This is indicated by China's Gini coefficient – the measure of how economic output is shared across a population. In the 1980s, when the egalitarian, yet low, income distributions of the Maoist era continued to influence earnings, the Gini coefficient was below 30, indicating relatively higher income equality than most countries. However, by the 2010s, the coefficient had risen to well above 40 – higher than the US and countries such as Brazil that have very unequal income distributions. China's economic growth has come at the cost of concentrating a large share of these gains in the hands of a small group of citizens. The greatest variations have been between the east and west of the country, and between more remote rural areas and the largest cities.[11] Increasingly, China is becoming a 'multi-speed' economy, and hence market.

Even though these disparities have produced greater income inequalities, they also create internal trading opportunities that will contribute to domestic growth and should, over time, raise growth rates in poorer parts of China. Companies in more prosperous areas, typically eastern China, where entrepreneurs are concentrated and account for a higher proportion of businesses and economic activity, sell products and services to the less prosperous parts of western China that are now seeking to catch up, and so still generally have higher growth rates than the national average. Higher growth rates combined with lower incomes and GDP levels offer opportunities for domestic market expansion for Chinese businesses, although the price and quality of goods and services will be lower than those in wealthier parts of the country. China has its own 'pyramid' of consumers, with many customers towards the bottom of it, as well as a growing number towards the top. These differentiated customer groups generate multiple market opportunities for businesses. Internal trading amplifies increases in incomes in less developed parts of China, subsequently growing these internal markets as less well-off residents increase their personal consumption.

In addition, some foreign investors and local businesses are relocating away from the coast to inland cities, where labour and land costs are lower. The move inland has accelerated as flows of migrant labour from the inland countryside to the coast and big cities have slowed. Along the coast, wages have tended to rise, as the availability of migrant workers has tightened and as demands for higher salaries have led to inflation in pay. This in turn accentuates differences in wage and land costs between the coast and less developed inland areas. A shift inland to benefit from these lower costs creates local economic development opportunities for those areas where investment is concentrated. Cities such as Chengdu, Chongqing and Xian are benefiting particularly with this shift inland of business investment, and have become vibrant economic growth nodes in their own right. However, it should be stressed that the vast proportion of foreign investment still goes to the Pearl River Delta, Yangzi River Delta around Shanghai-Pudong, and Bohai economic area incorporating Beijing and Tianjin.[12]

As national growth slows and labour costs rise along the coast, further moves of investment inland are likely to generate higher growth rates in some parts of western China – mostly the larger cities – that should allow these places to catch up with the prosperous coast, at least to some extent. This will be driven by state investment and policies to incentivise private investment inland, as well as decisions by businesses to either relocate or set up subsidiaries away from the coast.[13] Although it is unlikely that all or even most parts of western China will converge with the east coast in terms of growth and prosperity, higher growth in the western cities and their immediate hinterlands could reduce the gap with the coast, as incomes rise at a faster rate in these urban areas. The extent to which actual income levels can rise, and the degree to which parts of the west can reduce the economic gap with the coast, will determine the future value and scale of the domestic Chinese market, and hence the country's capacity to generate sustained internal growth. If the west continues to lag behind the coast, China's domestic growth potential will be more limited. If the gap continues to be large, or grows even larger, future prospects for growth will be even more limited.

Road, rail, air and digital connections can help domestic convergence and improve economic growth in less developed parts of China. Infrastructure investment is positively associated with higher levels of GDP and contributes to economic growth, although there is a debate as to whether such investments stimulate or respond to growth. In addition, there is some debate about the economic value of individual projects, even if the overall macroeconomic effects are positive.[14] China has a legacy of very large, high-cost projects that have had unclear or poor economic returns when examined on a case-by-case basis. However, enhanced connectivity will improve domestic flows of goods and people.

Although much of this transport and communications development has focused on wealthier parts of the country, expenditure on infrastructure in the west is increasing, especially since the advent of the 'One belt one road' policy to open up trading links through the old Silk Roads.[15] Should this policy be pursued as a key means for China to build overland, as well as maritime, economic links with countries in Eurasia and Europe, western China will be a major beneficiary of high levels of domestic state investment. If this arises, western China is likely to converge more quickly with the more developed east coast.

National investment in infrastructure has tended to follow three patterns. First, investment in infrastructure has placed strong emphasis on connectivity with Beijing as the capital. The high-speed train network and internal domestic flight paths attest to this focus on linking local places with the capital. This may not make economic sense, especially when these locations are distant from Beijing. A capital-centric approach does not recognise the economic geography of China, where concentrations of economic activity and competitiveness lie along the coast, especially around Shanghai and to the south. However, it makes symbolic and political sense, as it reinforces the importance of the capital and its status as China's most important city.

Second, infrastructure investment has been heavily concentrated along the coast and in eastern parts of China, such as Guangdong province and the lower reaches of the Yangzi River. These parts of China are well connected with international trade links and supply chains, and often have ports, roads and distribution centres that are comparable with those in highly developed economies. Much of this investment has focused on improving the flow of goods and people into and out of these specific areas within China. It has also tended to join up settlements within these coastal growth nodes, thereby linking them together and into international supply and travel networks. As a result, these investments have not strengthened internal connectivity beyond the growth nodes anywhere near as much as they have linked these nodes to other markets and international trade flows.

Third, infrastructure has tended to link up local areas, typically by connecting adjacent or proximate cities and the settlements around them. This creates local markets that comprise multiple cities, but does not necessarily improve connectivity with other parts of China. Examples include the Pearl River Delta and its connections with Hong Kong, Shanghai's improving links with settlements along the Yangzi River, and the Beijing–Tianjin corridor. By bringing these areas closer together through investment in high-speed rail and roads, these areas become localised economic entities in their own rights. They are all examples of localised network connections improved by infrastructure investment. However, they tend not to be as effectively linked with other economic areas and settlements within China.

The distribution and travel connections between Hong Kong, the Pearl River Delta and Guangzhou are highly developed and constantly being upgraded and expanded. These links are much more developed than links between Guangdong province and other parts of China, even though Guangzhou is on the main north–south rail line. Multiple forms of transportation – including rail, roads and shipping – have more closely linked the Pearl River Delta and Hong Kong, reducing travel times and congestion considerably. In mid-China, cities such as Hangzhou and Suzhou are increasingly linked with Shanghai and Pudong, which in turn are investing in airport and maritime connectivity with the global economy. Although Shanghai and Beijing are very well linked by air and rail, the connectivity between Shanghai and the lower Yangzi River, on the one hand, and other parts of China, on the other hand, is much less developed than links within this economic area. As investment reinforces these internal linkages in a small number of economic areas, income and GDP differences are likely to grow more in these localised areas than in less connected parts of the China. Over time, China is likely to become a series of local economies, comprising multiple large cities and, to an extent, their hinterlands, within which GDP and overall development is higher than in less connected parts of China.

For these reasons, national distribution is still challenging. Although transport is better than it has been historically – because of massive investment in high-speed rail and domestic flights – China does not yet have a well-connected national distribution and travel infrastructure that enables efficient travel between second- and third-tier cities and their hinterlands. Instead, multiple self-contained economic units are increasingly well connected within themselves, internationally and with Beijing. However, many of these local economic areas are less effectively connected with each other. By improving local connectivity, often by linking up proximate cities or areas where there are concentrations of business activity, China has become a vast market broken up into local concentrations of customers and economic activity. Each of these is a large market, with sizeable populations of consumers and businesses, and levels of output that in some cases compare favourably to the economies of other countries.

Notable examples of these 'local' markets are:

- Greater Beijing and the Beijing–Tianjin corridor, sometimes known as the 'Bohai Basin economic area', when this includes cities such as Tangshan and the ports on the Bohai Sea. With both cities now connected by high-speed train (taking around 40 minutes to travel between them) and improved port facilities on the coast, this is an increasingly connected and powerful economic area. It contains many of the SOEs that have been relocated out of Beijing and Tianjin to smaller cities and towns.
- Greater Shanghai and the Yangzi River Delta: High-speed train connections to Hangzhou, Suzhou and other cities (such as Changzhou and Wuxi), as well as improved road communications along the Yangzi River, have created an increasingly connected economic area, in particular linking up air, rail and road connections through multi-modal transport hubs.
- The Pearl River Delta, Hong Kong and Guangzhou: This is one of the longest-standing local economic areas, and a focus of government policy to develop an export economy from the early days of reform. High-speed rail, major highways and port and distribution facilities increasingly connect these three areas. As a single entity, this area would be one of the world's largest economies. It is dominated by private enterprises and accounts for a large share of China's exports and inward investment.

- Chongqing–Chengdu growth corridor: Both rapidly developing cities in their own rights, investment in high-speed rail and highways has brought these cities closer together and integrated smaller settlements between them into what is emerging as a single economic development area. Direct commercial air connections have been restricted in order to move travellers onto the rail and road connections that have been developed, creating better connectivity within this economic area.

There are other emergent local development areas in China, including a Shenyang–Dalian corridor in Liaoning province, which incorporates nearby industrial cities, such as Anshan; the coastal cities of Fujian province; the cities around Wuhan in central China; and Shandong province's coastal and inland industrial cities. Should the belt and road initiative continue to be pursued, then a further corridor may emerge between Xian and Lanzhou, incorporating cities in between, such as Baoji. This possible economic node is putative at this point, although it would bring together the two largest cities in north-eastern China.

Overall, these emerging economic areas are smaller (although still significant in their own right) and in earlier stages of integration than the more developed examples outlined above. They are likely to emerge as nationally important local economic development areas over the coming decade, as investment improves their internal connectivity. These sub-national economic entities are likely to grow by absorbing smaller settlements around them. As such, they will become more attractive locations for indigenous and international businesses, and will attract domestic and foreign investment as they emerge as important economic nodes inside China.

The fragmentation of the Chinese domestic market is most apparent when considering internal logistics and distribution networks. There are few national logistics companies, and the sector is composed of myriad smaller businesses that operate locally. This creates a dispersed logistics sector, with many small players and few national integrators. Moreover, supply chain management and support services are under-developed in China, with little expertise in this aspect of logistics, even though China supplies almost all of the major global original equipment manufacturers (OEMs) and multinationals with a vast proportion of their goods. Although there are some large logistics firms (such as Li and Fung), they tend to be focused on exports and international supply chains, and spatially concentrated in the Pearl River Delta and greater Shanghai area. A small number of logistics companies (such as Eternal Asia) are building national distribution networks; however, these have been relatively recent developments. Entering China as a national market is constrained by a fragmented and under-developed logistics industry, as well as by the existence of multiple local economic entities.

Thus, China represents a conundrum in terms of the scale and level of connectivity of its internal domestic market. As a single national state (with strong government control and a population that is highly integrated culturally), China is the world's largest market. Demand and consumer tastes are relatively homogenous, creating potential opportunities to generate high volumes of business and sales across the country as a whole. However, in practice, variable and locally focused transport connections and distribution networks mean that, at this point in its development, China is not one single, huge market. Instead, it comprises a series of local economic development areas that are increasingly well integrated internally, but generally not as well connected with other parts of China – in particular other local markets. Some areas are likely to be more linked to overseas markets and international supply chains than to some other parts of China. The challenge for businesses operating in China is to build presences in multiple local markets within the country, and to support the development of national networks that cross these somewhat insulated units in order to secure a significant presence and market share across the whole country.

The effects of liberalisation and state control on markets

Since the start of the reform period in the late 1970s, one of the most consistent and fundamental changes to China's economic system has been increasing liberalisation of markets. Over that period, the state has moved from directly controlling almost all of the economy to relinquishing control over production and sales decisions, and leaving these considerations to the market. As the state has retreated from direct control of the economy, it has created institutions – with varying success – designed to regulate and govern market exchange.[16] The partial introduction of institutions required for effective market exchange, and their varying capabilities, has at times stimulated state intervention and has also created a volatile economy that is subject to bubbles and boom-and-bust cycles that reinforce this volatility. However, this has not stopped the move of the state away from direct intervention in and control of production and consumption. Increasingly, particularly after the financial downturn of 2008, state interventions have focused on improving governance, stimulating and improving macro-economic conditions, and sanctioning corruption and other non-productive forms of extraction. This can be seen in recent fiscal and monetary interventions, as well as in Keynesian stimuli since 2008. These actions have been designed to boost economic activity by improving incentives for businesses to grow and consumers to increase purchases.

In most markets in China, liberalisation will continue, thereby offering greater flexibility for enterprises to compete. This will reduce the constraints on individual businesses, but will also likely encourage more entrants. As a result, competition will be intense and the quality of products and services offered by Chinese businesses – alongside their understanding of the Chinese market, its customers and cultural values – will make entry by foreign businesses challenging. This is yet another Chinese conundrum. As personal prosperity rises, thereby creating demand for more expensive goods and services, competition will also rise, as indigenous businesses and foreign entrants seek to exploit these expansions in China's consumer economy. In other words, as one of the world's largest markets grows even larger, the intensity of competition will make more challenging the ability of individual companies to benefit from this expansion.

However, some markets will continue to be shaped and protected by the state. Oil and gas, telecommunications, the internet and the media will all continue to be sectors where the state is highly active and controlling, both directly and indirectly. In protected sectors, market liberalisation is much less likely and, if it does arise, it will be gradual and determined by the state. In the short- to medium-term at least, and possibly over a longer period, certain industries in China will be state dominated and controlled because they are of strategic importance to the government. Energy is a good example of this because ensuring sufficient power generation to enable economic growth is a primary government concern. China is dependent on oil for its continued growth, yet it has insufficient domestic oil reserves, which emphasises the importance of energy security to the Chinese government. Sectors that affect the performance of the economy or can affect the government's reputation are the most closely controlled. As a result, media and telecommunications are protected because the government is careful to control public opinion about the party and monitor potential sources of competition and conflict.

In addition, the Chinese government owns just over 100 very large SOEs that receive high levels of patronage and protection from the state. Supporting these companies and ensuring they have dominance in their markets is a priority for the state, and influences economic policymaking, as well as decisions by central and local governments. In some sectors, such as energy, almost all key businesses are state owned. This can lead to very close ties between these businesses and government officials. The three state oil companies – China National Petrochemical Company, China Petrochemical (or SinoPec) and China National Offshore Oil Company – are intimately linked with the state. Individuals move between senior positions in huge SOEs such as these and high-ranking positions in the government, thereby reinforcing these links. Similarly, the state has close and controlling relations with the major public banks in China. These businesses and the sectors they dominate are of strategic importance to the state, and will subsequently receive support and protection as considered necessary. Private enterprises that seek to compete against these SOEs, especially in protected sectors, will face challenges and the risk of intervention by the state in order to protect its own corporate interests.

Chinese-style competition

China now has highly competitive markets in most sectors, with many businesses producing and offering improving products, services and experiences. This section explores several common patterns of Chinese competition that are evident in many sectors and markets, each of which have implications for the dynamics of these markets and for the strategies of non-Chinese businesses seeking to compete in China.

Clustering and copycatting

When a business becomes successful in China, a typical reaction is for other businesses to start up that mimic the successful enterprise. These new businesses note the success of the existing venture and copy the business model. As a result, the profit margins of the original enterprise can fall quickly, unless there is sufficient demand to cater for multiple new entrants. This is generally the case in sectors where start-up costs are low, and it is common for restaurants and retailers of products such as household goods and do-it-yourself materials. In most Chinese cities, there are now streets where different businesses that sell the same or very similar products are located. For example, one can walk down a street where there are many shops selling floor and wall tiles, and then turn into another street where shops are selling taps and shower heads.

This 'copycatting' is generally good for customers because it drives down price and pushes businesses to compete more intensively for custom. Over time, it can become beneficial for the businesses too, as they diversify their product range and build complementary foci for their business offer. Taking the example of tiles used above, over time, different retailers on the same street generally start to offer varying styles and materials that are different to other retailers in the same area. This allows some differentiation and ensures that customers have a much wider choice than if all the shops offered broadly the same products. As a result, small clusters emerge, with similar yet increasingly differentiated products and services offered by multiple providers all operating close to each other. These clusters – focused on consumers and small businesses – can be seen in cities and large towns across China.

Copycatting can also be seen in the manufacturing and business-to-business sectors. For example, in the Pearl River Delta, there are locations where manufacturing companies and computer assembly businesses cluster and compete against each other. This provides greater flexibility for the supply chains in this part of China, and keeps costs low. One of the longest-standing and best-known examples of clustering is Wenzhou, which has been a hotspot of private enterprise since the early 1980s. Wenzhou is a world leader in cigarette lighter manufacturing, and has significant clusters in shoe production and small electrical equipment. Both of these clusters, and almost all of the local economy, are composed of private enterprises.[17]

Copycatting can be seen in other industries, including (notably) solar power and wind energy, as well as heavy industry, such as iron and steel. As China strategically developed its solar power industry, supported by central and local governments, many enterprises rushed into this boom industry, thereby creating overcapacity. Although this level of entry and copycatting has established China as the world's largest producer of solar photovoltaic equipment, it has generated excess production capacity. This has led to rationalisation of this industry, with firms closing as enterprises have become insolvent and stopped trading because of price-cutting and insufficient demand to buy all the equipment being produced. From a national perspective, copycatting in emerging and strategic markets has established China as a world leader in many of these sectors. For the individual enterprise, copycatting has created a boom-and-bust cycle that has forced many businesses to close because of excess capacity.

China has a second dimension to this form of mimicry, or copycatting, called '*Shanzhai*'. Literally meaning 'the mountain fortress occupied by outlaws or bandits', this is the fake economy of copying branded products. The *Shanzhai* economy is rife in China, with local companies quickly producing fakes or mimics of a wide range of products soon after they are launched. This ranges from the latest smartphone to fake foods and medicines that can place consumers at real personal risk. As with most aspects of China, *Shanzhai* represents a form of dynamic response to rapid economic growth that has positive and negative aspects. For non-Chinese businesses, *Shanzhai* is a major problem when trading and negotiating with China. It represents an erosion of global brands and a loss of intellectual property that is challenging to businesses and (in the minds of many policymakers, especially those in Western economies) breaches the fundamental bases of international trade and effective market governance.[18] In China itself, *Shanzhai* has been characterised as both positive and negative, indicating some ambivalence.[19] Many commentators have also pointed out that non-Chinese tourists are often avid buyers of 'knock-off' products when travelling in China.

Three specific aspects of *Shanzhai* can illuminate the ambivalence within China to what has been characterised by global agencies and developed economies as a major problem and constraint on deeper economic cooperation. First, it reflects a highly entrepreneurial and opportunistic business sector. Second, reverse engineering expensive and highly branded products, such as electronic devices and luxury goods, allows Chinese businesses to produce copies that they can then sell quickly in a country where more people aspire to these high-end products than can actually afford them. Third, copying high-specification products through reverse engineering builds the technical, design and (over time) innovative capacities of businesses. Indeed, a common feature of the emergence of the East Asian 'tiger' economies since the 1950s has been a transition from copying Western (typically US) products to incremental innovation that emerged from improving the capacity to reverse engineer complex and high-specification products. China appears to be going through a similar phase in its economic development as did economies such as Japan, South Korea and Taiwan.

As well as *Shanzhai* copies, growing consumer demand has triggered new products that have been targeted at lower income individuals and families. Two particular examples are Xiaomi and Huawei, both of which have secured large market shares in China for their smartphones. Xiaomi started producing a smartphone that resembled the iPhone in 2011, and quickly grew to become one of the largest manufacturers in China and the world. It offered a relatively high-specification smartphone at much lower prices than leading brands such as Apple. Huawei developed its Honor brand of lower cost and lower specification smartphones in order to sell to lower income individuals in China and overseas in emerging economies.

This is not to downplay the negative effects of *Shanzhai*, which can be highly problematic for both consumers and businesses. When *Shanzhai* leads to the production and sale of fakes that are damaging to consumers – as has been the case with baby foods – its effects are highly negative and can lead to injury and death. This fake economy sits outside the legal system and is subsequently not subject to the quality assurance and standards of genuine products. Poor-quality fakes, as well as products that are physically damaging to those who buy them, have been a feature of China's economic growth, as unscrupulous entrepreneurs have sought to generate profit in under-regulated and fast-changing markets. In addition, for international businesses, *Shanzhai* leads to loss of intellectual property and sales that have both long- and short-term effects. These threats make China an unwelcoming and challenging market, both to sell into and compete with.

China knowledge and Chinese language

China's business and consumer markets are well established and have grown considerably in recent years. Even with the reduced levels of annual economic growth experienced in China most years since 2009, business and consumer demand continue to grow. Chinese entrepreneurs are well positioned to take advantage of this growth. They understand their markets well, and have more insight into the nature of this demand than businesses based outside China or with a subsidiary presence in the country. They have established and grown their businesses within China, and are embedded in their markets. Moreover, their primary language is mainland Mandarin Chinese (Putonghua), which is the national *lingua franca* and is distinct from dialects and variants spoken in overseas Chinese communities. This gives indigenous entrepreneurs an advantage over overseas Chinese businesspeople seeking to start or grow businesses in China.

Thus, business models that are China-specific (rather than aimed at more than one international market or adapted from other markets to the Chinese context) are more likely to be successful. Wahaha is a producer and seller of health and nutrition drinks that is focused almost exclusively on the domestic market, where it is the dominant brand in its product category. However, the company's products are tailored to the Chinese market and are subsequently less attractive in other countries, thereby constraining the scope for expanding overseas.

One example of a sector where local knowledge and language offer significant advantages to Chinese enterprises is in online services and entertainment. Unlike most other major economies, other than the USA, China has a group of indigenous internet service providers that have outperformed leading global brands, such as Google, eBay and Facebook. Companies such as Alibaba, Sohu and Tencent have created very successful businesses of real scale by focusing on China as their core market. They have recognised the constraints regarding online access and expression imposed by the Chinese government, and have worked within these parameters. This is unlike major international providers and brands, such as Google, which were unable or unwilling to adapt their offer to China's distinctive political and economic context. The 'Chinese firewall' created protected conditions for a domestic digital economy to emerge, populated by businesses that have achieved significant scale. Companies such as Alibaba and Tencent count their users in the hundreds of millions.

There are many examples of very successful businesses that have based their business model on China, and in doing so have outperformed established and successful non-Chinese businesses seeking to enter the country. These businesses, especially in complex industries, such as online services and entertainment, are upgrading their offer and online capacity, and subsequently have the potential to maintain their leadership in their Chinese markets, and expand into other countries in the future. They have developed brands that are well established in China, and in many cases outperform non-Chinese brands.

Manufacturers moving up the value chain

A growing number of successful Chinese businesses are developing branded products and technologies. Historically, many businesses, and especially private enterprises, grew by becoming subcontractors that manufactured at low cost for export. They drove the 'made in China' phenomenon that delivered cheap goods and products to consumers in other countries through much of the reform period in China (and indeed still does). The businesses that were successful not only manufactured at low cost, but also improved their quality, reducing the proportion of defects and imperfections to among the best levels internationally. By entering and succeeding in global supply chains, China's manufacturers became high-quality and low-cost producers of industrial products and consumer goods.

Increasingly, these companies have started to develop their own products and are seeking to build their R&D and innovation capabilities. Often reverse engineering the products they manufactured under contract or license, many of these companies identified improvements they could make themselves and, over time, developed alternative designs that could compete with the products they were making for other companies. These businesses are well placed to compete internationally because they can combine low-cost, high-quality production with an increasing innovation capability. As they develop and refine their products, they will become more competitive, both domestically and internationally.

This trend has been reinforced by a growing pattern of acquisitions of foreign businesses by both private and state-owned Chinese enterprises. In many cases, Chinese businesses have been seeking to secure technology from these acquisitions to apply to their own businesses. Initially, many acquisitions did not lead to the transfer of technologies, in part because of a lack of capacity in the acquiring company to absorb the know-how, techniques and processes that drive technological innovation. However, there is increasing expertise in capturing and harnessing technologies as Chinese businesses become more experienced in technology transfer.[20]

Moving up the value chain is a desirable strategy for many Chinese manufacturers that are experiencing higher production costs. Wages have risen in China and other costs are increasing, such as land, construction and welfare compliance requirements. The average costs of production have risen particularly along the coast, in areas such as the Pearl River Delta. Although large global corporations can move their production in China from the coast to inland provinces and cities, many private enterprises are tied to the communities and locations within which they were founded, and within which the founder entrepreneurs live, work and in many cases were born. These private enterprises are less mobile as a result, and must subsequently adopt or develop higher levels of innovation and technology in order to sustain margins as production costs rise.

'Follow the leader': lower cost, acceptable quality, improving design and technology

Although manufacturers are moving up the value chain, to create their own products and offer integrated solutions, these moves do not necessarily place these businesses at the top of technology expertise in their industries. Instead, many Chinese businesses and sectors have developed a strategy of producing products that are of acceptable (but not the best) quality and technological design, yet are cheaper than higher quality international benchmarks. An example of this is Chinese motorbikes that are not as good quality as their Japanese competitor products, for example, yet are cheaper and of sufficient quality to be durable and useable. Another example is earthmoving equipment, whereby Chinese producers manufacture vehicles that are of sufficient standard to undertake the required removal and construction work, yet are not as expensive or high specification as global leaders, such as Caterpillar. In both motorcycles and earthmoving equipment, China now has a leading market share and dominates many Asian markets.

This is a shift away from the low-cost, lower quality strategy seen in China and the other emerging economies of East Asia during their early years of economic growth. Instead, the approach is to produce something that is 'almost as good as' the benchmark product, yet less expensive. By way of example, a product may be considered – by consumers and the manufacturer – as 75 per cent of the technical specification of a market leader, yet could be profitably sold at 60 per cent of the price. In comparative terms, this gives these manufacturers a market advantage because the specification outperforms the price.

There are examples of this strategy in consumer products across China, such as in household goods and whitegoods. For example, many of China's television producers have moved from low-cost, lower quality to a 'follower'-type strategy, as described above. Although Haier now produces higher quality white goods, in the earlier stages of development, the company sought to improve quality from a low starting point and, in terms of after-sales maintenance and care, continues to be considered by some reviewers to be of lower quality than premium brands. However, the emphasis of Haier on improving quality and being innovative in working practices and product design indicates that the company is seeking to move closer to premium international brands, while still retaining a price advantage.

Many clothing companies in China adopt a 'follower' strategy, moving closer to international design standards, while maintaining a price advantage. Toread – one of the leading outdoor wear producers and retailers in China – is an example of how this 'follower' strategy can lead to rapid increases in performance and at the same time improvements in the design and quality of clothing. The company benchmarks itself against international active outdoor clothing companies, such as Columbia and The North Face in the USA. Although it recognises that these types of companies develop materials and designs that are superior to Toread and many other competitors, the company has sought to use materials and designs that move it closer to its international benchmarks. At this stage, the company is seeking to move closer to these quality benchmarks, while maintaining the price advantage generated by lower production and materials costs.

Successful Chinese businesses – initially in manufacturing, yet increasingly in other sectors – have massively improved the quality of their products. 'Made in China' today indicates products that are of much better reliability, specification and performance than previously. The fast-growing 'follower' businesses in China are now improving their design and creating more innovative products, albeit generally not quite at the level of international benchmarks. This strategy indicates that these enterprises are building their capacity to innovate. This is very different to the low-cost, low-quality production approach that typified much of 'made in China' in the 1980s and 1990s.

China's innovators

Alongside the 'follower' strategy of tracking international benchmarks, there are an increasing number of businesses, typically private, in China that are truly innovative – both domestically and globally. Many of China's leading web-based internet service providers – some of which we discussed earlier in this chapter – have developed innovative provider models that have secured major market share and large user numbers domestically. As well as Alibaba, Sina Weibo and Sohu, Tencent's app innovations (including in particular WeChat) and those of other ventures (such as Didi Chuxing – a merging of two services to become China's 'Uber') have created an online communication and trading environment that is more advanced than in most other countries.

One of the strongest examples of business as well as product innovation has been in the handheld smartphone sector. The emergence of Xiaomi – established in 2011 and, by 2014, the third-largest producer of smartphones in the world – has stimulated new ventures that have grown at explosive rates. Oppo and Vivo have followed Xiaomi in developing their own handsets, with the former succeeding in international low- to middle-income markets, and both becoming top-five producers in China. All three firms have created highly successful smartphones that have generated sales in the tens of millions in China. As well as developing distinctive new products, these companies' business models have been innovative. Xiaomi is focused on lower income, more rural consumers – hence the name, which literally means 'little millet' or 'rice' – and has a business model that cuts the price of the handset, yet generates profits from after-sales support, services and enhancements. Oppo has started to compete with Apple's iPhone as a prestigious smartphone. These enterprises are innovative in terms of both their business models and products, and are highly sensitive to demand and market dynamics. With their local knowledge of consumers and production, they are considerable competitors to major global brands, such as Apple. In some sectors – particularly consumer electronics and online services – Chinese enterprises are at the forefront of innovation globally.

Opportunity seizers

China remains a dynamic and turbulent market, where new ventures start and close on a regular basis. This 'churn' in business formation means that the individual entrepreneurial venture itself is quite fragile, even though the overall emergence of entrepreneurs as the primary generator of China's wealth and employment continues. In other words, there is a divide between the overall positive effects of a fast-growing economy on private enterprise formation, and the uncertainties and risks of setting up a venture in this uncertain environment.

Often, in these conditions, entrepreneurs find that the original proposition they developed does not quite work in the way they had hoped or expected, or that demand has changed quickly, making the initial product or service obsolete. In this environment, sticking with a business plan will not work and can place the enterprise at risk. Instead, being focused on market opportunities and the nature of customer demand – and how both keep changing – is a logical and understandable reaction. Entrepreneurs who are successful in this way react to the market and how it changes, and in doing so can fundamentally alter their business. Some of these businesses can grow quickly to become considerable businesses in their own right.

China is full of micro-sized household enterprises that change and adapt their business, as well as large companies that completely refocus within markets, or move from one market to another as their primary activity and income source. These enterprises are highly entrepreneurial, in the sense that they change their business model depending on evidence and their understanding of demand and opportunities to generate profit. However, these firms do not have a clear vision or strategy, and certainly do not follow an agreed and fixed business plan in order to achieve business success. Instead, they move to exploit opportunities as they arise, even if this means changing the business or moving it away from its existing model and approach. Businesses of all sizes follow this opportunity-seeking strategy in China. This makes these businesses highly adaptable and able to respond to changing market dynamics and patterns. However, their business model is often unclear and they may reorient their whole business without warning or expectation.

International expansion

A growing number of Chinese businesses are developing substantial market shares and presences outside China and, increasingly, globally. Some of these companies, such as Haier and Lenovo, are now market leaders worldwide, with the former producing more whitegoods than any other company globally, and the latter being the world's second-largest manufacturer of personal computers. Independently managed SOEs, such as Konka, TCL and Changhong, are among the largest television manufacturers in the world. China's huge SOEs are also expanding internationally, acquiring resources and businesses, as well as exporting products and establishing production and logistics centres globally.

In recent years, there has been an explosion in acquisitions of companies, assets and resources by Chinese businesses – both public and private – in countries worldwide. This includes farmland in the Ukraine, mines in Africa, vineyards and luxury goods producers in France, Mittelstand family businesses in Germany, and high-tech firms in the UK and US. There are many reasons for international acquisitions; however, in most cases, the acquisition and then use of technologies, brands or other assets back in China is cited as a primary reason for buying companies in other countries.[21]

As well as relatively well-publicised examples of Chinese businesses that are expanding and competing internationally, there are an increasing number of less well-known companies that have globalised their businesses. Often, these businesses have secured a dominant market share in a niche sector. Examples of businesses that are the largest or almost the largest in global niche markets include Hengtong Optic-Electrics (optical fibres and cables), Hikvision (security cameras and closed-circuit television systems), Wanfeng Auto (car wheels) and Zhongding (rubber sealing parts for the automotive industry).[22] Each of these four businesses has focused on a particular niche market that is not dominated by existing global corporations.

There are an increasing number of industries in which China is developing or has secured a leading position globally. Examples include motorbikes, earthmoving equipment, solar photovoltaics, cell and smart phones, and whitegoods. Although some of these industries are dominated by international manufacturers that have located in China – often from Taiwan, Japan, Korea and Hong Kong – others are dominated by Chinese companies. This chapter has already noted the recent emergence of Chinese producers of smartphones, both domestically and globally. What is most interesting about many of these globalising Chinese businesses is that they focus on very different markets. Some may sell their products into all nations, competing effectively with competitors in the most developed economies in the world (such as Lenovo). Other Chinese businesses sell to middle-income countries, such as India and Thailand, while others focus on lower income countries in South Asia and Sub-Saharan Africa.

In several cases, the presence of overseas Chinese businesses – especially those from Hong Kong, Singapore and Taiwan – is worth considering. Some of these inward investors created the conditions for China's own smartphone companies to emerge, and have close working relations with them. For example, Foxconn has been long established in China, especially in the Pearl River Delta, and has become one of Apple's largest suppliers. It has manufactured for Huawei (the leading

Chinese electricals and electronics business) for many years, and more recently has gone into partnership with Xiaomi to manufacture in India. There is an interdependence between these international businesses and the emerging Chinese tech companies that are starting to build global as well as domestic Chinese market shares.

In general terms, there are two ways in which Chinese enterprises have gone global. First are Chinese businesses that have built strong market shares in their domestic market and, based on that foundation, have started to internationalise their operations. Examples include iSoftstone, a software company that started in China and has since secured Fortune 500 clients in the US and other countries, and Ctrip, an online travel booking service that is expanding its English language site and extending its booking service to countries outside China. In the case of iSoftstone, market share was built in China by securing major contracts with some of the largest companies in the country. International expansion occurred once the company had built a strong domestic presence and could demonstrate the capacity and capability to deliver major information technology projects for large companies. In the case of Ctrip, internationalisation has occurred because they have followed their customers, who increasingly are choosing to holiday and travel overseas, rather than just in China. The explosion in international tourism by Chinese travellers has pushed Ctrip into other countries as demand has soared for hotels, flights and arranged holidays.

The second way in which Chinese enterprises have gone global encompasses businesses in manufacturing and engineering that have successfully grown by exporting their products through global supply chains and OEMs. As has been noted in this chapter, based on this success, many of these businesses have started to develop their own branded products, and are subsequently becoming less reliant on OEMs and their brands to sell products. Wanfeng Auto Wheel is an example of a business that grew by supplying wheels to other branded companies, and then began developing its own brand to sell overseas. These businesses created successful business models through contracting to OEMs, and are now applying these models to their own branded products.

There may also be a third pattern of international expansion emerging. A small yet growing number of Chinese businesses appear to be trying to become global businesses that have a presence in multiple countries. The most notable example is Lenovo, which explicitly describes itself as a global business, and has research centres in the US and other countries. The key to identifying these businesses is to examine whether they are establishing or already have R&D facilities outside China that contribute to the innovation and new product development activities of the parent business. As these R&D centres become increasingly important, they will move the focus of investment in the business out of China and to the countries in which these centres are located.

Notes

1 Barro, R. 2016, 'Economic growth and convergence, applied especially to China', NBER Working Paper No. 21872, NBER, http://www.nber.org/papers/w21872 (viewed 3 June 2017).

2 Wildau, G, Cadman, E, Yang, Y & Kavanagh, L 2016, 'The Chinese economy at a glance', https://ig.ft.com/sites/numbers/economies/china (viewed 3 June 2017).
3 Yang, K 2015, 'The significance of new company registration policies in China', China Policy Institute, Nottingham University, https://cpianalysis.org/2015/02/05/the-significance-of-new-company-registration-policies-in-china/ (viewed 3 June 2017).
4 Atherton, A 2015, 'China's move to entrepreneurship: will the private sector continue to grow?' China Policy Institute, Nottingham University, https://cpianalysis.org/2015/02/06/chinas-move-to-entrepreneurship-will-the-private-sector-continue-to-grow-in-the-future/ (viewed 3 June 2017).
5 http://www.economist.com/node/14299720 (viewed 3 June 2017)
6 Kikkawa, T 1995, 'The formation and functions of enterprise groups', *Business History*, vol. 37, no. 2, pp. 44–53.
7 Hankyoreh 2012, 'Top ten *chaebol* now almost 80% of economy', *Hankyoreh*, 28 August, http://www.hani.co.kr/arti/english_edition/e_business/549028.html (viewed 3 June 2017).
8 Liu, P 2016, 'China opens the door a bit further', *AB Magazine*, ACCA, http://www.accaglobal.com/uk/en/member/member/accounting-business/insights/china-fdi.html (viewed 3 June 2017).
9 Atherton, A & Gao, Z 2016, *China's next 100 global giants: 2016 edition*, ACCA, London, http://www.accaglobal.com/content/dam/ACCA_Global/Technical/Future/pi-china-global-giants.2016.pdf (viewed 3 June 2017).
10 Liao, H & Wei, Y 2016, 'Space, scale and regional inequality in provincial China: a spatial filtering approach', *Applied Geography*, vol. 61, pp. 94–104.
11 He, S, Bayrak, M, & Lin, H 2017, 'A comparative analysis of multi-scalar regional inequality in China', *Geoforum*, vol. 78, pp. 1–11.
12 Zhao, X, Chan, C & Ming, N 2012, 'Spatial polarization and dynamic pathways of foreign direct investment in China 1990–2009', *Geoforum*, vol. 43, no. 4, pp. 836–850.
13 Cheng, S 2006, 'From East to West: the evolution of China's FDI preferential policies', *Journal of the Washington Institute of China Studies*, vol. 1, no. 1, pp. 66–70.
14 Banerjee, A, Duflo, E & Qian, N 2012, 'On the road: access to transportation infrastructure and economic growth in China'. Working Paper, Massachusetts Institute of Technology, http://economics.mit.edu/files/7782 (viewed 3 June 2017); Ansar, A, Flyybjerg, A & Lunn, D 2016, 'Does infrastructure investment lead to economic growth or economic fragility? Evidence from China', *Oxford Review of Economic Policy*, vol. 32, no. 3, pp. 360–390.
15 Mansharamani, V 2016, 'China is spending nearly $1 trillion to rebuild the Silk Road', *PBS News*, 2 March, http://www.pbs.org/newshour/making-sense/china-is-spending-nearly-1-trillion-to-rebuild-the-silk-road/ (viewed 3 June 2017).
16 Atherton, A & Newman, A 2016, 'The emergence of the private entrepreneur in reform era China: re-birth of an earlier tradition, or a more recent product of development and change?', *Business History*, vol. 58, no. 3, pp. 319–344.
17 Nolan, P & Dong, F 1990, *Market forces in China: competition and small business – the Wenzhou debate*, Zed Books, London, UK.
18 Mertha, A 2005, *The politics of piracy: intellectual property in contemporary China*, Cornell University Press, Ithaca, NY.
19 Lin, Y-CJ 2011, *Fake stuff. China and the rise of counterfeit goods*, Routledge, New York, NY.
20 Li, J, Li, P & Wang, B 2016, 'Do cross-border acquisitions create value? Evidence from overseas acquisitions by Chinese firms', *International Business Review*, vol. 25, no. 2, pp. 471–483.
21 Zheng, N, Wei, Y, Zhang, Y & Yang, J 2016 'In search of strategic assets through cross-border merger and acquisitions: evidence from Chinese multinational companies in developed economies', *International Business Review*, vol. 25 no. 1, pp. 177–186.
22 Atherton, A, Huang, Q & Gao, Z 2014, *China's next 100 global giants*, ACCA Global Futures Academy, http://www.accaglobal.com/content/dam/acca/global/PDF-technical/futures/pol-afa-cngg-chinas-next.pdf (viewed 3 June 2017).

6
FINANCING ENTREPRENEURSHIP IN CHINA

Introduction

Access to adequate financial capital is an important determinant of the performance, growth and subsequent survival of new ventures and small and medium-sized enterprises (SMEs).[1] This is especially the case in China, where access to adequate sources of both formal and informal financing has an important influence on the growth of Chinese private SMEs.[2] However, entrepreneurs in China have faced constraints in the availability and provision of finance throughout the reform period; although this has improved recently.

In the early stages of the opening up and reform period in China there were very few channels through which entrepreneurs could finance their business activities. They typically financed their businesses using personal savings, borrowing from friends and family, and informal financing. However, in the last 20 years the financial landscape has changed completely as a result of financial market reform, the introduction of competition into the banking sector and the establishment of new financing mechanisms such as venture capital, angel investment and microfinance. According to the EY G20 entrepreneurship barometer, China now ranks highly in terms of access to funding for entrepreneurs; significantly higher than developed economies such as Japan, Germany and France and just behind the United Kingdom and the United States of America (USA).[3] However, it is important to note that the EY G20 barometer was focused on a small group of relatively large and successful private enterprises, so it does not reflect the true state of enterprise financing in China. For most private enterprises the sources of finance remain limited, with a small venture capital sector focused mainly on the big cities, and relatively underdeveloped forms of small and micro business financing in many parts of China.

Because many private enterprises, especially smaller ones, have faced challenges in securing finance from formal sources – in particular state banks – informal finance has been of central importance for many entrepreneurs. 'Shadow' banking and finance, through informal, often underground organisations has played a central role in funding private sector emergence and growth through much of the reform period. These sources continue to be important today, especially for smaller and micro-enterprises.

In this chapter the main informal and formal entrepreneurial financing mechanisms used by SMEs in China will be examined. Research on what factors improve entrepreneurs' access to external sources of financing will then be scrutinised.

Financing mechanisms for Chinese enterprises

Informal sources of financing

In the early years of opening up and reform, in particular, entrepreneurs relied overwhelmingly on informal sources to finance their business activities. Facing exclusion from the banking sector, which lent predominantly to state-owned enterprises, entrepreneurs used alternative financing channels such as retained earnings, interpersonal lending from friends and family, underground financing networks in their local communities and trade credit.[4] Whereas underground financing refers to that obtained from quasi-legal forms of lending outside the formal banking sector,[5] trade credit refers to financing obtained through accounts receivable. Due to a lack of institutional support for the private sector, informal financing has served as the main financing mechanism for private SMEs, and continues to be important today in many regions of China. It was particularly important for private sector development in China during the early years of opening up and reform, when it represented the only available form of finance for many private businesses.

Informal financing acts as a source of financing for many SMEs that find it difficult to obtain credit from the banking sector due to demand-side issues; in particular, high levels of asymmetric information resulting from a lack of a credit history and poor accounting practices. Private enterprises only emerged at a large scale in China in the early 1980s, as household and informal enterprises were encouraged to stimulate the consumer economy and 'sideline' sectors not covered by the state. In the early years of their emergence, in particular, these businesses were new and so lacked a credit history on which banks could base lending decisions. In addition, many private enterprises have not used fully formal accounting procedures throughout the reform period, especially those run by an owner–manager or family. In these cases, the practice has been to hold the money close, and not to overly distinguish between business expenditure on the one hand, and personal or household expenses on the other. Larger private enterprises and those seeking external finance have adopted more transparent and formal accounting practices in recent years, particularly since accession to the World Trade Organization, which came with a commitment to greater convergence with international business norms.

China has also experienced 'supply-side' issues that have constrained funding to the private sector. These arise in part from the pre-reform legacies that existed in state banks, which did not make credit decisions before the reform era began. They lacked the skills and techniques to make lending decisions in an economy that was shifting from the structures and thinking of a planned economy, where resources were allocated centrally, to a marketised economy where firms compete for customers and resources. In the early years of the reform period, bankers lacked the credit assessment, product development and deal-structuring expertise of banks operating in market economies. They had learned how to become bankers in an era when banks provided cash to state-owned enterprises on the command of party officials based on centrally planned production quotas. Banking, in other words, was state-controlled funding of production in state-owned enterprises, rather than providing credit based on assessment of the ability and likelihood of a business to generate sufficient surpluses to service and repay debt. To this day, state banks provide finance to state-owned enterprises, both to enable them to grow and also to cover deficits and underperformance that prevents them generating the surpluses to service debt or other forms of finance. They still understand, and operate within, state frameworks and dynamics that can trump standard banking procedures driven by commercial considerations. This can make it difficult for these banks to understand and empathise with the world of the entrepreneur and the financing needs of private enterprise.

It is not surprising that in these circumstances, informal sources of finance became the primary means for entrepreneurs to fund their businesses through the early reform era in particular. Informal financing mechanisms provide a means by which entrepreneurs can capitalise on their reputation to access adequate funds and are especially important as a source of funds for entrepreneurs in rural areas, where the banking sector is less developed.[6] A number of studies have examined the prevalence of informal financing in China. For example, Tsai's work highlighted the role played by informal financing in supporting entrepreneurship across Southeast China.[7] She found that informal financing mechanisms were diverse and varied from region to region. Li surveyed entrepreneurs across regions of China about their use of informal financing.[8] He found that it was viewed as critical to enterprise success in light of constraints in accessing adequate financing from the banking sector. Other research by Xiao and colleagues examined the financing behaviour of high-technology SMEs in China over a decade. They found that informal financing was prevalent during all stages of business development, and that bank and venture capital were rarely used, even as a firm matured.[9] This suggests that SMEs in an emerging economy such as China do not have the same access to formal sources of financing as those in more developed institutional contexts. It also indicates that informal financing is an important means of funding business growth for private entrepreneurs.

Researchers have begun to examine the effects of informal financing on the financial performance of SMEs. Using data obtained from a nationwide survey in 2007, Yiu and colleagues established that the informal financing mechanisms of underground financing and trade credit had positive effects on the profitability of private SMEs, whereas formal financing in the form of bank loans did not.[10] They argue this may result from the fact that informal financing is more beneficial than formal financing as it is more flexible and timely. Degryse and colleagues found that although informal finance is associated with a higher sales growth rate for small firms and can complement formal financing, it is associated with a lower sales growth rate for large firms.[11] In explaining these results they argue that although informal financing may enhance the growth of enterprises in their start-up and growth stages due to the advantages informal financiers have in screening applicants and tracking their performance, these advantages do not scale up with firm size and may even be detrimental for the performance of large firms due to higher interest rates and inherent costs.

Informal financing is also likely to work better for smaller firms, because the amounts of finance they are seeking are generally much lower than those for larger firms. Given the informal nature of local finance in China – which is based on lending circles and underground banks in many places – the ability of an informal funder to mobilise large amounts of finance is limited. This points to a 'supply-side' constraint that limits the size of credit offered to entrepreneurs as they grow their businesses. After private enterprises reach a certain size, it is likely that many if not most informal finance entities will not be able to mobilise sufficient funds or will be overly exposed to this single transaction and so will be reluctant to offer finance. At this point, larger, growing private enterprises are more likely to seek out formal finance, even if banks and other providers privilege state-owned enterprises.

In the following sections we examine the main informal financing mechanisms, which include personal savings, interpersonal financing from friends and family, underground financing and trade credit.

Personal savings and interpersonal financing from friends and family

In the early stages of opening up and reform in China, entrepreneurs were unable to access formal sources of debt financing, and underground financing mechanisms were not always accessible in many areas of the country.[12] As a result, entrepreneurs in China typically started their businesses using their own savings and with the help of extended family networks, friends and close business associates. Such sources of financing are relatively cheap as they are based on strong relational ties and trust between the parties, and do not require collateral. However, they might not always lead to optimal outcomes. Research suggests that such sources of financing should only be used as a last resort as they may limit the willingness of the entrepreneur to take risks, for fear this may affect the livelihoods of themselves, friends and family members.[13] In addition, many entrepreneurs are also reluctant to accept financing from close contacts as this may require them to reciprocate the support provided by supplying funds when the other person needs to borrow in the future.[14] They may choose to borrow funds from outside their immediate network to avoid incurring such costs. That said, for many entrepreneurs in China, asking friends and family for money to start up or grow a business may be the only choice, or the most accessible of a very limited range of options. This is likely to be the case for smaller and less formal enterprises in rural areas where informal and 'underground' finance is less available. More recent research by Liao and colleagues found that the use of personal savings and interpersonal financing from friends and family was widespread among entrepreneurs in Hubei Province, and that entrepreneurs who use significantly more of this type of finance were typically female, with longer working experience and high school education or less.[15]

Underground financing

Underground financing developed quickly in the 1980s to support the growth of the private sector in China during the opening up and reform period.[16] Although it was not officially sanctioned by government authorities, in many areas of the country local officials turned a blind eye to it and it grew rapidly in the early years of reform, especially in South-east China where there was a developed private economy. Multiple forms of underground financing developed in China during the early years of opening up and reform, including credit associations, money houses and pawnbrokers. Credit associations, also known as contractual or cooperative associations were a common form of informal financing. In each association, 10–15 people would contribute money to a collective pot that would be rotated to the members in turn or to the member willing to pay the highest interest rate to their fellow members.[17] These lending circles provided high levels of governance of underground finance, with households monitoring the borrowing of members of these lending circles, as neighbours as well as co-investors. During the 1980s, money houses emerged across South-east China. In money houses, brokers acted as intermediaries between those with extra cash on hand and business people who were short on money. After undertaking a risk evaluation, the broker would decide to extend credit and obtain commission for arranging the deal.[18] Pawnbroking is another informal financing mechanism that was and continues to be widely used by Chinese entrepreneurs. In return for credit, entrepreneurs pawn their assets for a period of time after which they are required to pay back the sum they had borrowed plus interest to have their assets returned. Compared to formal sources of finance, underground financing tends to be expensive as lenders charge high rates of interest. However, it is very flexible in the sense that entrepreneurs can borrow money for very short periods when they have cash flow problems.

Trade credit

While underground financing is at best quasi-legal in that it is not regulated by government authorities, trade credit is legal.[19] Such credit is derived from transactions with suppliers or customers, such as through accounts payable, accounts receivable and pre-payment. Research has highlighted the importance of trade credit as a source of informal financing for private SMEs to fund their business activities in the face of financial discrimination from the banking sector.[20] It was especially important as a source of financing during the early stages of opening up and reform, as state-owned enterprises redistributed credit to private enterprises with less privileged access to loans, but it has become less important over time as access to formal sources of financing have improved.[21] Trade credit appears to have been replaced to some degree in recent years by the emergence of a factoring sector in China that offers credit against future invoice values based on orders secured. There has also been extensive and increasing availability of hire purchase and leasing as means of ensuring that cash flow is sufficient to finance key investments.

Case study – informal financing in Wenzhou

As highlighted in Chapter 4 of this book, the city of Wenzhou in Zhejiang Province is considered by many as the birthplace of private entrepreneurship in China. Among other factors, the success of entrepreneurship in Wenzhou can be put down to the development of a large informal financial sector, which sprung up to support entrepreneurship in the 1980s. In the early period of opening up and reform, entrepreneurs in Wenzhou had access to a wide range of mechanisms from which to obtain capital for and grow businesses that were not officially sanctioned by the Chinese government. These mechanisms were documented by Tsai in her book *Back Alley Banking* and include trade credit, pawnshops, professional money lenders, middlemen, credit associations and private money houses.[22] The success of the informal financial sector in Wenzhou has attracted the attention of central government on numerous occasions over the last 30 years. As financial innovations developed in Wenzhou and other cities in Zhejiang Province, the central government would take note and act by either cracking down on such practices or sanctioning them as reforms, often claiming that they had proposed them in some form in the first place. Much of what went on in Wenzhou was used by regulators as a basis on which to reform the banking system, and influenced the establishment of a commercial banking system in the 1990s and the introduction of regulations that allowed the establishment of small-loan companies in 2012.[23] Although it is difficult to calculate the exact proportion of financing obtained outside the formal financial system in Wenzhou, it has been estimated that more than 90 per cent of capital flows in the early 1980s were accounted for by the informal sector.[24] Although informal financing is less prevalent today, it still accounts for a significant proportion of enterprise financing in Wenzhou. Recent figures released by the government authorities revealed that around 57 per cent of private enterprises in Wenzhou have borrowed from outside the formal banking system.[25] In other words, in one of China's most developed hotspots for entrepreneurship, more than half of the funding used by entrepreneurs is informal. This indicates both the endurance of this form of finance, and also the ongoing challenges that private enterprises, especially those that are small, face when seeking formal finance.

Formal sources of financing

Bank lending

In the early years of opening up and reform, the overwhelming majority of financing from the state-owned banking system was directed to state-owned enterprises. Moreover, much of this funding was offered on soft rather than strict commercial terms, with variable and often low levels of repayment. However, as the government implemented reform of the banking sector to allow the establishment of commercial banks, and former state-owned SMEs were sold off throughout the 1990s under the *Zhuada Fangxiao* ('Keep the Big, Let Go of the Small') policy, a greater proportion of credit from the banking sector was directed towards the burgeoning private sector as a means of hastening economic development. This shift to private enterprises was enhanced through existing relationships between banks and recently privatised former state-owned enterprises. As these businesses became private, those that involved management buyouts or equivalent transfers of ownership to the incumbent management team were able to maintain historical ties with state banks.

The government implemented three major stages of banking sector reform during the 1980s and 1990s. The first and second stages of banking sector reform in the 1980s led to the establishment of a central bank and four specialised state-owned banks (the Bank of China, the China Construction Bank, the Agricultural Bank of China and the Industrial and Commercial Bank of China). Under this system the People's Bank of China became the central bank. Following this in the 1990s additional reforms led to the creation of a three-tier banking system, which consisted of the central bank, the four specialised state-owned banks which became commercial banks, three policy banks (the Agricultural Development Bank of China, the China Development Bank and the Export-Import Bank of China) which took over responsibility for financing state projects, over 100 commercial banks and thousands of credit cooperatives.[26] Additional reforms that were introduced more recently as part of China's accession to the World Trade Organization have also allowed foreign banks to establish branches in China and purchase shares in Chinese banks.

In recent years, state banks have been encouraged by central government to lend more to the private sector, and to smaller businesses. This represents a shift away from lending to large state-owned enterprises for many banks, and also demands different skills in terms of credit assessment, relationship management, and empathy with different kinds of organisation and business strategy. Today the banking sector is a much more important source of debt financing for many SMEs in China, although there continue to be indications that private enterprises find bank funding more difficult to acquire than state-owned enterprises. Despite this, the total value and volume of state bank lending to entrepreneurs has increased rapidly in recent years, and appears likely to continue to do so. For many enterprises the banking sector acts as the main, if not only source of formal external capital, in part because other forms are scarce or not widely available in China.[27] Unlike sources of equity financing, bank lending allows entrepreneurs to raise capital without losing control over their businesses.[28]

However, SMEs still continue to face discrimination vis-à-vis state-owned enterprises in obtaining access to bank loans. Commentators point out that despite the reforms introduced over the last three decades the Chinese banking system is still relatively inefficient compared to other economies, even those in a similar stage of development.[29] This arguably results from weaker investor protection systems and accounting standards, and continued government intervention in the banking system to encourage lending to be directed towards state-owned or controlled enterprises. Although the Chinese government established more than 200 guarantee agencies across the country in the 2000s to assist private organisations in accessing credit, this did not lead to a significant redistribution of credit in their favour.[30] Financiers continued to prefer to lend to larger and established state-owned or controlled firms which are less risky lending propositions due to their affiliation with government and higher levels of transparency. Recent surveys also suggest it is difficult for entrepreneurs to get loans from banks as a result of complex procedures, strict collateral requirements and high costs.[31] Consequently, entrepreneurs find it harder to get access to bank financing than larger organisations, especially those under state-ownership or control, and continue to use informal financing to meet some of their financing needs.[32] Research generally supports the viewpoint that private SMEs are discriminated against by the banking sector.[33] For example, recent figures indicate that compared to the amount of Gross Domestic Product contributed by private SMEs the amount of bank lending they receive is disproportionately low.[34]

However, other researchers argue that discrimination might be less of a problem than these figures suggest, and may be down to the unwillingness of entrepreneurs to seek external financing. A recent survey of SMEs in Beijing who had recently sought financing found that most applicants were successful in acquiring bank financing. On average they found that SMEs received two-thirds of financing they applied for. They also found that non-exporters, manufacturing enterprises and limited liability enterprises were more successful in obtaining bank loans than exporters, service sector enterprises and single-owner enterprises respectively, and that larger enterprises were more likely to apply for finance in the first place.[35] This may be due to the 'discouraged borrower' effect, which suppresses applications for formal finance by SMEs because they do not expect to acquire it.[36]

Venture capital

By the start of the 21st century the Chinese government realised it needed to do more to support entrepreneurship across China. Previously government had supported SMEs, especially those in high-technology industries, by facilitating financing from banks, reducing tax burdens and directly subsidising research and development. However, such strategies alone were not enough to meet the financial needs of many start-ups. In order to facilitate access to private sources of funds for high-technology start-ups in the late 2000s and improve their growth potential, the government began to understand the importance of venture capital as a financing mechanism.[37]

In July 2007 the Ministry of Finance and Ministry of Science and Technology jointly developed the *Interim Regulation on Managing the Venture Capital Guiding Fund for High-Tech SMEs* (the *Interim Regulation*). This document highlighted four ways in which regional and local governments could work with private investors to direct money towards high-technology enterprises through the co-investment of public and private funds. This included government contributing initial capital to a venture capital fund, co-investment by private venture capital firms and government in high-technology enterprises, provision of subsidies by government to private venture capital firms and the provision of guarantees by government to private venture capital firms.

As a result of these changes and growing interest from foreign venture capital firms in the Chinese market, the venture capital industry has grown substantially over the last decade. According to the Price Waterhouse Coopers *Private Equity/Venture Capital 2014 Review* the number of investments by venture capital firms increased from 694 in 2008 to 1,334 in 2014.[38] The report also revealed that China accounted for around 9 per cent of global venture capital funds. According to recent figures, Chinese entrepreneurs rate access to venture capital in China as being reasonable, at 3.5 on a scale where 1 is impossible and 7 is very easy.[39] This is above the G20 average of 3.0.

There is growing agreement amongst researchers that there are marked differences in how venture capital is practiced between China and the West due to cultural and regulatory differences.[40] For example, Bruton and Ahlstrom found that venture capital firms in China were more likely than Western firms to use their social networks to select enterprises in which to invest due to higher levels of asymmetric information than in the West due to a lack of transparent accounting and reporting practices. They also found that venture capitalists in China were less likely to use board membership and legal channels to monitor and review their investments than in the West, but more likely to spend significant time on the ground with the entrepreneur. Based on interviews with venture capitalists in the early 2000s, Tan and colleagues established that domestic venture capitalists provided fewer value-added services, were less active in monitoring and were less likely to retain veto rights than foreign venture capitalists.[41] In contrast, they typically concentrated more on monitoring the financial performance of their investments. Wu and colleagues found that domestic venture capitalists were more likely to invest in traditional industries than foreign venture capitalists who were more likely to invest in non-traditional industries such as the information technology sector.[42] They also found that domestic venture capitalists preferred to invest in more mature firms and in the first round of equity financing. In contrast foreign venture capitalists preferred to invest in start-ups and in later rounds of equity financing. Finally, they established that although foreign venture capitalists outperformed domestic venture capitalists in the past in successfully exiting their investments, in recent years the performance gap has closed and domestic venture capitalists have now surpassed their foreign counterparts. This is the new generation of venture capitalists in China who are more educated and are using more advanced techniques to monitor their investments than in the past, whilst benefitting from local knowledge.

Examining the investment behaviour of foreign and domestic venture capitalists, Fuller found evidence of three distinct patterns by venture capitalists investing in technology start-ups in China.[43] He argued that these differences in investment behaviour arise from differences in the institutional environment in which venture capitalists honed their skills. The first pattern he found was that venture capital firms founded by non-ethnic Chinese were more likely to invest in service-oriented firms that were technology-light. He argued that this resulted from the fact that such firms had little exposure to markets in which formal protection of intellectual property was weak, and therefore feared making investments in technology-intensive firms on behalf of their customers as their customers might lose out if the technology was stolen or copied by competitors. The second pattern he found was that foreign venture capital firms established by ethnic Chinese were more likely to invest in firms that were technology-intensive. He argued that this was because they had greater knowledge of informal mechanisms to protect intellectual property, and felt more comfortable working in an uncertain legal environment where the creation of intellectual property was an important part of the business. The third pattern he found was that government-backed venture capital firms tended to invest in state-directed projects or opted out of investing into technology start-ups altogether. He argued that this was because such firms are under state-direction and act as investment vehicles for state-backed projects and state-owned firms rather than technology-intensive start-ups. Compared to economies such as the USA, the share of government sponsored venture capital investment is higher in China, accounting for around a quarter of the total. This type of venture capital generally underperforms that of private venture capital as many of them lack the expertise and operational mechanisms to identify and manage investments in high-technology enterprises.[44]

Research has begun to examine the effects of different sources of venture capital on the performance of Chinese SMEs. Using data on manufacturing businesses from 1998 to 2007, Guo and Jiang found that although investment by venture capitalists improved the productivity of enterprises shortly after investment, its long-term effects were minimal.[45] In addition, they found that foreign venture capital and syndicated venture capital investments added more value to enterprises than domestic and non-syndicated venture capital. Examining the effect of venture capital investment on the success of SMEs' initial public offerings in the period from 2004 to 2010, Jiang and colleagues found that venture capital-backed public offerings have higher premiums, lower initial underpricing and higher market reaction.[46] They also found that initial underpricing was more prominent for SMEs backed by younger venture capitalists and there was no difference in the levels of initial underpricing of SMEs backed by foreign and domestic venture capitalists. Tan and colleagues looked at the effects of venture capital on the performance of SMEs after their initial public offerings on the stock exchange in the years 2004 to 2008.[47] They found that domestic venture capitalists neither added value to SMEs in the initial public offering process nor improved their operating performance. Compared to non-venture capital-backed enterprises those backed by venture capital had lower levels of underpricing in initial public offerings and weaker operating performance both before and after the initial public offering.

Angel investment

Although venture capital is the most commonly used form of private equity financing in China, we have witnessed the growth of smaller-scale angel investment in recent years. Compared to venture capitalists who tend to be selective, angel investors tend to enter in the seed to early stages of business growth and are therefore less risk averse and selective. According to the 2013 China Angel Investment Annual Report survey conducted by Venture China we have witnessed a growth in angel investment from 72 start-ups in 2008 to 262 new ventures in 2013.[48] Most of the angel investment goes into high-technology start-ups located in zones such as Beijing's Zhongguancun where many angel investors have set up incubators to support their early stage investments.

Case study – ZhenFund

ZhenFund is an early stage angel investment fund based in Beijing China. It was founded in 2006 by the co-founder of New Oriental Education Group, Xu Xiaoping, who is one of the most successful angel investors in China, winning awards such as 'Most Respected Angel Investor' and 'Angel Investor of the Year'. In 2012 ZhenFund teamed up with American private equity group Sequoia Capital to launch one of the largest angel investment funds in China and expand the scale of their investment activities. It concentrates its investment in the areas of e-commerce, social networking, online education and entertainment. Over the last decade it has invested in start-ups such as LightIntheBox (an online retailer), Jumei (an online beauty product retailer) and Jiayuan (a dating website).

The Chinese stock market

Apart from the two main Chinese stock exchanges in Shanghai and Shenzhen which were established in 1990 and 1991 respectively, two additional stock exchanges (the Small and Medium Enterprise Board and ChiNext) were later set up to provide small and medium-sized private enterprises with improved access to external sources of equity financing.

In 2004, the Small and Medium Enterprise Board was established by the Shenzhen Stock Exchange. Although similar listing requirements apply to the SME

Board as the main board, it operates under a separate trading system and stock price index.[49] By mid-2015 over 750 enterprises had listed on the SME Board.

Following this in 2009, China's equivalent of the NASDAQ Stock Exchange, ChiNext, also known as the Growth Enterprise Board, was established by the Shenzhen Stock Exchange. In its first year of operation over 100 enterprises were listed on ChiNext, and by mid-2015 over 450 enterprises had listed. Compared to more established stock exchanges, ChiNext seeks to attract faster growing, more innovative enterprises, especially those in high-technology and internet sectors, by having less stringent listing requirements.

Despite the presence of domestic stock exchanges, some of the larger internet enterprises in China have decided not to list in China, preferring to list directly on stock exchanges in Hong Kong or overseas. A growing number of them have listed in the USA, with NASDAQ being a preferred destination. These include the search engines Baidu and Qihoo 360, e-commerce platform Alibaba and travel agency Ctrip. For example, Alibaba undertook a $25 billion initial public offering on NASDAQ in 2014. Internet enterprises have typically favoured a listing on NASDAQ rather than the mainland or Hong Kong to get around stricter listing requirements that require enterprises to show a profit for three years.

However, the popularity of NASDAQ has waned in recent years as investors realise that American investors face difficulties in understanding the business models that Chinese enterprises adopt. This has led to increased interest amongst Chinese enterprises to list on Chinese exchanges such as ChiNext. The introduction of government regulations to limit foreign shareholder control of enterprises in key technology sectors has also led to domestic listings becoming more popular in recent years.

Microfinance

Over the last two decades we have witnessed the rapid expansion of the microfinance industry in China. Microfinance refers to the provision of financial services to low-income clients who lack access to formal financial services without requiring them to provide collateral. It has been widely recognised as a tool for fostering entrepreneurship amongst low-income populations, especially in rural areas of the world. The types of products provided by Chinese microfinance institutions include loans, savings accounts and insurance. Today there are over 10,000 microfinance providers in China and take the form of microcredit companies, village and township banks, rural credit cooperatives and banks, non-governmental organisations (NGOs) and peer-to-peer lenders.

Although microfinance was introduced in China at the beginning of the 1990s through international aid programmes for poverty alleviation, the central government only formally recognised the role microfinance may play as a tool to foster entrepreneurship in rural areas of the country towards the end of the 1990s.[50] Given limited access to the formal banking system, policy makers saw the potential of microfinance to support rural entrepreneurs with limited credit history and few assets to leverage as collateral. Following trials conducted by the Chinese Academy of Social Sciences in the early 1990s, the central government encouraged local governments and financial institutions to support the development of microfinance organisations in rural areas.[51] This led to a rapid growth in the number of microfinance institutions operating in China, especially after 2008 when the government issued its *Guidelines for pilot microloan companies*.[52]

Today the lion's share of microfinance institutions in China are microcredit companies. However, most of these are not traditional microfinance providers as they typically lend to more established SMEs in urban areas of the country, rather than low-income entrepreneurs in rural areas.[53a] According to Accion's Centre for Financial Inclusion, only 10 per cent of these target low-income segments of the population.[53b] Similarly, most commercial banks tend to focus on lending to more established SMEs and not to low-income entrepreneurs. As such, a significant proportion of what is termed 'microfinance' in China, particularly that provided by local banks, is in fact not this type of credit, but rather is small-scale lending to local individuals and businesses using standard retail and business banking products. Actual microfinance, in the way that this term is used in countries with lower per capita incomes than China's, is less evident in China than may appear at first glance. However, there is microfinance provision in less developed parts of the country, which plays an important role in providing credit to low-income individuals and households. In rural areas of the country, village and township banks, rural credit cooperatives and the Postal Savings Bank of China provide the overwhelming majority of microfinance services to low-income populations. Although some non-government organisations operate microfinance schemes in rural areas of the country, their scale is limited and few are sustainable, relying on donations rather than an operating surplus to operate.[54]

Research has begun to examine the effect of microfinance on entrepreneurship in China. Using data from rural households, Jia and colleagues found that unlike credit from the banking system and informal networks, access to microfinance led farmers to increase the time they worked on off-farm entrepreneurial activity. They also found that the effects were much stronger for poorer households. These findings provide initial evidence that microfinance is effective in fostering entrepreneurship in China.

Peer-to-peer lending and crowdfunding

In the last few years we have witnessed an explosion in the number of lenders entering the peer-to-peer lending and crowdfunding markets as a result of the growth of e-commerce in China. The peer-to-peer industry in China is now the largest in the world and is rapidly growing year by year.[55] Large internet companies such as Alibaba and JD.com have also entered the peer-to-peer lending industry, providing online savings accounts and microcredit to entrepreneurs via the internet.[56] Alifinance, the peer-to-peer financing arm of internet giant Alibaba, offers loans to entrepreneurs of up to several million RMB without the need for collateral. They evaluate loan applications using transaction data from loan applicants obtained through their own e-commerce platform. Another internet giant, JD.com, launched a crowdfunding platform in 2015 in conjunction with Grameen Bank China. This partnership will use JD.com's crowdfunding platform to raise money to establish Grameen Bank China's on-ground operations, and provide micro-loans for rural entrepreneurs.

Case study – Positive Planet China

Positive Planet China is an NGO that is part of the Positive Planet Group (previously known as PlaNet Finance) – an NGO that supports the development of microfinance in more than 35 countries across the globe. In 2013, it received the *Best Socially Responsible Microcredit Company* award from the China Microfinance Association. In more than 20 Chinese provinces it has provided technical assistance to financial institutions to establish and improve their microfinance businesses through teaching them best practice with respect to strategy, process optimisation, risk management and governance. Its clients range from commercial banks, to village and township banks and NGOs. Specific projects undertaken by Positive Planet China include working with Huishang Bank to establish the largest microfinance operation in Anhui Province, and with Harbin Bank to set up one of the first commercial microfinance operations in China. Positive Planet China also runs two microfinance institutions in Western China through its subsidiary Microcred. These institutions serve as a model from which their clients can learn best practice to implement into their own organisations. Through its *Microfinance Plus* programme, Positive Planet China also works with its clients to implement projects in the fields of financial education, health and sustainability, alongside the provision of microfinance. For example, it has helped deliver financial education to women across rural China with the aim of promoting good money management and financial planning, and has partnered with local telecommunications providers to introduce technologies that provide low-income populations with pricing and market information.[57]

Accessing external financing

There has been growing research examining which factors influence the use of external sources of financing by SMEs. Most studies considered firm-level determinants using finance-based theories such as the pecking order theory, which proposes that businesses will use internal sources of financing before seeking external debt and then external equity. For example, examining the firm-level determinants of the capital structure of SMEs in Zhejiang Province as predicted by the pecking order theory, Newman and colleagues found that size and profitability influenced debt levels in line with predictions from the pecking order theory.[58] However, they also found a negative relationship between asset structure and debt, which indicates the limited use of formal bank financing by Chinese SMEs, and a highly 'truncated' pecking order. Other research using data from SMEs across China has revealed differences between the use of debt between enterprises with single and multiple owners. In this research, Newman and colleagues found that single-owner enterprises faced a more constrained pecking order than those with multiple owners, given they used significantly less external debt and relied mainly on internal sources of financing.[59]

Researchers have also begun to examine the link between social and political capital and entrepreneurs' access to external financing.[60] For example, using data on over 60,000 private SMEs from across China in the period 2000–2006, Du and colleagues found that entrepreneurs can improve access to short-term debt by adopting strategies aimed at building social capital such as entertaining and providing gifts to others in their social network. However, they found that such strategies did not improve access to long-term debt. In contrast, obtaining political affiliation (i.e. developing strong formalised ties with the government) improved SME access to long-term debt. These findings highlight the importance of nonmarket strategies to resource acquisition in China, where formal institutional frameworks are less developed, and firms are reliant on informal mechanisms to reduce asymmetric information between themselves and potential lenders. Talavera and colleagues found that social and political capital influences entrepreneurs' access to loans from commercial banks.[61] Using data from SMEs across China in the period 2004–2006, they found that entrepreneurs who were members of the Communist Party, those who spent time building social relationships with others and those who contributed to charities were more successful in obtaining loans from commercial banks. Similarly, Li and colleagues found that membership of the Communist Party helped entrepreneurs to obtain loans from banks or other state institutions, and was especially important to firm performance in regions of China with weaker market institutions and weaker legal protection.[62] Examining the influence of political participation on access to finance from the banking sector, Guo and colleagues found that private enterprises who were owned by members of the Communist Party were able to obtain significantly more bank loans than those who were not owned by members of the Communist Party, after constitutional amendments in the early 2000s to support development of the private sector.[63] Prior to this, private enterprises owned by party members were no more likely to obtain bank loans than those not owned by party members. However, more recent data suggest the influence of Communist Party membership on acquisition of debt might be on the wane. Using data from a survey of private SMEs in 2012, Ma and colleagues found that joining government-controlled business associations or becoming a member of the Communist Party did not help entrepreneurs to obtain more loans from banks.[64] However, they found that when entrepreneurs became deputies of the People's Congress or the People's Political Consultative Conference they were more likely to obtain loans from banks. Finally, Feng and colleagues found that enterprises controlled by entrepreneurs who participate in politics exhibit superior post-initial public offering performance and are subject to less underpricing at the time of initial public offering.[65] Together, these studies suggest that although becoming a member of the Communist Party historically provided entrepreneurs an advantage in gaining access to formal sources of finance, increasingly in today's China, only a senior position in the party brings such benefits.

Zhang found that entrepreneurs' use of different sources of debt financing depended on the resources inherent in their social networks.[66] He established that the more business or political contacts entrepreneurs possessed, the greater the likelihood that they would use formal sources of debt financing; and the more urban ties they possessed the greater the likelihood that they would use informal sources of debt financing. In addition, he found that business ties had a greater influence on the use of formal financing for older firms and in regions of the country where institutional trust was higher. Chen and colleagues found that although enterprise performance improved the access of private enterprises to bank loans from the 'big four' banks it did not improve access to bank loans from other commercial banks.[67] They also found that firms who spend more on building social capital are awarded more loans and perform better as a result.

Research findings to date suggest that social and political capital remains influential in assisting entrepreneurs to obtain external sources of debt financing in an institutional context where the legal system is underdeveloped and the Communist Party continues to exert significant control over the economy.

Notes

1 Alsos, G, Isaksen, E & Ljunggren, E 2006, 'New venture financing and subsequent business growth in men and women led businesses', *Entrepreneurship Theory & Practice*, vol. 30, no. 5, pp. 667–687; Huynh, K, Petrunia, R & Voia, M 2010, 'The impact of initial financial state on firm duration across entry cohorts', *Journal of Industrial Economics*, vol. 58, pp. 661–689; Yiu, DW, Su, J & Xu, Y 2013, 'Alternative financing and private firm performance', *Asia Pacific Journal of Management*, vol. 30, pp. 829–852.
2 Degryse, H, Lu, L & Ongena, S 2015, 'Informal or formal financing? Or both? First evidence on the co-funding of Chinese firms', Working Paper, http://dx.doi.org/10.2139/ssrn.2023751 (viewed 19 February 2015).
3 Ho, T & Qi, M 2013, *The EY G20 Entrepreneurship Barometer 2013: China*, Ernst and Young, Beijing.
4 Tsai, K 2009, 'Beyond banks: the local logic of informal finance and private sector development in China', in J Li & S Hsu (eds), *Informal finance in China. American and Chinese perspectives*, Oxford University Press, Oxford, pp. 80–103.
5 Tsai, K 2002, *Back-alley banking: private entrepreneurs in China*, Cornell University Press, Ithaca, NY.
6 Hsu, S 2009, 'Introduction', in J Li & S Hsu (eds), *Informal finance in China. American and Chinese perspectives*, Oxford University Press, Oxford, pp. 3–11.
7 Tsai, K 2002.
8 Li, J 2006, *The survey of underground financing in China*, Shanghai Renmin Press, Shanghai.
9 Xiao, L 2011, 'Financing high-tech SMEs in China: a three-stage model of business development', *Entrepreneurship & Regional Development*, vol. 23, no. 3–4, pp. 217–234; Xiao, L & North, D 2012, 'Institutional transition and the financing of high-tech SMEs in China: a longitudinal perspective', *Venture Capital*, vol. 14, no. 4, pp. 269–287.
10 Yiu, DW, Su, J & Xu, Y 2013.
11 Degryse, H, Lu, L & Ongena, S 2015.

12 Liao, J, Ye, Q, Pistrui, D & Welsch, HP 2009, 'New venture financing: an empirical investigation of Chinese entrepreneurs', in J Li & S Hsu (eds), *Informal finance in China. American and Chinese perspectives*, Oxford University Press, Oxford, pp. 104–124.
13 Degryse, H, Lu, L & Ongena, S 2015.
14 Zhang, Y 2015, 'The contingent value of social resources: entrepreneurs' use of debt-financing sources in Western China', *Journal of Business Venturing*, vol. 30, no. 3, pp. 390–406.
15 Liao, J, Ye, Q, Pistrui, D & Welsch, HP 2009.
16 Tsai, K 2002.
17 Tsai, K 2002.
18 Jiang, S 2009, 'The evolution of informal finance in China and its prospects', in J Li & S Hsu (eds), *Informal finance in China. American and Chinese perspectives*, Oxford University Press, Oxford, pp. 12–38.
19 Yiu, DW, Su, J & Xu, Y 2013.
20 Ge, Y & Qiu, J 2007, 'Financial development, bank discrimination and trade credit'. *Journal of Banking & Finance*, vol. 31, no. 2, pp. 513–530.
21 Cull, R, Xu, LC & Zhu, T 2009, 'Formal finance and trade credit during China's transition', *Journal of Financial Intermediation*, vol. 18, no. 2, pp. 173–192.
22 Tsai, K 2002.
23 Wei, L, McMahon, D & Orlik, T 2012, 'Wenzhou reforms point to clean up of China's financial system', *The Australian Business Review*, 29 March; Zhou, X & Hornby, L 2012, 'China gives go-ahead to Wenzhou financial reforms', *Reuters*, 28 March.
24 Liu, YL 1992, 'Reform from below: the private economy and local politics in the rural industrialization of Wenzhou', *The China Quarterly*, vol. 130, pp. 293–316.
25 'Let a million flowers bloom' 2011, *The Economist*, 10 March.
26 Jiang, S 2009.
27 Milana, C & Wu, HX 2012, 'Growth, institutions, and entrepreneurial finance in China: a survey', *Strategic Change*, vol. 21, pp. 83–106.
28 Chen, D, Ding, S & Wu, Z 2014, 'Effect of foreign ownership on cost of borrowing: evidence from small and medium-sized enterprises in China', *International Small Business Journal*, vol. 32, no. 6, pp. 693–715.
29 Allen, F, Qian, J, Zhang, C & Zhao, M 2012, 'China's financial system: opportunities and challenges', National Bureau of Economic Research, Working Paper No. 17828, National Bureau of Economic Research, Cambridge, MA; Riedel, J, Jin, J & Gao, J 2007, *How China grows: investment, finance and reform*, Princeton University Press, Princeton, NJ.
30 Liao, J, Ye, Q, Pistrui, D & Welsch, HP 2009.
31 Yiu, DW, Su, J & Xu, Y 2013.
32 Zhang, Y 2015.
33 Cong, J 2009, 'Chinese informal financial systems and economic growth: a case study of China's small and medium-size enterprises', *Public Policy Review*, vol. 5, no. 1, pp. 63–88; Ding, S, Guariglia, A & Knight, J 2013, 'Investment and financial constraints in China: does working capital management make a difference?', *Journal of Banking & Finance*, vol. 37, no. 5, pp. 1490–1507; Poncet, S, Steingress, W & Vandenbussche, H 2010, 'Financial constraints in China: firm-level evidence', *China Economic Review*, vol. 21, pp. 411–422.
34 Fagan, M & Zhao, S 2009, 'SME financing in China: the current situation, problems and possible solutions', *International Journal of Entrepreneurship & Small Business*, vol. 8, no. 2, pp. 171–185; Firth, M, Lin, C, Liu, P & Wong, SML 2009, 'Inside the black box: bank credit allocation in China's private sector', *Journal of Banking & Finance*, vol. 33, pp. 1144–1155.
35 Wang, J, Robson, P & Freel, M 2015, 'The financing of small firms in Beijing, China: exploring the extent of credit constraints', *Journal of Small Business & Enterprise Development*, vol. 22, no. 3, pp. 397–416.
36 Kon, Y & Storey, D 2003, 'A theory of discouraged borrowers', *Small Business Economics*, vol. 21, no. 1, pp. 37–49.

37 Tan, Y, Huang, H & Lu, H 2013, 'The effect of venture capital investment – evidence from China's small and medium-sized enterprises board', *Journal of Small Business Management*, vol. 51, no. 1, pp. 138–157.
38 Price Waterhouse Coopers 2015, *PWC private equity/venture capital 2014 review*, PWC, Hong Kong.
39 Ho, T & Qi, M 2013.
40 Bruton, GD & Ahlstrom, D 2003, 'An institutional view of China's venture capital industry: explaining differences between China and the West', *Journal of Business Venturing*, vol. 18, no. 2, pp. 233–259.
41 Tan, J, Zhang, W & Xia, J 2008, 'Managing risk in a transitional environment: an exploratory study of control and incentive mechanisms of venture capital firms in China', *Journal of Small Business Management*, vol. 46, no. 2, pp. 263–285.
42 Wu, S, Ren, T, & Yang, H 2015, 'Fund ownership, investment preference, and performance: the venture capital industry in China', in D Cumming, M Firth, W Hou & E Lee (eds), *Developments in Chinese entrepreneurship: key issues and challenges*, Palgrave Macmillan, New York, NY, pp. 153–197.
43 Fuller, DB 2010, 'How law, politics and transnational networks affect technology entrepreneurship: explaining divergent venture capital investing strategies in China', *Asia Pacific Journal of Management*, vol. 27, pp. 445–459.
44 Milana, C & Wu, Z 2012.
45 Guo, D & Jiang, K 2013, 'Venture capital investment and the performance of entrepreneurial firms: evidence from China', *Journal of Corporate Finance*, vol. 22, pp. 375–395.
46 Jiang, P, Cai, CX, Keasey, K, Wright, M & Zhang, Q 2014, 'The role of venture capitalists in small and medium-sized enterprise initial public offerings: evidence from China', *International Small Business Journal*, vol. 32, no. 6, pp. 619–643.
47 Tan, Y, Huang, H & Lu, H 2013.
48 Liu, M, Shi, Y & Wu, Z 2015, 'Angel investor's affiliations and investment returns in China', in D Cumming, M Firth, W Hou & E Lee (eds), *Developments in Chinese entrepreneurship: key issues and challenges*, Palgrave Macmillan, New York, NY, pp. 59–75.
49 Jiang, P, Cai, CX, Keasey, K, Wright, M & Zhang, Q 2014.
50 Jia, X, Xiang, C & Huang, J 2013, 'Microfinance, self-employment, and entrepreneurs in less developed areas of rural China', *China Economic Review*, vol. 27, pp. 94–103; Turvey, CG & Kong, R 2010, 'Informal lending amongst friends and relatives: can microcredit compete in rural China?' *China Economic Review*, vol. 21, no. 4, pp. 544–556.
51 Park, A & Ren, C 2001, 'Microfinance with Chinese characteristics', *World Development*, vol. 29, no. 1, pp. 39–62; Tsai, KS 2004, 'Imperfect substitutes: the local political economy of informal finance and microfinance in rural China and India', *World Development*, vol. 32, no. 9, pp. 1487–1507.
52 Britzelmaier, B, Kraus, P & Xu, Y 2013, 'Microfinance institutions in China: development and challenges to their sustainability', *Strategic Change*, vol. 22, pp. 67–78.
53a Jia, X, Xiang, C & Huang, J 2013, 'Microfinance, self-employment, and entrepreneurs in less developed areas of rural China', China Economic Review, vol. 27, pp. 94–103
53b Riecke, J 2014, 'China's microfinance landscape: nonprofits, microcredit companies, rural financers, and Alibaba', Accion Centre for Financial Inclusion, Blog, 23 September 2014.
54 Riecke, J 2014.
55 Aveni, T 2015, *New insights into an evolving P2P lending industry: how shifts in roles and risk are shaping the industry*, Positive Planet, Beijing.
56 Rabinovitch, S 2013, 'Alibaba digs deep for Chinese banking treasure', *Financial Times*, 25 August.
57 Positive Planet China, Beijing, http://www.positiveplanet.ngo/en/our-manifesto/ (viewed 24 May 2017).
58 Newman, A, Gunessee, S & Hilton, B 2012, 'Applicability of financial theories of capital structure to the Chinese cultural context: a study of privately owned SMEs', *International Small Business Journal*, vol. 30, no. 1, pp. 65–83.

59 Newman, A, Borgia, D & Deng, Z 2013, 'How do SMEs with single and multiple owners finance their operations differently? Empirical evidence from China', *Thunderbird International Business Review*, vol. 55, no. 5, pp. 531–544.
60 Du, J, Guariglia, A & Newman, A 2015, 'Do social capital building strategies influence the financing behavior of Chinese private small and medium-sized enterprises?' *Entrepreneurship, Theory & Practice*, vol. 39, no. 3, pp. 601–631.
61 Talavera, O, Xiong, L & Xiong, X 2012, 'Social capital and access to bank financing: the case of Chinese entrepreneurs', *Emerging Markets Finance & Trade*, vol. 48, no. 1, pp. 55–69.
62 Li, H, Meng, L, Wang, Q & Zhou, LA 2008, 'Political connections, financing and firm performance: evidence from Chinese private firms', *Journal of Development Economics*, vol. 87, no. 2, pp. 283–299.
63 Guo, D, Jiang, K, Kim, BY & Xu, C 2014, 'Political economy of private firms in China', *Journal of Comparative Economics*, vol. 42, pp. 286–303.
64 Ma, G, Rui, OM & Wu, Y 2015, 'A springboard into politics: do Chinese entrepreneurs benefit from joining the government-controlled business associations', *China Economic Review*, vol. 36, pp. 166–183.
65 Feng, X, Johansson, A & Zhang, T 2014, 'Political participation and entrepreneurial initial public offerings in China', *Journal of Comparative Economics*, vol. 42, pp. 269–285.
66 Zhang, Y 2015.
67 Chen, Y, Liu, M & Su, J 2013, 'Greasing the wheels of bank lending: evidence from private firms in China', *Journal of Banking & Finance*, vol. 37, pp. 2533–2545.

7
CHINESE BUSINESS CULTURE AND ENTREPRENEURSHIP

Introduction

When interacting with Chinese entrepreneurs, it is important to understand the influence of Chinese culture on how they undertake business. In order to do this, this chapter first highlights the key philosophical and ideological influences on Chinese culture, and considers how they have shaped the values, norms and behaviour of the Chinese. It then examines the key cultural dimensions that have been shown to differentiate the Chinese culture from other cultures. Following this, alternative approaches to understanding Chinese culture are scrutinised, and geographical and generational cultural diversity in China highlighted. Finally, the chapter investigates the influence of Chinese culture on entrepreneurs' business practices.

Philosophical and ideological influences on Chinese culture

Before examining the main features that distinguish Chinese culture from other cultures and how they influence the ways in which Chinese entrepreneurs undertake business, it is important to understand the main philosophical and ideological influences on Chinese culture. The following sections examine the influence of Confucianism, Daoism, Communism and globalisation on Chinese culture.

Confucianism

Confucianism is a philosophical doctrine based on the ideas of the Chinese philosopher Confucius, who lived around 500BC.[1] It establishes a series of moral, social and behavioural norms to govern human interactions and social relationships in society. Confucianism is based on the assumption that human beings are fundamentally good and can strive to improve themselves through hard work and acquisition of knowledge. It highlights the importance of five main ethical virtues: *Ren* (humaneness), *Yi* (righteousness), *Li* (ritual norms), *Zhi* (wisdom) and *Xin* (integrity). The first virtue, *Ren*, stresses that human beings should be compassionate and benevolent to others.[2] According to Confucius, *Ren* refers to the good feelings that arise when being altruistic and acting in the interests of others. The second virtue, *Yi*, stresses the moral importance of upholding righteousness and doing what is right. It refers to a human being's ability to recognise what is right and good, and determine the correct way to act in different circumstances. The third virtue, *Li*, stresses the importance of establishing and abiding by etiquette and norms.[3] In his work, Confucius established a system of rules or a code of conduct that governs personal interactions and determines how people should properly act in their daily lives. The fourth virtue, *Zhi*, refers to the innate ability of an individual to distinguish right from wrong. Without this ability, individuals are unable to recognise what is right and good, and how they should act in their daily lives. Finally, the fifth virtue, *Xin*, stresses the importance of keeping to one's word and being trustworthy. According to Confucius, *Xin* is an indispensable virtue for human beings because it acts as the basis for human interaction.

Under Confucianism, harmony is viewed as the primary goal of one's social life. Confucius argued that, in their daily lives, people should strive to achieve harmony with themselves and in personal relationships with other people.[4] According to Confucius, this can be achieved through practising *Ren, Yi* and *Li*. In order to maintain harmony, Confucius also stressed the need for a hierarchical structure of human relationships to govern individuals' behaviour in any given social context. He created a set of 'five cardinal relationships' (*Wu Lun*) and described the obligations that the parties in each relationship have with one another.[5] These relationships are between ruler and subject, parents and children, older siblings and younger siblings, husband and wife, and friends.

According to the *Wu Lun* doctrine, Confucius argued that each member of the relationship has mutual obligations to the other, and fulfilling these obligations will lead to a harmonious society.[6] For example, he argued that the ruler must protect the safety of his or her subjects, and the subjects must be loyal in return. Similarly, he argued that, while parents have a duty to raise and educate their children, children have a duty to support parents in their old age. He argued that husband and wife must work together to build an environment in which their children are raised and the elderly are cared for. Among siblings, he argued that older siblings must care for their younger siblings, while younger siblings should respect their older siblings. Finally, he argued that friends must help one another when in difficulty. Examining the set of five cardinal relationships, Confucianism evidently stresses hierarchy and familism. As explained later in this chapter, this has resulted in a culture that is high in power distance, where individuals with higher levels of seniority in social relationships are treated with deference by those with lower levels of seniority, through the use of humble language and appropriate non-verbal behaviour.

Confucius also advocated the principle of 'rule by man' over the legalist principle of 'rule by law'. Rule by man assumes that senior decision makers are of good ethical character and make decisions wisely. Confucian dominance over legalism ensured that the rule by man principle has become an engrained part of Chinese culture. For a long time, China had no developed legal system and no civil law to protect people's interests. If a dispute arose, the local ruler would decide how to solve the conflict. Today, Chinese people still tend to prefer mediation, rather than legal means, to solve disputes. This is especially evident in business dealings between entrepreneurs.

Confucianism has remained a strong influence on Chinese society for the last 2,000 years, and is arguably the most important philosophical influence on Chinese culture.[7] For example, Gordon Redding argued that Confucianism is the 'most appropriate single-word label for the values which govern social behavior' among Chinese people.[8] Until the fall of the imperial system in China at the beginning of the 20th century, students seeking a position in government were required to study Confucian teachings and pass exams on Confucianism. Although Confucianism was renounced during the Cultural Revolution as being old fashioned, in recent years, China has witnessed a resurgence of Confucianism.

In response to the inequalities that China experienced due to rapid economic growth in the reform period, the government authorities reintroduced ideas from Confucian thought into their policy making during the 2000s in an attempt to manage growing social unrest.[9] In doing so, they advocated the need to maintain a harmonious society as a key objective for China's socioeconomic development, and stressed that it was no longer productive to focus on economic growth alone.[10]

The promotion of a harmonious society by Hu Jintao's government led to the reintroduction of Confucian philosophy to the education system and training for party officials. Maintaining a harmonious society was highlighted as one of the key national goals for the Communist Party. The Chinese government has also sought to promote Chinese Confucian values overseas through establishing Confucius Institutes in numerous countries. By the end of 2014, there were more than 475 Confucius Institutes established in partnership with universities in over 70 countries.[11]

Daoism

Alongside Confucianism, Daoism (sometimes called Taoism) is considered one of the two great philosophical influences on Chinese society.[12] Daoism emphasises living in harmony with the Dao. Translated literally as 'the way' or 'the path', the Dao refers to the unexplainable force behind everything that exists. It is generally agreed that Daoist thinking originated from the work of Laozi, who wrote the key text – the Daodejing – on which subsequent thinking has been built. In his work, Laozi also introduced the concept of Yin and Yang, which emphasises the need to maintain a balance between competing extremes in order to maintain social harmony.[13] Other Daoist philosophers include Zhuangzi.

Daoism emphasises the importance of serving others without expectation of personal gain, while remaining humble. It rejects traits that are often valued in the West, such as assertiveness, aggressiveness and competition.[14] Daoism highlights the need for humans to maintain balance in their lives, live in harmony with the natural environment and maintain good relationships with other people. In addition, Daoism promotes flexibility by emphasising the need to alter one's behaviour to suit changing situations.[15] Daoism conflicts with Confucian thinking by rejecting the need for rigid rules and hierarchical relationships to govern social interactions. In doing so, it highlights the need for individuals to act spontaneously without the need to conform to social norms and rely on the structures imposed by society.[16] It also differs from Confucianism in that it does not emphasise the need to look up and be loyal to others in positions of greater power. Although Daoism has arguably had a weaker influence than Confucianism on Chinese culture, its impact on Chinese culture is evident, especially in relation to the ease with which Chinese people adapt to changing external circumstances and their attitudes towards risk.

Communism

After coming to power after World War II, the Communist Party, under the leadership of Chairman Mao, attempted to eradicate Confucian thinking from the minds of the Chinese people.[17] Through political campaigns and mass mobilisation programmes, the party highlighted the importance of being loyal to the party, and attacked the Confucian values of hierarchical subordination. This was achieved through a series of campaigns that emphasised the importance of treating women equally to men, and the need to struggle against those in positions of power. For example, during the period of the Cultural Revolution, Chinese youth were encouraged by the party to denounce their reactionary elders and even reject their own families in exchange for the comradeship of the Communist Party.[18] Leaders of the party called for the destruction of the 'four olds': old customs, habits, culture and ideas. In many parts of the country, this politicisation of society led to the erosion of traditional loyalties and associations, which were replaced with the new 'family' of party comradeship. Although Confucian thinking was not removed completely, people's cultural values and norms changed considerably through exposure to Maoist doctrine. It was not until the late 1970s that society returned to some level of normality, and people were no longer attacked for holding Confucian values. However, the experience of the Cultural Revolution led to a generation of people who were less trusting of others than previous generations. It also arguably weakened people's willingness to be subordinate to those in higher positions of authority.

Globalisation

There is general agreement that Chinese culture has changed dramatically due to China's integration into the global economy, since the introduction of the opening-up and reform policy in the late 1970s.[19] Over the last three decades, there has been an acceleration in interactions in the cultural and business space between China and the rest of the world. China has been one of the world's largest recipients of foreign direct investment (FDI) in the last two decades. At present, there are half a million foreign-invested companies located in China and over 80 per cent of Fortune 500 companies have subsidiaries there.[20] In addition, a growing number of Chinese people are travelling overseas for education. In 2013, over 700,000 people left China to study overseas, many focusing on business-related subjects.[21] This increased interaction with foreign cultures has led to the adoption of foreign business practices, and caused the Chinese people to question their traditional ways of acting. As highlighted later in this chapter, the younger generation of Chinese people – who have been most influenced by globalisation through advances in technology and interactions with people from overseas – are more educated and global minded, and less traditional than their predecessors. Compared to previous generations, they are more likely to think and act in an individualistic manner, are less deferential to those in positions of power, and demand more involvement in decision making.[22]

Key dimensions of Chinese culture

This section examines the key cultural dimensions that have been identified by scholars such as Hall, Hofstede and Trompenaars, and discusses how Chinese culture is ranked among these dimensions.

Hall's high/low-context dimension

The anthropologist Edward Hall presented a theory of culture based on how information is transmitted by people within a given society – that is, how people communicate with one another.[23] He drew a distinction between high- and low-context cultures, and used this to differentiate cultures. According to Hall, high-context cultures are cultures where less must be explicitly said or written because there is shared meaning and understanding between people. In such cultures, the individual internalises meaning and information, so that less needs to be said and written explicitly. In order to understand the meaning of what is being communicated, there is greater reliance on non-verbal cues, which might include the speaker's tone of voice, facial expressions, gestures and eye contact. High-context cultures tend to be more collectivistic, as the bonds between individuals within society are generally much stronger than in low-context cultures. In contrast, low-context cultures are cultures in which more has to be said or written because there is little shared meaning or understanding between people. In such cultures, verbal communication is highly valued and there are explicit rules regarding how people should act.

Like most cultures in Asia, the Chinese culture is generally considered a high-context culture, where messages are indirect and the meaning of words can be understood by the context in which they are spoken. Messages are interpreted with reference to the environment, situation and non-verbal behaviour of the sender. The receiver tends to share the same knowledge, assumptions and values as the sender, making it relatively easy to understand the message. In contrast, Anglo-Saxon cultures such as the US, UK and Australia are typically considered low-context cultures. Growing research has highlighted key differences between high- and low-context cultures, consistent with Hall's conceptualisation. For example, research on individuals from China, Korea and the US found that the Chinese and Korean participants acted in a way consistent with Hall's description of high-context cultures, and that the US participants acted in a way consistent with Hall's description of low-context cultures.[24]

Hofstede's cultural dimensions

In the late 1960s and early 1970s, Geert Hofstede undertook one of the largest ever cross-cultural surveys, using data from 80,000 IBM employees located in multiple countries around the world.[25] From this data, Hofstede identified four values in which cultures varied: individualism/collectivism, power distance, uncertainty avoidance and masculinity/femininity. Additional research identified a fifth dimension: long-term versus short-term orientation. Hofstede's work suggests that China is a collectivistic culture that ranks high in power distance, ranks low in uncertainty avoidance, ranks relatively high in masculinity and has a long-term orientation.[26] The following sections introduce each of Hofstede's cultural dimensions, and identify how China ranks in each of these dimensions.

Individualism/collectivism

Hofstede classified China as a highly collectivistic culture.[27] In such a culture, people typically consider group interests over individual interests, tend to stress the importance of collaboration and consultation over competition, and strive to maintain harmony in relationships.[28] Compared to individualistic cultures, there are typically higher levels of in-group trust, a greater preference for equality in the distribution of rewards, and a general preference for conflict avoidance.[29] This arguably results from the influence of Confucianism, which stresses the importance of harmony, treating everybody equally, and showing respect for others.

However, while relationships with colleagues are cooperative for in-groups, Chinese people can be cold or even hostile to out-groups. This makes collectivism in China very different from that in other Asian Confucian-based societies, such as Japan or Korea, where members of the out-group are often treated with greater respect than members of the in-group – that is, unlike in China, there is a phenomenon of collectivism that exists outside of immediate familial and friendship circles. Indeed, some authors have begun to critique the notion that China is a collectivistic society, arguing that Chinese people are typically more concerned with maintaining relationships with the people connected to them – mostly for self-serving reasons – and are less concerned about striving and sacrificing to improve the wellbeing of others in the group more generally.[30] As a result, collectivism in China has been referred to as 'familial collectivism', where individuals treat those in their family and immediate circles with respect, yet treat outsiders with distrust and suspicion.[31] This arguably results from the turmoil that arose from the Cultural Revolution and the early period of opening-up and reform, where individuals realised the only people they could trust were close family and friends.

Power distance

Researchers have classified China as a high power distance or hierarchical culture.[32] Power distance refers to the extent to which people in a given society accept that power is distributed unequally. The influence of power distance in Chinese organisations has been well researched. For example, researchers have established that Chinese people react less negatively than people from lower power distance cultures when provided with lower levels of decision-making power.[33] Other researchers have examined how high levels of power distance have shaped work behaviours in Chinese organisations. For example, they highlighted the prevalence of paternalistic leadership in Chinese organisations, which refers to a top-down leadership style emphasising follower obedience combined with benevolence.[34]

Although research in the West has generally found the authoritarian dimension of paternalistic leadership to have a negative influence on employee performance, the findings in China are mixed, suggesting that Chinese people are more accepting of top-down leadership styles that discourage employee autonomy and participation.[35] The use of paternalistic leadership practices is evident in many Chinese SMEs, especially in more traditional network-based enterprises, where the older generation of founder entrepreneurs typically maintain control over decision making and involvement in the day-to-day running of the business. However, entrepreneurs running newer innovation-based enterprises increasingly realise the need to provide autonomy and participation in decision making to enhance the motivation and commitment of a newer generation of employees who have different values from previous generations.

Uncertainty avoidance

According to Hofstede's framework, China is a culture low in uncertainty avoidance.[36] Uncertainty avoidance refers to the extent to which a culture prefers to avoid ambiguity and considers the way in which it deals with uncertainty. In low uncertainty avoidance cultures, such as China, people are generally comfortable with change and taking risk. They tolerate greater ambiguity and are flexible in how they respond to issues that may affect them at work. In contrast, in high uncertainty avoidance cultures, people prefer rules to guide their behaviour, emphasise compliance and obedience, and are less flexible.

The low uncertainty avoidance culture in China may have resulted from the influence of Daoist ideology, which highlights the need to tolerate ambiguity and adapt to changing circumstances. There is general agreement among researchers that low uncertainty avoidance cultures are more conducive to entrepreneurial activity than are high uncertainty avoidance cultures.[37] This may explain why there are high rates of entrepreneurial activity in China. Although it is generally accepted by researchers that China is a society low in uncertainty avoidance, other researchers disagree with Hofstede's findings, arguing that it ranks high on uncertainty avoidance. For example, the GLOBE study identified China as a culture high in uncertainty avoidance.[38]

Masculinity/femininity

Researchers have classified China as a culture relatively high in masculinity.[39] In such a culture, people tend to endorse assertiveness and competition, and are more success oriented than in feminine cultures, where people prefer to compromise and cooperate. In masculine cultures, such as China, financial and material achievements are highly valued. This leads people to prioritise work over family and personal commitments. As a result, there is general agreement among researchers that masculine societies are more conducive to entrepreneurial activity than feminine cultures.[40] This may explain why there are high rates of entrepreneurial activity in China.

Long/short-term orientation

Working alongside Michael Bond, Hofstede uncovered a fifth dimension: long-term orientation (also known as 'Confucian Dynamism') in addition to the original four dimensions. In their research, Hofstede and Bond found that individuals from Confucian-based societies, such as China, typically focus on long-term, rather than short-term, objectives.[41] Compared to individuals in cultures where there is a short-term orientation, individuals in cultures with a long-term orientation, such as China, tend to think more about the future than the present, and emphasise the values of thrift and perseverance, rather than satisfying immediate needs. In a business context, this leads Chinese entrepreneurs to focus on long-term objectives and take time to build business relationships, rather than focusing solely on short-term objectives.

Trompenaars' cultural dimensions

Working with Charles Hampden-Turner, Fons Trompenaars, like Hofstede, developed a set of dimensions to classify cultures based on 15 years of training managers and academic research.[42] Similar to Hofstede, he developed a dimension of individualism/collectivism. However, he added a number of alternative dimensions examining how people engage with other people, with time and with the environment. The following sections introduce a number of key dimensions that are particularly relevant to China. The first four dimensions relate to how people engage with others.

Particularism/universalism

China has been classified as a particularistic culture by Trompenaars and other researchers.[43] Trompenaars defined a particularistic culture as one governed by relationships, rather than rules.[44] Such cultures often have an absence of rules to govern behaviour, and relationships determine what is achieved in business and society.[45] Decisions are often made with regard to circumstances and are not always based on uniform rules. In contrast, a universalistic culture is one in which laws are extremely important and rules are more important than relationships.

In particularistic cultures, such as China, conducting business requires a great deal of time to be invested in building relationships. Particularism is clearly evident in the importance placed on personal relationship (*guanxi*) in China when making decisions.[46] The particularistic structure of Chinese culture permeates the business and personal lives of Chinese people, and is often argued to result from Confucianism, which stresses the importance of rule by man over rule by law.[47] However, other authors have questioned the influence of Confucianism on *guanxi*-based practices, arguing that the use of such practices results from the institutional uncertainty that has characterised China's opening-up and reform period since the late 1970s.[48]

Ascription/achievement

China is widely considered an ascription culture, where importance is attached to individuals' personal characteristics, such as age, education, professional qualifications and family background (rather than past achievements), when considering a person's ability.[49] In ascription cultures, an individual's status in the eyes of others is determined by their seniority and position within the organisation. For Chinese people, titles are indicative of one's status and demand recognition by others when engaging in business negotiations.[50] When undertaking business in ascription cultures, such as China, Trompenaars highlighted the need for individuals to give face to and respect the status of the other party in business negotiations, and ensure that senior members of their organisation lead business dealings as a sign of respect to the other party. The importance assigned to status (ascription) in Chinese society arguably results from the influence of Confucianism, which emphasises the need to respect others who are more senior in the hierarchy.

Neutral/emotional

Under Trompenaars' framework, China is considered a relatively emotional culture – a culture in which emotions are openly and freely expressed. In emotional cultures, people tend to greet each other with enthusiasm, smile a great deal and talk loudly. In contrast, in a neutral culture, people keep their emotions in check and do not always express their true feelings. Although it is typically considered acceptable to show one's emotions in public in China, in the workplace, this is generally dependent on one's position in the organisational hierarchy. As China is a face-based culture, it is not generally considered appropriate to show one's emotions – especially negative emotions – to people in more senior positions, as this may cause them to lose face.

Specific/diffuse

China is considered a diffuse culture, in which people see an overlap between their personal and work lives.[51] In diffuse cultures, people tend not to keep their work and personal lives separate, and may spend time outside work hours with their colleagues and customers. Compared to specific cultures, where people tend to separate their personal and work lives, people in diffuse cultures are more comfortable discussing personal issues at work and business issues on social occasions. In China, as in other diffuse cultures, revealing facts about one's personal life during business dealings is seen as important to exhibit one's character and develop trust to the other party in business negotiations.[52] As a result, business transactions in diffuse cultures are often time consuming, and business is only undertaken when the two parties have spent time together, getting to know each other on a personal level. As a result, before undertaking business, Chinese entrepreneurs typically invest time to get to know personally the people with whom they are doing business.

Sequential/synchronous

As well as examining how people engage with others, Trompenaars established that a major difference between cultures is how people engage with the concept of time.[53] According to Trompenaars, China is a synchronous culture – a culture in which people view the past, present and future as being interwoven. In synchronous cultures, people are flexible, tend to undertake more than one activity at the same time, and view schedules as less important than relationships. Compared to sequential cultures, where people place a high value on punctuality and planning, people in synchronous cultures typically views plans and commitments as flexible. People from sequential cultures must recognise that, in synchronous cultures, such as China, plans might change at the last minute and Chinese people might not always abide by strict guidelines.

Internal direction/external direction

Trompenaars also argued that another dimension in which cultures vary is the extent to which people believe they can control the environment or the environment controls them. This is labelled 'internal direction' versus 'external direction'.[54] According to Trompenaars' framework, China is a good example of a culture characterised by external direction.[55] In such cultures, people typically believe that the environment controls them, and they must work within the confines of their environment to achieve their goals. The focus on external direction has its roots in Daoism, which advocates living in harmony with the natural environment.

Holistic approaches to the study of Chinese culture

Some researchers have criticised the approach taken by Hofstede and Trompenaars in measuring national culture using a series of cultural dimensions.[56] They argue that scholars should not try to simplify culture through applying bipolar, context-free and static frameworks, and that culture – especially Eastern culture – is more complex than such frameworks may suggest. Drawing on Chinese philosophy, scholars such as Tony Fang argue that culture is inherently paradoxical and that individuals in all cultures may act in different ways, depending on the situation they are facing.[57] In his seminal work, Fang argued that paradoxical values coexist in any culture, and work to reinforce and complement each other to shape a holistic, dynamic and dialectical nature of culture.[58] He argued that, like all people, Chinese people can be both individualistic and collectivistic, be masculine and feminine, and act with both high and low power distance at different times, depending on the context. In other words, we must be cautious not to over rely on cultural dimension frameworks, and base our assessment of a culture on its ranking in a set of dimensions, as such frameworks paint too simplified a view of culture. However, despite criticisms of the approaches adopted by Hofstede and Trompenaars to measure culture, we must recognise that they provide an important starting point from which to view Chinese culture.

Geographical and generational diversity

Cultural dimensions frameworks such as those espoused by Hofstede and Trompenaars have also been criticised for failing to consider geographical diversity in China, and for assuming that all Chinese people have the same cultural values. Given that China borders countries as diverse as India, Vietnam, Afghanistan, Russia and North Korea and comprises 56 ethnic groups, viewing China as a single unified culture is problematic. Although the major ethnic group, the Han Chinese, accounts for over 90 per cent of the Chinese population, other ethnic groups comprise a significant proportion of the population in provinces, such as Yunnan, and autonomous regions, such as Xinjiang and Tibet. There is also significant religious diversity in China, with a growing number of people identifying themselves as Christian or Muslim. Recent research indicates that there is even significant cultural diversity among the Han Chinese, depending on where they originate in China.[59] A survey of over 1,000 individuals from six areas of China established that Han people in the north of China are more individualistic, more aggressive and less reliant on others than those in the south.

Cultural dimensions frameworks have also been criticised for not considering generational differences, and for failing to examine how Chinese culture has adapted as a result of political, social and economic change.[60] The institutional transformation that occurred during the opening-up and reform period, introduction of the 'one-child policy' in the early 1980s, and technology revolution of the past 20 years have all exerted significant influence on the cultural values of young Chinese people. As a result of the one-child policy, most young people in China born after 1980 grew up without siblings and were the sole focus of their parents' attention at home. Due to being raised in a technologically advanced era, they are also more digitally literate than their predecessors and more connected to the outside world through the internet. Such changes have made the younger generation of Chinese people – who are more educated and have a more global mindset than the older generation – less respectful of traditional culture, more individualistic and autonomous, and less deferential to hierarchy than their parents' generation.[61]

A growing body of research suggests that the cultural values endorsed by the younger generation are very different to those endorsed by their predecessors. For example, in comparing the values of Chinese managers from different generations, Ralston and colleagues found that the younger generation of Chinese managers valued individualism more and were less likely to adhere to Confucian values than the older generations.[62] In a Gallup survey undertaken over 10 years, McEwen and colleagues also found that young people who are more educated and connected with the rest of the world demonstrate a desire to stress their individuality and increasingly embrace Western values.[63]

Influence of culture on the business practices adopted by Chinese entrepreneurs

Given the significant cultural diversity across different geographic regions of China and different generational cohorts, as highlighted in the previous section, it is important for non-Chinese people to be cognisant of these differences when dealing with Chinese entrepreneurs. In general, the experience of undertaking business with the older generation of Chinese entrepreneurs operating network-based enterprises is likely to be different to the experience of business with the new generation of entrepreneurs focusing on innovation-based and social models of entrepreneurship. The older generation of Chinese entrepreneurs are likely to be more traditional in how they approach business, and more influenced by Confucian thinking. For example, they are more likely to value the need to build long-term relationships with business associates built on trust and reciprocity, less likely to delegate decision making to those lower in the organisational hierarchy, and more likely to consider the long term when making business decisions. Older entrepreneurs will typically view themselves as the patriarch/matriarch of the business, and tend to treat employees as members of the family.

In contrast, the newer generation of Chinese entrepreneurs are likely to be less influenced by traditional Chinese thinking when undertaking business. Compared to previous generations, they tend to be more open to new ideas, act in an individualistic manner, and exhibit a greater willingness to delegate decision making to their subordinates. The younger generation of entrepreneurs will be more likely to trust those from outside their immediate social network and happier to rely on contracts to govern business dealings. In some ways, it is easier for non-Chinese people to work with the younger generation of entrepreneurs, as they are more globally minded, flexible and open to alternative ways of working.

Conclusion

This chapter has highlighted the key philosophical and ideological influences on Chinese culture and considered the extent to which they have shaped the values, norms and behaviour of Chinese people. Following this, this chapter examined how Chinese people rank across the different cultural dimensions proposed by scholars such as Hofstede and Trompenaars, and examined alternative approaches to understanding Chinese culture, before investigating the extent of cultural diversity in different geographical regions and across different generational cohorts. Finally, this chapter discussed the influence of Chinese culture on Chinese entrepreneurship. Based on the insights into China's culture provided by this chapter, Chapter 9 sets out a series of recommendations for non-Chinese people wishing to undertake business with Chinese entrepreneurs.

Notes

1. Chan, GKY 2008, 'The relevance and value of Confucianism in contemporary business ethics', *Journal of Business Ethics*, vol. 77, pp. 347–360.
2. Henning, A 2016, 'Daoism in management', *Philosophy of Management*, forthcoming. doi:10.1007/s40926-015-0024-4.
3. Henning, A 2013, 'The ethical background of business in China: an outline', in S Khan & W Amann (eds), *World humanism: cross-cultural perspectives on ethical practices in organizations*, Palgrave Macmillan, Basingstoke, pp. 194–207.
4. Cheung, C & Chan A 2005, 'Philosophical foundations of eminent Hong Kong Chinese CEOs' leadership', *Journal of Business Ethics*, vol. 60, pp. 47–62.
5. Ip, PK 2009, 'Is Confucianism good for business ethics in China?', *Journal of Business Ethics*, vol. 88, pp. 463–476; Wang, CL, Tee, DD & Ahmed, PK 2012, 'Entrepreneurial leadership and context in Chinese firms: a tale of two Chinese private enterprises', *Asia Pacific Business Review*, vol. 18, no. 4, pp. 505–530.
6. Lin, LH, Ho, YL & Lin, WHE 2013, 'Confucian and Taoist work values: an exploratory study of the Chinese transformational leadership behavior', *Journal of Business Ethics*, vol. 113, no. 1, pp. 91–103.
7. Fan, Y 2000, 'A classification of Chinese culture', *Cross Cultural Management: An International Journal*, vol. 7, no. 2, pp. 3–10; Pun, KF, Chin, KS & Lau, H 2000, 'A review of the Chinese cultural influences on Chinese enterprise management', *International Journal of Management Reviews*, vol. 2, no. 4, 325–338.
8. Redding, G 1993, *The spirit of Chinese capitalism*, Walter De Gruyter, Berlin.
9. See, G 2009, 'Harmonious society and Chinese CSR: is there really a link?', *Journal of Business Ethics*, vol. 89, pp. 1–22.
10. Zhuang, J 2008, 'Inclusive growth toward a harmonious society in the People's Republic of China: policy implications', *Asian Development Review*, vol. 25, no. 1–2, pp. 22–33.
11. Hartig, F 2015, 'Communicating China to the world: Confucius institutes and China's strategic narratives', *Politics*, vol. 35, no. 3–4, pp. 245–258.

12 Hansen, C 2007, 'Daoism', *Stanford Encyclopaedia of Philosophy*, http://plato.stanford.edu/entries/daoism/ (viewed 8 March 2016).
13 Bai, X & Roberts, W 2011, 'Taoism and its model of traits of successful leaders', *Journal of Management Development*, vol. 30, no. 7/8, pp. 724–739.
14 Lee, YT, Han, AG, Byron, TK & Fan, HX 2008, 'Daoist leadership: theory and application', in CC Chen & YT Lee (eds), *Leadership and management in China*, Cambridge University Press, Cambridge, pp. 239–271.
15 Cheung, C & Chan, A 2005.
16 Henning, A 2016.
17 Atherton, A & Newman, A 2016, 'The emergence of the private entrepreneur in reform era China: re-birth of an earlier tradition, or a more recent product of development and change?', *Business History*, vol. 58, no. 3, pp. 319–344.
18 Vogel, E 1965, 'From friendship to comradeship: the change in personal relations in Communist China', *The China Quarterly*, vol. 21, pp. 46–60.
19 Tung, RL, Worm, V & Fang, T 2008, 'Sino-western business negotiations revisited – 30 years after China's open door policy', *Organizational Dynamics*, vol. 37, no. 1, pp. 60–74.
20 Fang, T 2012, 'Yin Yang: a new perspective on culture', *Management and Organization Review*, vol. 8, no. 1, pp. 25–50.
21 UNESCO 2016, 'Global flow of tertiary-level students', UNESCO Institute for Statistics, http://www.uis.unesco.org/Education/Pages/international-student-flow-viz.aspx (viewed 14 March 2016).
22 Zhang, ZX, Chen, ZX, Chen, YR & Ang, S 2014, 'Business leadership in the Chinese context: trends, findings, and implications', *Management and Organization Review*, vol. 10, no. 2, pp. 199–221.
23 Hall, E 1976, *Beyond culture*, Anchor Books, Doubleday, New York.
24 Kim, D, Pan, Y & Park, HS 1998, 'High- versus low-context culture: a comparison of Chinese, Korean, and American cultures', *Psychology and Marketing*, vol. 15, no. 6, pp. 507–521.
25 Hofstede, G 1981, *Cultures and organizations: software of the mind*, Harper Collins, London.
26 Hofstede, G 2001, *Culture's consequences: comparing values, behaviors, institutions and organizations*, Sage, Thousand Oaks, CA.
27 Hofstede, G 2001.
28 Lin, X & Miller, SJ 2003, 'Negotiation approaches: direct and indirect effect of national culture', *International Marketing Review*, vol. 20, no. 3, pp. 286–303.
29 Friedman, R, Chi, SC & Liu, LA 2006, 'An expectancy model of Chinese-American differences in conflict-avoiding', *Journal of International Business Studies*, vol. 37, no. 1, pp. 76–91; Kim, TY & Leung, K 2007, 'Forming and reacting to overall fairness: a cross-cultural comparison', *Organizational Behavior and Human Decision Processes*, vol. 104, pp. 83–95.
30 Brewer, MB & Chen, Y 2007, 'Where (who) are collectives in collectivism: towards a conceptual clarification of individualism and collectivism', *Psychological Review*, vol. 114, no. 1, pp. 133–151.
31 Ip, PK 2009.
32 Hofstede, G 2001.
33 Brockner, J, Ackerman, G, Greenberg, J, Gelfand, MJ, Franscesco, A, Chen, Z, Leung, K, Bierbauer, G, Gomez, C, Kirkman, B & Shapiro, D 2001, 'Culture and procedural justice: the influence of power distance on reactions to voice', *Journal of Experimental Social Psychology*, vol. 37, pp. 300–315.
34 Chan, SCH, Huang, X, Snape, E & Lam, CK 2013, 'The Janus face of paternalistic leaders: authoritarianism, benevolence, subordinates' organization-based self-esteem, and performance', *Journal of Organizational Behavior*, vol. 34, no. 1, pp. 108–128; Cheng, BS, Chou, LF, Wu, TY, Huang, MP & Farh, JL 2004, 'Paternalistic leadership and subordinate responses: establishing a leadership model in Chinese organizations', *Asian Journal of Social Psychology*, vol. 7, no. 1, pp. 89–117.

35 Chen, XP, Eberly, MB, Chiang, TJ, Farh, JL & Cheng, BS 2014, 'Affective trust in Chinese leaders: linking paternalistic leadership to employee performance', *Journal of Management*, vol. 40, no. 3, pp. 796–819.
36 Hofstede, G 2001.
37 Lee, SM & Peterson, SJ 2000, 'Culture, entrepreneurial orientation, and global competitiveness', *Journal of World Business*, vol. 35, no. 4, pp. 401–416.
38 Sully de Luque, M & Javidan, M 2004, 'Uncertainty avoidance', in RJ House, PM Hanges, M Javidan, P Dorfman & V Gupta, (eds), *Culture, leadership and organizations: the GLOBE study of 62 societies*, Sage, Thousand Oaks, CA, pp. 602–653.
39 Hofstede, G 2001.
40 Lee, SM & Peterson, SJ 2000.
41 Hofstede, G & Bond, MH 1988, 'The Confucian connection: from cultural roots to economic growth', *Organizational Dynamics*, vol. 16, no. 4, pp. 4–21.
42 Trompenaars, F 1993, *Riding the waves of culture: understanding cultural diversity in business*, Nicholas Brearly, London, UK.
43 Noronha, C 2009, 'Culture and business in Asia', in H Hasegawa & C Noronha (eds), *Asian Business and Management*, Palgrave Macmillan, Basingstoke, UK, pp. 101–124.
44 Trompenaars, F & Hampden-Turner, C 1997, *Riding the waves of culture: understanding diversity in global business*, McGraw-Hill, New York.
45 Michailova, S & Hutchings, K 2006, 'National cultural influences on knowledge sharing: a comparison of China and Russia', *Journal of Management Studies*, vol. 43, no. 3, pp. 383–405; Wang, X & Ma, L 2011, 'What change, what stay: the mix picture of value system of Chinese business managers', *Chinese Management Studies*, vol. 5, no. 4, pp. 422–430.
46 Ip, PK 2009.
47 Michailova, S & Hutchings, K 2006.
48 Atherton, A & Newman, A 2016.
49 Trompenaars, F & Hampden-Turner, C 1997.
50 Pang, CK, Roberts, D & Sutton, J 1998, 'Doing business in China – the art of war', *International Journal of Contemporary Hospitality Management*, vol. 10, no. 7, pp. 272–282.
51 Wang, X & Ma, L 2011.
52 Sully De Luque, MF & Sommer, SM 2000, 'The impact of culture on feedback seeking behavior: an integrated model and propositions', *The Academy of Management Review*, vol. 25, no. 4, pp. 829–849.
53 Hampden-Turner, CM & Trompenaars, F 2000, *Building cross cultural competence: how to create wealth from conflicting value*, Yale University Press, New Haven, CT.
54 Trompenaars, F & Hampden-Turner, C 1997.
55 Wang, X & Ma, L 2011.
56 Ambler, T, Witzel, M & Xi, C 2009, *Doing business in China*, Routledge, Abingdon.
57 Fang, T 2005, 'From "onion" to "ocean": paradox and change in national cultures', *International Studies of Management and Organization*, vol. 35, no. 4, pp. 71–90; Fang, T 2012; Faure, GO & Fang, T 2008, 'Changing Chinese values: keeping up with paradoxes', *International Business Review*, vol. 17, pp. 194–207.
58 Fang, T 2012.
59 Talhelm, T, Zhang, X, Oishi, S, Shimin, C, Duan, D, Lan, X & Kitayama, S 2014, 'Large-scale psychological differences within China explained by rice versus wheat agriculture', *Science*, vol. 344, no. 6184, 603–608.
60 Fang, T 2005.
61 McEwen, W, Fang, X, Zhang, C & Burkholder, R 2006, 'Inside the mind of the Chinese consumer', *Harvard Business Review*, vol. 84, no. 3, pp. 68–76; Zhang, ZX, Chen, ZX, Chen, YR & Ang, S 2014.
62 Ralston, DA, Egri, CP, Stewart, S, Terpstra, RH & Yu, K 1999, 'Doing business in the 21st century with the new generation of Chinese managers: a study of generational shifts in work values in China', *Journal of International Business Studies*, vol. 30, no. 2, pp. 415–428.
63 McEwen, W, Fang, X, Zhang, C & Burkholder, R 2006.

8

DEALING WITH THE GOVERNMENT

Introduction

Although the Chinese state has become less directly involved in controlling enterprises and their operational decisions (with the exception of certain state-owned and state-sponsored enterprises), it still plays an important and highly influential role in China's economy. The Chinese government can influence markets through close control of state-owned enterprises (SOEs) and large corporations that are floated on stock exchanges, yet still owned by the state. Certain sectors that are considered strategically important, such as energy, are still controlled tightly by the government, and significant support is given to giant SOEs in these industries. The state also intervenes in the day-to-day operations of other enterprises when it wishes, dictating certain decisions or placing responsibilities or requirements on otherwise independent businesses.

This chapter explores the nature of the state in China and its interactions with entrepreneurs. The analysis focuses on three broad themes. The first theme is the nature of government in China, including its structure and particularly the relationship between the Communist Party of China and the government. The second theme is current enterprise policy in China, and the extent to which this is sufficiently supportive to have a substantive influence on the growth prospects of private enterprises. The third theme is the relationship between the state and entrepreneurs, and particularly whether the state views the private sector as the principal driver of economic development in China's 'new normal' of lower overall growth.

The nature of government in China

The party and the state

The system of government in China is distinct, and its particular feature is the primacy of the Communist Party over the government. The Chinese government formally has four components: the National People's Congress (NPC), the State Council, the state judiciary or Supreme Court, and the People's Liberation Army (PLA). In essence, the NPC has little actual power, and invariably votes for the legislation proposed to it by the executive State Council. It also votes for the president of the People's Republic of China. The judiciary and China's court system are also less powerful, with little tradition of the state and its organs complying with legislation.

This leaves the State Council and the PLA. The key executive body of the State Council is the Politburo Standing Committee, which is an organ of the Chinese Communist Party. This small group, currently of seven people, meets weekly and makes all major executive decisions for the Chinese state. The Politburo Standing Committee is chaired by Xi Jinping, who is concurrently President of the People's Republic of China, General Secretary of the Chinese Communist Party, and chair of the China Military Commission (CMC), which oversees the PLA. This consolidates power across the main organs of the Chinese government in one individual, who chairs the Standing Committee. For such a large and complex country, China is in effect ruled by seven people, with Xi Jinping having significant concentration of power in his hands through the multiple roles he holds. This consolidation of roles was seen to the same or a greater extent in previous leaders, with the exception of Deng Xiaoping in his later years. When Deng stepped down from his other official roles, he remained chair of the CMC, and subsequently had control of the PLA after having nominally retired from public office.

On almost every occasion, senior figures in Chinese government are also senior members of the Chinese Communist Party. In terms of hierarchy and decision making, the party has precedence over the government. The Politburo Standing Committee is both a part of the Communist Party and the primary decision-making entity in China. The pre-eminence of the party is seen throughout China's administrative structures, where the party secretary is more senior than the president, chair or chief executive of the organ of the state to which they both belong. The superiority of the party over the government extends across all aspects of state governance and decision making. One minor yet highly symbolic representation of this is the allocation of number plates in municipalities and provinces. In all cases, the party secretary and deputy secretaries have higher registration numbers than the mayor or governor. This publicly announces the higher position of the party above the government within China.

Ministries, commissions and parallel entities

Under the State Council are the ministries and other administrative entities of China's government. In terms of formal organisation, China's ministries reflect those of many other countries, although the exact configuration is particular to China. These ministries have central functions in Beijing and subsidiaries at provincial, municipal and district levels across China. Thus, they represent vertical pillars reporting up from local level to the province and then to Beijing exclusively through their ministerial reporting lines. This can create silos within the Chinese state that are difficult to cross, as ministries define their goals and advancement of their interests and their officials' careers by their own areas of responsibility.

Partly to address this, China has established a series of cross-cutting commissions over time. These commissions report to the State Council, and have equivalent status to ministries. The most relevant is the National Development and Reform Commission (NDRC), which has overall responsibility for the economic development of China, including macroeconomic policy, economic restructuring and rebalancing, major infrastructure projects, and the opening up the west policy. These responsibilities give NDRC far-reaching powers to engage across ministries and to take an overview of China's economy and its future development. It also places the NDRC in potential conflict or difference of opinion with ministries that it feels are engaged in the NDRC's overall national development remit.

Alongside the formal structure of government, most ministries and other national state entities have created parallel entities that sit outside the governance frameworks. This gives ministries and other state entities the flexibility to operate outside – yet alongside or parallel to – the formal procedures and policies of government. There have been successive campaigns to remove these parallel entities. For example, in the late 1990s and early 2000s, 'social organisations' (*shehui jigou*) – in which ministerial officials held mirror roles – were closed down. In successive periods of the reform era, ministry think tanks and research units have also been closed down or moved to other parts of government. However, these parallel non-governmental organisations continue to operate and provide ministries and other state organisations with less official routes for policy development and implementation.

Central, provincial and local government

As well as the potential for competition and difference between ministries at national level, there are spatial variations in government that can produce internal rivalries. Alongside ministries and other government bodies reporting to the State Council are the administrative bodies that are responsible for China's provinces, four major municipalities and five special administrative regions. These bodies cover the geography of China, and have provincial status in the government. China's third spatial level of government is local. In practice, local government comprises cities, districts and counties, with counties and districts tending to be rural. Each city, district and county reports to the provincial government, which in turn reports to Beijing.[1] There are four classes of cities: tier 1 (the largest cities), tier 2 (large cities), tier 3 (smaller cities) and tier 4 (cities of county standing). There is, therefore, considerable variation in the size and economic importance of cities across China.

This multi-tier government within a centralist state dominated by an autocratic party has created tensions and spatial variations over time. In the early years of reform, local governments tended to enjoy significant autonomy. This was beneficial in many parts of China because central edict or policy could be adapted to local conditions. In extreme cases, local governments did not implement national policy that they believed would either be of little benefit to their locality or could have negative consequences. In addition, local governments often undertook their own initiatives and encouraged or at least tolerated local experimentation.

De-collectivisation and the transfer of agricultural production to households occurred spontaneously in several rural parts of China in the late 1970s and early 1980s – most notably in Anhui and Sichuan provinces. Collectives had become unpopular among most farmers, in large part because they could not sufficiently credit the efforts of individual households and their specific contributions to total yields. Generally, the local governments in the rural parts of China where farmers were de-collectivising and beginning to farm land at a household level did little to prevent this, and observed these experiments with interest. When this phenomenon began to generate much improved yields, local government officials reported these changes as positive local reforms. Provincial and then central government sent 'investigation teams' to examine these cases, and pronounced them successful and to be encouraged elsewhere. Not long after, the last collectives were dissolved and farmers started to farm land for themselves – in many cases, the strips they had cultivated before the communists took power in 1949.[2]

For private enterprises, the autonomy of local government tended to be beneficial. In most cases, local governments were motivated to boost the economic development of their administrative area and, as private enterprises emerged, these businesses became key partners in development. Relationships with privatised SOEs and township and village enterprises (TVEs) were often long-standing, with most local governments having TVE bureaus within them that oversaw these enterprises and negotiated contracts with private entrepreneurs who took over their management. There is evidence that, even when local officials rewarded their own family and social group, support for private entrepreneurs extended beyond their personal networks to include any enterprises that were successful and growing.[3]

Over time, the ability of local government to determine the development of their administrative areas began to create problems that accumulated to become national concerns – two of which are worthy of particular note. The first was an increase – if not explosion – in corruption by local officials. With high levels of local power and little scrutiny or sanctions by provincial or national government, local officials were able to extract resources and favours from individuals, households and organisations that either needed their approval or were seeking favours and opportunities. The combination of high levels of local autonomy and power held by small numbers of officials in localities across China reduced the risks of being caught in corrupt practices.[4] In recent years, local corruption has become one of the most important sources of protest and disturbance in China, especially in rural areas.

The second concern has been the accumulation of debt at levels that are not sustainable, either locally or nationally. Local government has become indebted at serious levels in most parts of China – for example, by issuing bonds in order to finance the construction of infrastructure and the trading of land for development. In most cases, local government does not have the funds to clear these debts, thereby placing the liability with central government. Recent changes to the financing of government in China seek to address these issues and control levels of local indebtedness.[5]

As a result of growing corruption and debt at local level, the Chinese government has increased central control over time. Starting with a 'soft centralisation' in the late 1990s and early 2000s, many regulatory government bodies and activities were moved from local to provincial level.[6] The recent crackdown on corruption has strengthened centralisation, with the national government taking a lead in investigating and punishing local and provincial government officials. Since the late 1990s, state control has become more centralised within the government apparatus in Beijing, with local and provincial governments losing much of the liberty to make their own decisions over this period. However, the scale of China provides centralisation with some pragmatic limits – given the country's size and the strength of local identities, the national government is unable to place local areas under direct and realisable control.

Therefore, China has a three-tier geography of government to administer the country and implement policy and state and party edicts. The relative dynamics between central, provincial and local government have changed during the reform period. In broad terms, local government was highly influential in the earlier years of reform, as the central government encouraged experimentation in policy implementation. Over time, the central government has reduced the autonomy of both local and provincial government, although there are limits to the extent that the centre can control different parts of China through the state apparatus.

Factions and debates inside the party

There is a temptation to view communist parties as monolithic entities that have a standard ideological line to which all members are expected to comply. In China, this representation is inaccurate and does not capture the breadth and extent of debate that exists within the Communist Party. This is not a recent phenomenon either, with differences of opinion being voiced within the party throughout most of its period of rule. These internal differences have been particularly acute at key points in the period of economic reform initiated by Deng Xiaoping.

In the early days of reform, in the late 1970s and 1980s, there was considerable debate and difference of opinion regarding strategies for China's economic development. Maoists held many senior positions in the party and government, and were strongly opposed to economic liberalisation. Although the reformers persuaded party members to support economic liberalisation, largely because of China's poverty, there were many resisters who opposed reform and sought to stop or slow it. Throughout the 1980s, voices for and against reform were heard within the party and, at different times in that decade, the anti-reformers were successful. A particular example is the anti-bourgeois liberalisation campaign in 1986, which followed a period of rapid economic, and limited social, liberalisation. Through most of this decade, the Politburo Standing Committee was split between pro- and anti-reformers, with experienced politicians who served under Mao holding influence over their colleagues.

Today's party has several factions within it that have different views about China's future economic development. There remains a more traditional part of the party, that looks back to more egalitarian times under Mao with nostalgia and sympathy. Factions also rise with successive Chinese leaders as they seek to fill key positions with officials they trust. Examples include the Shanghai faction around Jiang Zemin when he was premier, the youth league faction associated with Hu Jintao, and the neo-Maoist and the Tsinghua University groups – both of which are associated with Xi Jinping. Different factions are portrayed in different ways. For example, Xi Jinping and others who studied at Tsinghua University are seen as reaching out to the public, in contrast with the more remote and ostentatiously privileged 'Princelings', who are children and relatives of earlier senior party leaders. Although Xi Jinping is associated with the Tsinghua University group, which has been viewed as open to Western thinking, he has also aligned closely with the neo-Maoists and traditionalists in the party to assert the party's control and to attack excessive communication of Western values in universities and the press.

This highlights two key observations about the party. The first is that much of what occurs inside the party – particularly its inner sanctum – is internal and not clear or obvious to external observers. As such, the construction of cliques and factions is based on surmise and interpretation, and may not reflect actual power structures. The second is that the internal politics of the party are real, and there are different views and positions. For entrepreneurs in China, this is a significant issue because of indications that there are groups and individuals who still focus on the state-owned sector and are either sceptical of or not committed to supporting private enterprises. The neo-Maoists – who have been actively criticising advocates of Westernisation in the party and beyond – represent such a group, and have been resurgent as a result of Xi Jinping's recent reinforcement of Chinese values and the central role of the Communist Party. Although the technical assessments of China's economic growth have identified the private sector as central to future development, the politics of the party indicate that views about entrepreneurs vary and are polarised.

The five-year plan as a key planning framework for the state

One key mechanism for negotiating differences in opinions about economic development strategy in the party is the five-year plan, which can be seen as a statement of goals and priorities for medium-term development. A remnant from China's planned economy, the five-year plan now functions as a cross-government and party statement on the nature of economic development, in particular identification of the key issues and priorities for the plan period. Individual five-year plans in recent years have had clear and distinctive emphases that have highlighted key issues to address, as well as future aspirations.

The 13th five-year plan was introduced in March 2016 for the period 2016 to 2020. Many of its economic priorities continue themes from the previous two five-year plans, in particular rebalancing the economy away from manufacturing and infrastructure towards services and consumption, addressing China's serious environmental and pollution problems, seeking to sustain growth at levels that will continue to increase household incomes and per capita GDP, and addressing growing income inequalities. The plan also emphasises innovation as a driver for growth and productivity. It will focus on China's current preoccupation: avoiding the middle-income trap experienced by other countries, such as those in South America. These priorities have also been the core concerns of other recent five-year plans. Thus, the 13th five-year plan provides continuity with the previous two plans, giving a 15-year period where consistent economic development priorities have been pursued.

However, what has not been evident in previous five-year plans is recognition of the central role of private enterprises in sustaining and stimulating economic growth. Even though China's economy is now predominantly private, there has been little explicit prioritisation of entrepreneurship. In contrast, there is an ongoing focus on restructuring and developing China's remaining SOEs. However, innovation is more likely to be developed in private enterprises bringing new products and business models to the market, rather than by increasing SOEs' R&D budgets and intellectual property development targets. Moreover, private enterprises account for most of the economy and are continuing to grow. Thus, there is an argument that private sector development should be the principal economic priority of future five-year plans. Without continued growth of this sector, China will not meet its future development objectives.

Enterprise policy in China

The development of enterprise policy in reform-era China

Enterprise policy has evolved to reflect the changing economic challenges of different stages of China's reform period. In the early days of reform, small-scale 'household' enterprises were encouraged in both cities and rural areas. Household enterprises in rural areas were recognised as a means of reducing poverty, especially in areas where there was little alternative employment to agriculture, and returns from farming were low. In the cities, unemployment rose as children 'sent down' to the countryside in the early 1970s (as a way of defusing the Cultural Revolution) started to return to their urban homes.

Household enterprises were also encouraged in order to diversify the Chinese economy by developing 'sideline industries' in which SOEs were not particularly active. 'Sideline' industries in rural areas focused on diversifying away from core agricultural production to activities such as fishing and fisheries, crafts, textiles production, and services and activities to support diversification, such as local production of fertilisers. In the cities, sideline industries focused on the emergence of a household retail and services economy that did not exist before 1978. As a result, and because of their small scale, household enterprises tended to offer services and trades that did not require high levels of initial investment to start and did not require highly technical skills. They engaged in small-scale artisan-type production, as well as trading and the provision of personal services. The emergence and recognition of household enterprises created bicycle repairers, small shops, noodle and snack houses, handicraft artisans, fisheries and countryside traders, which in aggregate created a low-level service economy that allowed for some consumption by households in both urban and rural areas.

Although household enterprises were recognised in 1979, and subsequently represent one of the first initiatives introduced during the reform era, it took time to establish formal legislation to ensure they had legal status. Legislation was passed in 1981 for urban household enterprises, and then in 1984 for their rural counterparts. By that time, the number of these businesses had exploded and they were prevalent across the country. As was the case in the early years of the reform era, the actions and decisions of individuals – in this case, to start their own businesses – preceded formalisation of these types of economic activity by the party and legislature. Legislation and policy then tried to catch up with the rapid emergence of a quasi-formal private sector. These businesses were set up by entrepreneurs before a formal framework recognising their status and existence was in place.

As some of these household enterprises grew, they became medium-sized businesses, employing considerably more people than the initial household. This broke the nominal limit of seven employees imposed on household enterprises – in many cases, several times over. The ability of some private enterprises to grow rapidly so they were no longer considered micro- or small-scale businesses challenged views that these enterprises were focused on generating income for individual households. Rapidly growing private enterprises introduced the notion of profit generation, as they generated significant surpluses. They also started to employ individuals from outside the household, thereby breaking the association between the family unit and business. These private enterprises represented a form of capitalist enterprise that was quickly emerging in the early to mid-1980s. In response, the government recognised the existence of 'private enterprises' in 1988, defining them as businesses that were not state- or collectively owned, with more than seven employees. This legislation was passed alongside tax regulations for these businesses, indicating that the concern was regarding the generation of private profits by these enterprises and how the state could secure a share of these fast-growing surpluses.

In many ways, the underlying narrative of private sector development in reform-era China has been the rapid and unexpected emergence of new forms of entrepreneurship. The government and party have been forced to respond to these new forms of economic activity through introducing policy to recognise and regulate businesses that were already operating – in some cases, for some time. Particularly in the early reform period, new forms of entrepreneurship emerged, creating economic growth and opportunities for individuals to start to generate wealth. Initially, entrepreneurs tended to generate incomes that were often higher than employee salaries. However, these differences were relatively small because China was then still a low-income economy. However, by the 1990s and 2000s, entrepreneurs were generating and retaining significant earnings from their businesses.

Overall, the government's view of private sector development has been *laissez faire* in the sense that these forms of economic activity were tolerated and allowed to emerge, rather than suppressed. The state responded in most cases by formalising emerging forms of private enterprise, rather than attempting to control, regulate or shut them down. Thus, throughout the reform period, the Chinese government has been broadly permissive of private enterprise, rather than seeking to constrain or control the development of these types of businesses. This has allowed new forms of entrepreneurship to emerge at different points during the reform period.

After recognition of the 'private enterprise' as a larger type of entrepreneurial venture, there was little government policy focused on the private sector until the late 1990s. China was growing rapidly, foreign investment was increasing and opening up the export sector, and TVEs were generating significant growth in rural areas, where China's poorest people lived. Over this period, more people came out of the international definition of global poverty (at that time, earning less than $1 USD a day) in China than the rest of the world.

The government's focus on the private sector re-emerged when a growing number of both SOEs and TVEs started losing money and passing the liability for these losses back to the state as their owners. Restructuring the state-owned sector and sell-offs of TVEs during the ninth five-year plan from 1996 to 2000 created major unemployment problems, particularly in areas with heavy reliance on the state sector for employment. For example, in the industrialised provinces of Liaoning and Shandong, unemployment increased so rapidly that, for a period in the late 1990s in some cities, the majority of people in the labour market were either 'laid off' by their work unit or unemployed.

The private sector was considered the primary means of absorbing laid-off workers from SOEs, as well as people made unemployed from loss-making TVEs or losing their government jobs. As a consequence of this interest in the job creation and absorption capabilities of the private sector, there was growing recognition of private enterprises within government and policy. In 1999, the private sector was recognised formally as a national 'pillar' of the economy and society, largely because it was seen as a key source of job creation.[7] In 2000, the State Council recognised small and medium-sized private enterprises as the primary source of re-employment for workers dismissed or laid off from SOEs, and, in 2003, the SME Promotion Law was passed, which noted the role of the private sector in generating both employment and growth.[8]

However, private sector development only became an aspect of public policy because it offered a means of dealing with a major unemployment issue that had been created by SOEs. In other words, private enterprises were not considered a focus for policy themselves, but rather as a means of addressing problems generated by the state enterprises that were a primary focus of government policy. The 2003 SME Promotion Law was passed in order to create local systems to support private business start-up and growth across China. However, these systems were not established, largely because local government had little expertise in private sector development and no real interest in better understanding the needs of this sector of the economy as part of formal plans. A lack of formal budget allocation in the finances of municipalities and counties meant that any systems that were developed could not be funded through a recognised channel or budget item. Thus, the SME support systems mandated in the 2003 law had no confirmed source of funding to finance their creation.[9] Partial or non-implementation is a common feature of legislation affecting private enterprises. The 2007 National Property Law recognised and formally protected private ownership, yet this has not been consistently or robustly enforced.

Instead of refocusing on the emerging private sector – which, by the late 2000s, had become the largest employer and generator of economic output in China – the state has continued its support for large SOEs, and strengthened its policy of building these national enterprises into huge corporations, dominating their markets in China and increasingly internationalising their activities. Through the 2000s, there is little evidence that the state has refocused its policies on the private sector and its dominant role in generating growth. As the private sector becomes increasingly important and accounts for almost all economic activity, a mismatch has emerged between a policy focus on the state sector and the emergence of the private economy as China's driver of future growth.

An area in which there has been progress is the state's reduction in the barriers to becoming an entrepreneur. In May 2014, the Chinese government simplified the registration requirements to start a new business in the hope that this would encourage higher levels of new venture creation. The response was almost immediate, with registrations increasing in 2014 by almost half (+50 per cent) compared with 2013, according to the State Administration for Industry and Commerce, which registers new businesses. Although a proportion of these new registrations appeared to be businesses that were already trading, this increase in business start-ups is an encouraging sign that entrepreneurship has become desirable for many Chinese people. Simplifying business start-up procedures has been a policy focus in the European Union and US for some time, based on the premise that making it easier to start a venture will encourage more potential entrepreneurs to do so. The experience of China supports this proposition, and bodes well for future wealth creation as the population of new private enterprises grows.

Given the current concern about overall growth rates in China, a lack of emphasis on private sector development in policy development may seem strange. However, the reasons are logical and in many ways understandable. As noted earlier in this chapter, the predisposition of the Chinese state has been to recognise emerging forms of entrepreneurship and formally legislate in their favour. This permissive attitude to entrepreneurship has allowed the private sector to grow, without many enterprises experiencing high levels of direct intervention and control from the state. In addition, the Chinese government continues to face challenges with its national SOEs and other businesses, particularly the state banks. Thus, a continuing focus on the state sector is viewed as important to remove inefficiencies and problems in the Chinese economy. It appears that the current policy stance is that, because the private sector has been successful, it can be left to compete and thrive in an increasingly market-driven economy without significant state support.

The focus of enterprise policy in China

The focus of enterprise policy has revolved around several key themes, which were discussed in the previous section. Initially, small-scale enterprise was viewed as a means of creating new forms of economic activity that were not provided by the state sector, which tended to focus on large-scale production and manufacturing. By encouraging new enterprises to set up, the Chinese economy was able to diversify, thereby creating enhanced services for consumers and generating new opportunities for economic activity. In rural areas, the driver for encouraging household enterprises was to increase income levels, which were extremely low at the start of the reform period and continue to lag behind urban incomes to this day. In cities, the driver has been to create new jobs to absorb excess labour and reduce unemployment.

Over most of the reform period, until relatively recently, small private enterprises were conceived by the government as creators of new jobs in the economy and a source of economic flexibility. However, they have not been a core policy focus for the Chinese state. Instead, to some extent, the private sector appears to be considered a safety valve in the Chinese economy when there are problems in the state sector. Although the government recognises the need for a private sector – for employment and to create economic dynamism – there is only some engagement in policy making to actively stimulate entrepreneurship. Recently, private enterprises have started to be seen as sources of innovation, especially in consumer services and products. However, they have not yet been characterised in policy statements and documents as a major component and driver of the Chinese economy.

In many ways, this is understandable. The notion of private enterprise is distant from communist theory. The Chinese Communist Party is still committed to public ownership of the means of production, and private enterprises contradict this element of communist ideology. Although party members may view entrepreneurship as important to economic growth, and indeed many members have, at times, engaged in some form of entrepreneurship themselves, public proclamation that the economy of the People's Republic of China is privately owned and that entrepreneurs will drive future economic growth can be seen as a major ideological shift in the party's position.

Creating the right conditions for entrepreneurship

With the transformation of the State Economic and Trade Commission and parts of what was the State Planning Commission into the NDRC in 2003, the Chinese government indicated that the next phase in future planning for the economy would shift from trade convergence to macroeconomic management. Since then, the NDRC has become the central government unit that has taken on the role of 'state capitalist', as mapped out by Hu Jintao and Wen Jiabao. Its overall remit is to oversee economic policy, and it played a central role in stabilising the Chinese economy in 2008 to 2009 and 2012, when wider global effects slowed growth in China. It also has considerable powers within government because its remit includes signing off major capital projects, including those initiated and implemented by other ministries and government bodies.

As the most powerful state commission, the NDRC sits above the state's ministries and has the power to engage across government, should its remit allow. The role of the NDRC as macroeconomic planner and manager, as well as its close links to the State Council, places the commission at the heart of economic policy and decision making. It continues to steer government policy and spending on economic development. The implications for the private sector are clear. Although there will be no substantive framework to directly stimulate entrepreneurship and create a more level playing field for competition between the public and private sectors, the emphasis of government policy will be on creating conducive macro-economic conditions. If these conditions are positive, this will encourage more individuals to start businesses, and will enable existing private enterprises to grow and succeed through market competition. Thus, the approach is to create the enabling conditions for individuals to start and grow their own businesses, rather than to intervene directly.

A key component of creating the right conditions for growth will be the major capital projects signed off by the NDRC. Many of these seek to improve connectivity within China – for example, through creating a national network of high-speed rail and through creating development corridors linking up major cities. In principle, internal connectivity reduces the transaction costs of internal market exchange, thereby lowering the minimum return on trading within China. Improved connectivity connects markets and improves the mobility of labour as the costs and time associated with travel fall. The efficiency of this infrastructure – in particular investment in communications and travel – should create more enabling conditions for entrepreneurship.

Thus, China has adopted a model of macroeconomic and infrastructure development – rather than direct intervention – that should create improved conditions for entrepreneurs. This is in contrast to the 100 or so major national SOEs, which it continues to support directly. Given that these enterprises are part of the state, and private enterprises are neither controlled nor owned by the state, this distinction appears logical within the framework of a communist government developing a more marketised economy.

Innovation and high-tech businesses

Although the Chinese government appears to have adopted a broadly *laissez faire* approach to private sector development in China, there are some exceptions. The most notable is the encouragement of innovation and high-tech business start-up and growth. Components of a national innovation system are in place, in particular the development of a strong academic research base and public investment in R&D spending. However, these have not yet translated into improved innovation performance, as measured by patents filed and application of R&D to improve business performance.[10] Despite this, China has one of the fastest rates of increase in academic paper citations of any country worldwide, and will become one of the most cited countries in the world for its published academic research. This is the first step in building a science base that can translate this research into innovation and technology development.

Moreover, there are signs that R&D spending is starting to translate into innovation in some areas. For example, in consumer electronics and internet services, which are both private sector led, the emergence of companies such as Xiaomi, Alibaba and Tencent has created examples of high levels of product and service innovation that are encouraging other entrepreneurs to develop new products, services and business models. In addition, incremental improvements in manufacturing efficiency and quality are evident across China's global supply chains, concentrated in the Pearl River Delta, Pudong and the lower Yangzi River. Process improvements have made many of these manufacturers among the leanest worldwide.

However, the Chinese innovation ecosystem is still under-developed. In science-based innovation and in the ability of SOEs to harness acquired technology, China's track record is at best mixed, and in many cases weak. At present, the link between R&D and economic growth through business innovation is insufficiently developed, even though there is huge expenditure by the state in universities and public institutions. Although China has many high-tech development zones in its cities, which were originally conceived as environments within which research could be commercially exploited, most operate as locations for inward investors – either from overseas, or increasingly to attract companies away from the coast and into inland China.[11]

This is partly because the emphasis of state spending to encourage private innovation has focused on business start-ups, and has tended to involve creating incubators. Since the introduction of the Torch programme by the Ministry of Science and Technology in the late 1980s, Torch incubators and successor technology development facilities have been established in most parts of China. Although there have been some successes, the emphasis on new venture creation makes technology exploitation particularly challenging, as this tends to be undertaken by established and older businesses.

Thus, for the state to enable more private sector innovation, there would need to be R&D investment in established and successful enterprises. At present, the state spends heavily on universities and research institutes, and supports SOEs to both acquire technology and undertake their own R&D. It has also created the conditions to stimulate the emergence of industries such as wind turbine technology and photovoltaics. However, much of these top-down successes have been due to subsidies and financial inducements. What has been lacking is an innovation relationship between successful private enterprises and the state. Indeed, where attempts have been made to bring them together, they have tended to be ineffective, as the cultures of entrepreneurship and the state have not been able to unite.[12]

Relations between entrepreneurs and the government

In broad terms, government attitudes towards entrepreneurs are based on three perspectives. First, there is political recognition that private enterprises now dominate the economy and are subsequently important to China's future economic growth and achievement of the five-year plan objectives. Second, there is a view that private entrepreneurs operate in the market, and should subsequently work within the parameters of competition, without support from the state. Third, for many in the party, there continues to be an ideological concern regarding the private sector because it is a capitalist dynamic within the socialist market economy of China. Private enterprise, although now important to China, runs counter to the manifesto of the Chinese Communist Party and to the values of ideologically committed party members. These three perspectives are complementary in the sense that all three can be held by party members. Thus, they reflect a broad policy perspective regarding the private sector in China.

The resistance by government officials to supporting private enterprise extends beyond ideological concerns about the political economy of China to more pragmatic views about entrepreneurship. From a party and government perspective, entrepreneurs take risks in competitive market environments and, if successful, secure rewards. In doing so, they are likely to earn considerably more than most party officials, even at senior level. There is little incentive or rationale for government officials and members of the Communist Party to intervene in the market to help entrepreneurs make even more money for themselves. In addition, within the party and at many levels in government, there continue to be proponents of communism who are either sceptical about or hostile towards entrepreneurship. Neo-Maoists and traditionalists in the party are likely to argue against and resist cases for direct state promotion and support of private enterprises.

However, there will also be views within the party that private entrepreneurs now drive the Chinese economy and should be supported – not only politically, as was done by recognising their right to join the party, but also through policy and direct intervention. The outcome that makes the most sense in this context is the policy approach that has been adopted: of creating the right conditions for entrepreneurship, yet allowing the market to select those that are successful through their ability to compete and innovate themselves. Ideologically, this allows officials with different views of entrepreneurship to engage with this policy approach.

Corruption and expropriation by officials

The ability of entrepreneurs to generate large returns from their enterprises in a country controlled by the state partly explains the corruption and expropriation experienced by many entrepreneurs. This operates at many levels. Local officials may charge successful private businesses ad hoc and excessive tax for many reasons, including to fund local projects and to bolster the finances of local government. Local officials may also look for a share of an entrepreneur's profits, and will use their power locally to put pressure on that individual to pay. On relatively low salaries and living in a state and party system where they control many aspects of the economy and society, it is understandable that some officials feel they can extract resources from successful private enterprises.

The primary issue for entrepreneurship is that extraction of resources increases the costs of operating as a business, and subsequently suppresses profits. This is particularly challenging if multiple officials seek payments and kickbacks from businesses. Equally, a successful private enterprise may be charged additional taxes when local government budgets run low or new projects are proposed. Growing businesses have also been asked to take on additional staff – either friends and relatives of officials, or unemployed individuals unable to find employment. In each of these cases, which are relatively common in China, the costs of running a business increase, and the profitability of the business suffers accordingly. The price of resisting these interventions from the government may be greater than the costs of complying, given the high levels of autonomy of local government and the low levels of accountability and governance.

In some cases, the private enterprise is taken over completely once it has reached a certain size and established itself as a successful venture. Known colloquially as the 'fat pig policy', successful and profitable private enterprises are expropriated by government (typically local) and effectively nationalised. Such risks, although increasingly rare in contemporary China, may push entrepreneurs to develop strong links with key officials in the local government in attempts to prevent expropriation. They may also tend to discourage overly conspicuous consumption by successful entrepreneurs. The 2007 Property Law provides legal protection against the 'fat pig policy', and a means of redress if take-over occurs. However, it has been implemented variably and may be difficult to deploy if the local judiciary and government officials collude or work closely together.

'Guanxi' relationships between officials and entrepreneurs

Corruption does not flow in one direction. Many entrepreneurs cultivate relationships with key officials in the government, either to secure special advantages or as a defensive strategy. This form of *'guanxi'* (relationship building through the offer and exchange of gifts and favours) is well established in China, and there is an ongoing pattern of *guanxi* interactions between entrepreneurs and officials. Offering gifts, hospitality and payments to officials can develop closer relationships that can benefit the entrepreneur. This may be done to buy access to lucrative government orders and tenders. It may also have other advantages, such as easing planning and building applications or avoiding taxation.

In broad terms, entrepreneurs can develop a business strategy based on 'leaning on government' (*kao zhengfu*), where they seek close relationships with officials as the basis for growing their business. For these businesses, which benefit from close working relations with the government, *guanxi* becomes an important dimension of business activity. Wining and dining officials and building close relationships can create business opportunities that would not otherwise be available. Alternatively, an entrepreneur can develop relationships as a form of protection for the enterprise. With a sponsor in government, this may deter or prevent other officials from expropriating assets or resources from the enterprise. In these cases, strategic relations with powerful officials act as a form of insurance against expropriation.

Most entrepreneurs have relations with party officials, as they are important economic actors that can influence the future development of an enterprise. The more successful an entrepreneur and their business, the more likely they will have extensive interactions and subsequent relations with government officials. These relationships will be multifaceted. Some will be because certain officials have responsibility for economic development or planning in a certain location or sector in which the entrepreneur is a major economic and potentially social influence. Others will be because the entrepreneur's business gains from these relations, and there may be benefits for the officials in return. For nationally known entrepreneurs, officials may engage with them as part of their own social networks, or to engage in wider projects for which private support or sponsorship is deemed desirable.

As noted, there will be a range of views about entrepreneurs and private businesses held by the officials that engage with them. Some will be supportive and interested in the development of the business. Others will be neutral in the sense that they find the relationship with the entrepreneur useful or stimulating, but have little interest in engaging directly with their business. Yet other officials will be hostile – strongly or mildly – viewing private entrepreneurs as sitting outside the state and party system to which they belong and are wedded.

The political roles and significance of entrepreneurs in China

In China, economic decisions are still ultimately politically motivated or influenced because of the dominant role that the party continues to play. In 2001, entrepreneurs were invited to join the Communist Party and were recognised as a 'pillar' of society. The political and social symbolism of this invitation is high in China, where the party is powerful and dominates the media. Recognition of the importance of private enterprises has brought greater social prestige to entrepreneurs, who, earlier in the reform period, were often ignored or considered inferior to the state sector and other parts of society.

However, this recognition does not mean that the Communist Party has become a strong and active advocate of the private sector. Instead, as noted above, the state is relatively *laissez faire*, leaving the fortunes of individual businesses to the market. Political recognition of entrepreneurs as an important part of the economy and member of the wider socio-political structures of contemporary China is different to active promotion and support of the private sector. The former has occurred, while the latter has not. At the same time, the state actively supports SOEs and state banks where necessary, to the detriment or disadvantage of private enterprises.

The socio-political role of entrepreneurs in China is readily apparent under Xi Jinping. His anti-corruption campaign has moved from government officials and senior managers of SOEs to prominent entrepreneurs. In several high-profile cases, millionaire and billionaire owners of highly successful independent businesses have been taken in for questioning and disappeared temporarily from their businesses and family lives. In a country where relationships between entrepreneurs and officials are often intertwined, and where there may be the exchange or transfer of favours and resources, investigation into corrupt government officials is likely to lead to the entrepreneurs with whom they had relationships. Thus, despite wider social recognition and a legislative framework that enshrines the independence of private enterprises, entrepreneurs and the businesses they run ultimately fall under the influence and intervention of the state, if that is what officials decide.

Notes

1 There are five levels of sub-national government: province (or equivalent); prefecture; county or district; townships; and villages. However, the key prefectural governments tend to be cities, and townships and villages report into the country or district government. Moreover, townships and villages tend to receive relatively similar treatment and consideration.
2 Nolan, P 1983, 'De-collectivisation of agriculture in China, 1979–82: A long-term perspective', *Economic and Political Weekly*, vol. 18, no. 32, pp. 1395–1406.
3 Ruf, G 1998, *Cadres and kin*, Stanford University Press, Stanford, CA
4 Birney, M 2014, 'Decentralization and veiled corruption under China's "Rule of Mandates"', *World Development*, vol. 53, pp. 55–67.
5 Lu, Y & Tao, S 2013, 'Local government financing platforms in China: a fortune or misfortune?' *IMF Working Paper No. 13/243*, https://ssrn.com/abstract=2375564 (viewed 3 June 2017).
6 Mertha, AC 2005, 'China's "soft" centralization: shifting *tiao/kuai* authority relations', *The China Quarterly*, vol. 184, pp. 791–810.
7 Atherton, A 2008, 'From "fat pigs" and "red hats" to a "new social stratum": the changing face of enterprise development policy in China', *Journal of Small Business and Enterprise Development*, vol. 15, no. 4, pp. 640–655.
8 Atherton, A & Smallbone, D 2013, 'Promoting private sector development in China: the challenge of building institutional capacity at the local level', *Environment and Planning C: Government and Policy*, vol. 31, no. 1, pp. 5–23.
9 Atherton, A & Fairbanks, A 2006, 'Stimulating private sector development in China: the emergence of enterprise development centres in Liaoning and Sichuan provinces', *Asia Pacific Business Review*, vol. 12, no. 3, pp. 333–354.
10 OECD 2008, *OECD Reviews of Innovation Policy*. OECD: Paris, http://www.oecd.org/sti/innovation/reviews/china (viewed 3 June 2017).
11 Roth, E, Seong, J & Woetzel, J 2015, *Gauging the strength of Chinese innovation*. McKinsey Global Institute, http://www.mckinsey.com/insights/innovation/gauging_the_strength_of_chinese_innovation (viewed 3 June 2017).
12 Abrami, RM, Kirby, WC & McFarlan, FW 2014, 'Why China can't innovate', *Harvard Business Review*, vol. 92, no. 3, pp. 107–111, https://hbr.org/2014/03/why-china-cant-innovate (viewed 3 June 2017).

9

DOING BUSINESS WITH CHINESE ENTREPRENEURS

Introduction

In this chapter, the tone of the book changes from a commentary on entrepreneurs in China to a series of suggestions on how to work with these entrepreneurs and build a presence in that country. The emphasis is on offering suggestions and advice, and the tone is more direct. As with any set of recommendations, they are neither instructions nor prerequisites, but rather guidelines to consider and adapt. They should not, however, replace direct experience. The most effective means of learning about doing business with Chinese entrepreneurs is through direct engagement.

The importance of local knowledge

Understanding China, and in particular its specific characteristics and development trajectory, is essential for business success in that country. Although local knowledge is important in all overseas markets, China has its own particular context that is complex, changing and influential. It is distinctive in that it combines the following: rapid economic growth; an entrepreneurial environment where competition is high; a huge domestic market; growing demand from businesses and consumers; national confidence; a strong government; and high levels of sovereign wealth. This is a combination that does not exist in other emerging economies. For many Chinese entrepreneurs, it creates a confidence and self-belief that shapes relationships with foreign business people and companies.

The Chinese often talk to foreigners about their country's 'special characteristics' (literally national circumstances, or *guoqing* in Mandarin). In doing so, they are not only pointing out China's particular circumstances but are indicating that experiences gained elsewhere are unlikely to apply to China. Understanding this national situation is essential for successful entry into the Chinese market. Businesses and individuals that have not recognised and sought insight into the China context have found it much more difficult to succeed in their business goals.[1] This notion of a special context indicates that the rules of the game are determined within China; those entering it are expected to comply and play by these rules. Those that do will be recognised for working within China's special circumstances, and so will develop greater credibility with partners.[2]

China has a strong culture that shapes how individuals engage in business and how relationships are developed and deployed in ways that can help a business to prosper. These cultural values are distinctive to China and endow its citizens with national pride, patriotism and confidence. They also generate a strong sense of cultural identity that is shared by almost all Chinese people, who associate themselves with a dominant ethnic identity and strong social and spiritual values based on traditions that pre-date communist rule. A sense of Chinese identity was reinforced in Maoist China, when a distinctive form of communism was developed and the country turned in on itself, engaging little with the outside world. This was particularly the case after 1962, when ties were broken with the Soviet Union.

A strong Chinese culture, combined with a language steeped in historical and cultural references, creates a context where having some understanding of these values and the reference points is essential. A sense of Chinese history; an understanding of Confucian and other values in modern-day society; an empathy with China's view of itself in the world; insight into how Chinese society and the state work; and some ability to speak and understand Chinese will all improve the prospects for international businesses and business people to better understand China, and in doing so improve the prospects of success in this country.

Local knowledge of China therefore incorporates several dimensions: cultural understanding of the values and viewpoints of Chinese people; a knowledge of Chinese history and its symbolic meaning and sensitivities for Chinese people; knowledge of Chinese customs and social interactions; and an understanding of how quickly China, in particular its social values and perspectives, are changing. Each of these, although not directly focused on developing business in China, will prepare foreign investors and business people to operate in a country that is proud of what it has achieved since the late 1970s and is working through its role and significance in East and Southeast Asia, and also globally.

Although China is a broadly homogenous society – ethnically, linguistically and in terms of shared values – there are significant local differences in culture, language and how business is done. Aspects of these differences are enshrined in national stereotypes of different types of Chinese person, as defined by their original birthplace. Ask a Chinese person their views about how people behave and think depending upon where they come from, and they will give you very different characterisations of people from, for example, Shanghai, Guangzhou, Sichuan or the north-east of China. Differences in how people are characterised by their origin may focus on how they do business ('watch the Shanghainese and Cantonese'), how hard working they are or are not ('especially if they come from laid-back

Sichuan'), or how forthright and hard drinking they may be ('be careful drinking or getting into an argument with somebody from the north-eastern provinces of Liaoning, Jilin or Heilongjiang'). These are of course stereotypes, and so caricatures at best, but they capture something of the diversity of local characteristics in different parts of China, and of the varying behaviours of people who come from those places.

Local differences in China are socio-cultural and linguistic, but they also relate to how business is done. Taking the examples of stereotypes used in the previous paragraph, how business negotiations and agreements are undertaken varies from place to place across China. Guangdong and the Pearl River Delta are influenced by Hong Kong business practices and the procedures and approaches of global giants sourcing from that part of China. Conversely, the north-east region continues to have a heavier industry base, and a relatively greater proportion of state-owned entrerprise (SOE) activity, than the coastal or southern regions. The contrast between the northern and other areas is evident when considering the role the state plays in economic development and business practice. Differences in the extent to which these areas are open to the global economy are also clear. Localised practices for 'striking a deal' vary across China, for example. This presents two challenges for entrepreneurs and business people seeking to operate in China. The first is to develop some insight into what these practices are; the second is to be aware that these business practices vary across China – meaning that local knowledge of doing business in one place does not necessarily prepare a foreign business person or entrepreneur for doing business in other parts of the country.

Local knowledge extends beyond culture and values, to business structures and the organisation of economic activities. The extent of distribution networks, transport services and warehousing, for example, varies considerably across China. In the Pearl River Delta, these are well developed and heavily influenced by Hong Kong's expertise in logistics. Major global sourcing and partnering businesses, such as Li and Fung, have developed extensive sourcing, distribution and logistics across the Pearl River Delta. This is based on close and well-developed relationships with infrastructure operators and local producers. Strong logistics and procurement networks exist in this part of China because of its geographical proximity to Hong Kong and the shared Cantonese language. The involvement of Hong Kong companies in the Pearl River Delta is long standing, with many setting up manufacturing, sourcing and supply chain operations in the 1980s and 1990s.

Global supply chain integration, and the logistics and sourcing expertise this brings, tends to be highly concentrated in a few places in China, where most of the manufactured products exported from China are made. As well as the Pearl River Delta, there are major concentrations of logistics and distribution capability in other parts of China: the Pudong development area in Shanghai; coastal Fujian and Zhejiang provinces, focused on key cities such as Wenzhou; and around Suzhou and Hangzhou in the Yangzi River Delta. Outside these parts of China, which are highly integrated into global supply chains and markets, distribution and logistics capacity is variable and in places underdeveloped. In many parts of China, distribution networks are limited, serving only a local economic area. This is despite major public investment by government in the logistics and distribution infrastructure across China.[3]

Many global businesses source large proportions of their inputs or goods from China, taking advantage of historically low prices due in large part to labour costs that have been markedly lower than in more mature economies. In recent years, and particularly since World Trade Organization (WTO) accession in the early 2000s, these businesses have improved their logistics networks, extending their sourcing from the Pearl River to other parts of the country. One example is Wal-Mart, which sources from China most of what it sells in the US and other Western countries. Wal-Mart has been involved in sourcing from China for several decades, and has opened up a national network of stores within the country itself. The majority of its suppliers are located in the Pearl River Delta, where its global outsourcing headquarters is based. Even though Wal-Mart has an expanding national network of retailers, the vast majority of its sourced products still come from this traditional exporting heartland of Guangdong. Companies such as Wal-Mart, in other words, have high levels of knowledge of China's clusters of exported manufactured products in Guangdong and Shanghai, and a growing understanding of demand in cities across China. However, this knowledge is specific to the networks and locations they have developed as a core focus for their China strategy. In other words, Wal-Mart's local knowledge within China does not translate into expertise in all parts of China and does not offer access to suppliers and to local knowledge in parts of the country where Wal-Mart has been less or not active during its period of high activity in China.

In conclusion, China knowledge and an understanding of its 'special circumstances' is essential for business success in China. However, insight into the 'national condition' is insufficient because of local variation in business practices and structures. International businesses will also need to develop their understanding of these variations and specific conditions within each part of China in which they are active. In addition, businesses seeking to develop a national presence or to source from across the country will need to build their logistics networks in a context where this sector is underdeveloped.

The *guanxi* factor: networks and relationships in China

Alongside improving local knowledge, building relationships is an essential part of doing business in China. The art of developing relationships that enable business is known as '*guanxixue*' (literally the study of relations).[4] The term '*guanxi*' is broader, and indicates an individual's networks and relationships, as well as the ways in which people interact to build trust between each other. *Guanxi* can help individuals, if these relationships provide access that may be difficult otherwise, but in general terms reciprocity and trust govern *guanxi* relations. In general, *guanxi* represents relationships between individuals that are mutually entered into and indicate respect for each party. They can help develop business opportunities, but their reciprocal nature and their focus on building trust between individuals means that there will be long-term obligations, as well as expectations that both parties will treat each other fairly and in an open way. These expectations effectively operate as sanctions against behaviours that appear to overly advantage one party or that are damaging to the other party. As a result, the application of *guanxi* to business is limited by the performance of these obligations.

The notion of *guanxixue* is more ambiguous. Although it can be seen as an essential strategy for developing businesses and securing opportunities, it also bears a connotation that is somewhat negative.[5] *Guanxixue* can involve the use of bribes and favours for personal and business gain in ways that could be seen as either short-cutting formal approaches and negotiations, or as forms of corruption and securing of resources that otherwise would not be available. As such, *guanxixue* is both a means for entrepreneurs to extend their networks to enable the development of their business, and a strategy for securing favours and opportunities from others, often illicitly or informally.

Despite this ambivalence about the use of *guanxixue* in developing businesses, relationships are essential for business success in China and their development and management can generate opportunities for entrepreneurs as well as helping to avoid problems and difficulties. Chinese entrepreneurs tend to have extensive networks of relationships and work hard to nurture positive *guanxi* with customers, suppliers, financiers and other stakeholders. These networks of relationships help the business to function more smoothly, regardless of whether specific favours are exchanged or traded. If, for example, an entrepreneur has an urgent deadline placed on an order, positive relationships with key suppliers can help fulfil the order. In this way, relationships in China are very similar to those in other countries. Trust and understanding can enable business to be transacted based on goodwill and mutual understanding. Entrepreneurs in any environment, and country, develop and manage their networks in this way to reduce risk and the costs of doing business.

In China, relationships can also be defensive, in the sense that they are developed to reduce risks that may arise for the entrepreneur and their business. Relationships with government are often defensive, at least in part, even when those relationships are developed to secure advantage or opportunities from public officials. Strong *guanxi* with key government officials in the city or location where an entrepreneur operates can help prevent, or reduce, the risks and scale of kickbacks and other forms of extraction that still occur in contemporary China.[6] Good relations with officials also help the business to expand. For example, positive *guanxi* with foreign trade and economic development officials in local government can generate access to international investors and businesses enquiring about opportunities in China. Positive *guanxi* can also help secure permits from government including, for example, those to build or extend facilities.

For foreign business people and entrepreneurs seeking to enter China, *guanxi* is important, although *guanxixue* may present risks and challenges. Building local networks of suppliers and service providers will be essential, and ensuring that procurement is effective and efficient will entail development of links and relationships with local businesses. If a foreign business is seeking to sell within China, developing an in-country distribution, warehousing and sales network will also be important. Major businesses that have created national retail chains in China – such as Carrefour, Home Depot, IKEA and Wal-Mart – have tended to focus on the tier 1 cities of Beijing and Shanghai initially and then expanded to the more prosperous cities in eastern and southern China as a second phase of growth. Some of these businesses are now expanding further, to the west and north, as cities in these parts of the country have grown rapidly in recent years, whereas growth has slowed and operating costs have risen along the coast.

Even when seeking to export from China, foreign businesses will need to develop local networks of suppliers and service providers, and also of export distribution and shipping companies. In each case, the more developed the foreign business' network, the better it will be able to compete in either the domestic Chinese or export markets. Building good relationships with key contacts in other businesses will enable orders to be filled more quickly, procurement to function more effectively and, in the case of problems or urgent requirements, issues to be resolved more easily. Conversely, not having good relationships with suppliers, service providers and distributors or logistics companies can make a foreign business vulnerable to poor service or closure of one of these partner businesses. In a dynamic and fast-changing environment such as China, changes and unexpected events will happen that make the strength and breadth of local networks, and the relationships that underpin them, essential to ensure continuity of business operations.

Relationships with government are also important in a country like China, where the state continues to have influence and control over many aspects of the economy and society. At a basic level, having the appropriate permissions and licenses to operate in China requires application and registration with state bodies, including the National Development and Reform Commission (NDRC), the Ministry of Commerce (MOFCOM) and the State Administration for Industry and Commerce (SAIC). This will require some relationship building to secure permissions. In addition, most enterprises in China develop some relationships with the local government in the locations in which they are based or where they have significant activities. These relationships can help in many ways including, for example, when applying for planning permission; also ensuring that any risks of land acquisition are either anticipated or avoided.

Building a strong and wide network of relationships with key individuals in partner and stakeholder businesses and organisations is important when establishing a presence in China, and at times will be key to expanding the business as well as protecting it. However, the notion of *guanxi* is specific to China, and many Chinese people consider it to be embedded in their own culture. This makes it more difficult for non-Chinese entities and individuals to develop their own *guanxi* and to do so in a way that is aligned with these cultural norms and expectations. As a result, foreign enterprises have sought out partnerships and joint ventures with leading Chinese enterprises in part to leverage the *guanxi* relationships and networks that these businesses have already developed. Although attractive superficially, this driver for collaboration typically does not improve the *guanxi* of the foreign enterprise, for several main reasons. First, *guanxi* developed by a Chinese business is embedded in its own networks and reasons for developing relationships. These relationships are focused, in other words, on supporting and enabling the business that has developed them. Typically, they are highly personalised, often around friendships that develop between key individuals in the business and its partner organisations. These social and personalised relationships are difficult to transfer to others without effort. Second, existing *guanxi* may not be aligned to the objectives or needs of a joint venture or partner. Even if some aspects of existing *guanxi* can help, the new collaboration will need to build its own *guanxi* to ensure that the relational benefits these networks offer align with the new venture. Third, existing *guanxi* is not always either strong or effective, as it is the legacy of years of existing relationships being maintained. It is conceivable that in privatised SOEs, for example, most of the historical *guanxi* has been with state officials; in a market environment, different *guanxi* networks are needed.

Foreign entrepreneurs and enterprises that seek to develop long-term and successful presences in China therefore need to build their own networks and develop and manage the *guanxi* relationships that are important to the success and survival of their ventures. Tapping into the existing *guanxi* networks and relationships of Chinese individuals and enterprises will not always secure the right type of *guanxi* for a foreign enterprise operating in China. Developing a network of relationships and partnerships to support the business is hard work, and initially culturally opaque and confusing. Nonetheless, it is essential for success in the Chinese market.

Doing business with Chinese entrepreneurs

Local knowledge and good *guanxi* are key factors that underpin success in the Chinese market. However, they will not on their own ensure successful entry into the Chinese market and operation. In this section, four dimensions of business success in China are considered. These are:

- Understanding Chinese business culture
- Developing and sustaining relationships
- Developing a successful presence in China
- Dealing with the environment around you.

For each dimension, there are recommendations on how they can be achieved. Many of these dimensions reflect good practice for companies operating in the Chinese market, and all are particularly important when working with entrepreneurs.

Understanding Chinese business culture

As with any country, China has its own distinctive ways of doing business. As has been noted already in this chapter, the boundaries between business and social relationships are more ambiguous and fluid in China than in many countries. There are also expectations that Chinese entrepreneurs have of how other Chinese people will behave when doing business. These expectations do not necessarily apply to non-Chinese business people, and there is an understanding that individuals from very different cultures will not understand many if any of these ways of behaving when doing business. It is commonplace, especially in parts of China that have had exposure to other countries and other nationalities, for Chinese entrepreneurs to explicitly recognise this when meeting international business people.

However, demonstrating some understanding of Chinese business practices, and attempting to follow them, generally has a very positive effect and so can help develop stronger relationships. When developing relationships with Chinese entrepreneurs, making the effort to work within these cultural norms tends to be well received. As such, seeking to better understand and align with the following aspects of Chinese business culture can help with initial entry into China and also development of a stronger market presence. Suggestions for how to operate within the specific aspects of business culture are presented in the rest of this section.

Understand and practice Chinese social rituals

There are many social rituals in China. These start when people are first introduced, with consideration of social hierarchies, and they continue as relationships develop. At first introductions, the order in which a Chinese group will present themselves indicates their internal hierarchy, with the most important person presenting themselves first. At a first introduction, business cards are invariably exchanged, with both hands being used to give out cards. Increasingly, Chinese people bow slightly when first introducing themselves. They also seek to play down their importance, demonstrating modesty in front of their colleagues. Mirroring these behaviours is generally a good start to discussions.

Gift giving and exchange is an important part of Chinese social rituals, associated with instrumental *guanxixue* development of relationships but also as a part of many social interactions. To arrive empty-handed when invited to someone's house can be considered rude. For non-Chinese partners, gifts will be offered at each meeting, at least in the early stages of relationship development. In these early stages, the gifts can be formal and are often expensive so that they give both the giver and the recipient face. Over time, and as social relationships and business partnerships develop, gifts become less formal and need not be expensive or rare. Instead, they become a means of offering respect to the other party, and to open up opportunities to socialise and eat together.

Social rituals around eating are important and there are many different practices to heed. The most important host sits at the head of the table with their most important guest to their right and the second most important guest to their left. The second most important host typically sits opposite the lead host. If the guests are non-Chinese speakers, interpreters or people who can speak the other language will typically sit next to the first and second guests. Guests do not start eating until the lead host invites them to, and will be expected to remain at the table until a fruit plate arrives and the host indicates that the meal is finished. The host may give face to the guests by taking food off the common plates and putting it on the guests' plates. Typically, a single conversation is held during the first period of a dinner, with the lead host initiating it and doing much of the talking. Over time, both during a meal and after many meals, several conversations will break out and the formality will reduce – sometimes considerably.

Soon into your time developing relationships in China, drinking will become part of a dinner or lunch with prospective partners. Drinking is important because it shows a willingness to socialise with your partner and also to become drunk. This is considered important to let down any guards that are being presented and also to make the conversation flow more freely and become more open. Sometimes Chinese hosts will encourage their guests to drink a lot of alcohol before a key negotiation or discussion. More typically, hosts will want everybody to get drunk together to celebrate an agreement or to demonstrate that this is part of building a friendship as well as a business partnership. Refusing to drink, unless on credible medical grounds, is considered poor manners and is very likely to make the Chinese host unhappy with the guests.

Toasting each other is a key part of banquet and mealtime drinking. The lead host will typically begin with a toast and if it is a formal dinner will tend to lead future toasts, although other members of the group will offer formal toasts too. Responding with your own toasts is a matter of judgement. Not offering a single toast could be taken as a lack of commitment to the partnership. However, excessively toasting can imply that the guest wants to take over the lead social role during the meal. As relationships develop, meals become less formal and the tendency to drink changes and diminishes. A key point generally reached in the development of relationships is when the host and guest agree not to drink alcohol even when finishing a day's work. This is more likely to happen at lunchtime than in the evening, when there will typically be alcohol offered. The number and formality of toasts is likely to reduce as relationships improve. However, there are exceptions and in particular there can be heavy drinking to celebrate key milestones or achievements. Also, many entrepreneurs will at some point want to drink heavily with their partners to show their commitment to the relationship. During these dinners, there is a lot of toasting from all members of the hosting group and these meals can descend into continuous toasts as groups move around and between tables to drink with everybody at that meal.

These are just a few examples of the many social practices in China. The more time spent in China, the better developed will be a non-Chinese person's understanding of these practices and how to participate in them. The more you understand and participate, the greater will be the appreciation of your Chinese partner in return.

Avoid direct conflict, usually

In general, Chinese people tend to avoid confrontation and direct conflict. A preference not to engage in direct conflict makes sense when the two parties are seeking to develop long-term relationships. Because of these considerations, issues and concerns generally will be articulated indirectly or will be presented in such a way that blame is not overly placed on the other party. However, this does not mean that Chinese business people are not tough negotiators. They are ready to go into detail and examine contracts and agreements line by line and word by word, raising concerns and disagreements throughout. They are also prepared to not give ground and to supply multiple reasons why they cannot shift their position. This intransigence may be tactical as well as focusing on material concerns, in the sense that indicating a willingness not to compromise on every point positions the Chinese as a tough negotiator. There is also a tendency for some negotiators to fight hard on what appears to be a trivial point but then concede on it. Generally, this point precedes one that is much more important to the Chinese negotiator.

Although the preference is to avoid direct conflict, Chinese business people will use confrontation and anger as tactics if they feel this will work, or if they genuinely disagree with a point that is up for negotiation. Walking out of negotiations and bluffing the other party are common tactics. Although these behaviours may be tactical, they will also reflect genuine feelings and views held by the Chinese negotiator. Agreements that they feel overly benefit the other party will not be well received. In addition, there may be some national and cultural pride if negotiations with a non-Chinese potential partner lead to a perception that that party presents itself as in some way better than or superior to the Chinese entrepreneur. More confrontational negotiations often are followed by attempts to recover the relationship. Initially, there tends to be a cooling-off period, which can be quite brief. Then, substantive matters are discussed and often a compromise found. Where the Chinese party is still not ready to compromise or shift their position, there may be reasons for this intransigence that that individual is not sharing during negotiations. If the two parties are able to move beyond this sticking point, there will most likely be a social event – typically a dinner – to bring the parties together to socialise and in most cases drink and toast each other. This signals a longer-term interest in building the relationship, and in reaching agreement. However, if a Chinese entrepreneur feels the balance is not right between building the relationship and securing a good deal, responses may vary. In these cases, talks can break down or the entrepreneur will decide to resolve the situation by focusing on the deal. If the entrepreneur does not believe a deal can be reached, they will quickly lose interest and move on to other matters.

Don't rush negotiations and decisions

A standard negotiating tactic is to hold out on a visiting party until the day or evening before they leave and then present a deal that is advantageous to the Chinese entrepreneur or business person. Aware that many visiting delegations are eager to take news of progress back to their companies, presenting last-minute deals and changes to existing deals is common practice. As the trip draws to an end, the local partner may refuse to sign an agreement that has been discussed and negotiated unless changes are made. In general, refusal to concede to changes to a deal or agreement is a viable option, because the local Chinese business person knows they are using this as a negotiation tactic. It may need a further visit to China by the foreign party, but this may be worthwhile if the changes are too problematic.

Foreign – in particular Western – business people are often seen as impatient by the Chinese. This is somewhat ironic given the dynamism of economic growth in China makes many business decisions by Chinese businesses short term. However, this concern reflects a wider preoccupation with building relationships that was touched on earlier in this chapter. Demonstrating commitment to the relationship, regardless of short-term differences when negotiating agreements and contracts, removes perceptions of being interested in the short term, and as a result eases future negotiations with that partner.

Develop an awareness of non-verbal communication

Because the Chinese often avoid direct conflict, they are likely to show their displeasure or disagreement non-verbally. A common response when confronted by behaviour or a proposal they do not support, or even like, is to displace this negative response into other activities. A typical sign of displeasure is to start sending and receiving texts and emails on smartphones in meetings, or to start making calls themselves, with one hand cupped over the phone as they speak. Often, Chinese entrepreneurs will do this in meetings anyway, excusing themselves if they receive an urgent call. However, displeasure can be shown by making it clear that the use of digital communications distances the Chinese entrepreneur from the discussions being held. It is the change in behaviour that is key to this non-verbal signalling, not just the behaviour itself. Many non-Chinese business people miss these non-verbal cues to how a Chinese entrepreneur may actually be thinking, and can continue to make the point that is the cause of the tension in the belief that it has not been heard. Inevitably, this increases the level of disengagement.

The use of smartphones in meetings does not necessarily indicate displeasure or disagreement. The use of such devices is commonplace in China and individuals regularly check their accounts when in meetings. As such, when this disengagement behaviour becomes particularly obvious – for example, loss of eye contact for a considerable period combined with multiple telephone conversations or use of the device without a break – this is the point at which it is most likely that it is an expression of disagreement or displeasure. Non-verbal reactions may be even clearer: individuals may leave the meeting, claiming urgent business and not return to that particular meeting.

Recognise hierarchies and loci of decision making

China is still a hierarchical society and its businesses maintain – and indeed in many organisations, reinforce – this cultural trait. Often, the entrepreneur is the primary, if not the only, decision maker. This is especially the case in smaller and micro-sized private businesses, where the entrepreneur tends to be the business founder, owner and manager. Even in larger private enterprises, decision making tends to be highly centralised, with one or a small group of individuals – often the founders – making the key decisions. In other words, in any private business, there is likely to be a very small number of people who decide on the allocation of resources and strategic direction of the enterprise. In smaller businesses, this is likely to be one or two people. In larger private enterprises, it is unlikely to be many more than five or six, and often will be a smaller group. Gaining access to these key decision makers is therefore essential to build business partnerships with entrepreneurs. However, the concentration of decision-making power in such a small number of people means that many people are seeking to gain access to them, and so they are often difficult to meet. Intermediaries, as discussed later in this chapter, are a key means of gaining access to these individuals. Effecting the initial introduction, and persuading the entrepreneur that there is benefit in meeting again, are crucial points in the development of business relationships, and a presence, in China.

As with all things in China, generalisations about hierarchies and indeed other aspects of Chinese culture do not reflect all practices. A growing number of private businesses have actively sought to delegate decision-making responsibilities to a much wider group of staff. The rationale for this is multifaceted, but a key reason is to attract staff who want to lead their own businesses and business units within a company. Fosun, based in Shanghai, is a good example of this kind of business. Fosun is made up of multiple individual businesses, each run by their own chief executive office and management team, who have responsibility for the performance of their business. Another Shanghai-based company, Ctrip.com, moved to this approach in 2014–2015, allowing individual parts of the business to not only compete where they could, but also to use services outside the company even if those services were available within Ctrip.com. These more distributed organisational structures can arise when the founders or senior managers have worked in countries where there is a more delegated model for organisational leadership. They also arise because highly skilled, motivated and capable managers are difficult to recruit and retain in China, where the labour market is very volatile and individuals move jobs regularly to increase their salaries. In this context, finding ways to not only keep, but also promote and reward staff becomes increasingly important to sustain the business and its growth.

Accept you are not mainland Chinese

For Western entrepreneurs and business people, at first read this is an obvious statement. For overseas Chinese from neighbouring East and Southeast Asian countries, there is generally a recognition that although they are ethnically Chinese, they are also overseas Chinese and so not considered part of the mainland Chinese culture. Even in Hong Kong – part of mainland China since 1997 – most business people will confirm that they are seen as 'overseas' by most mainland Chinese people, and would also see their own business culture and practices as different. As individuals from outside mainland China live and work there, and become more familiar with its own special circumstances, they will better understand that country's particular context and circumstances. Over time, this familiarity will build into a much deeper understanding of Chinese culture and business practices. However, this expertise has its potential pitfalls, two of which are of note.

The first is that not being mainland Chinese means that non-Chinese business people – even 'old China hands' – will never be fully accepted regardless of their knowledge of China and Chinese and their long-standing experience of working in China. Even old China hands who have lived in that country for many years will be perceived as different, or 'other', regardless of their experience of and time working in China. This is social, in the sense that a non-Chinese resident does not have their own kinship group within China. Even if they marry a Chinese person and the wider family network accepts that person, they may still see them as outside the bloodline of the kinship group. It is also political, in that membership of the Communist Party in almost all circumstances is limited to mainland Chinese nationals (there have been some exceptions to this, but these have been largely honorary recognition).

The second way to avoid a pitfall is to recognise they are not from Mainland Chinese and to act accordingly. A common mistake made by non-Chinese who have worked in China for a long time is to start to believe that they understand the country and how it operates. Notwithstanding the wider question around whether any individual can understand a country as complex and dynamic as China, a view that you understand 'how China works' is both risky and deceptive. As an outsider, regardless of the time spent in-country, there will be conversations and decisions that will occur without the presence of the non-Chinese party that will affect these individuals. In addition, there will be wider conversations – about politics in particular, but also aspects of family life – to which a non-Chinese person will not be privy. Even when old China hands are included in conversations, the inferences and background is likely to remain opaque in many instances. The implication of this for all non-Chinese operating in that country is that they should constantly test pre-conceptions and perceptions, even when China becomes very familiar and their understanding of underlying dynamics and contexts improves considerably.

Developing and sustaining relationships

The discussion earlier in this chapter of *guanxi* and *guanxixue* highlighted the central importance of relationship development to business success in China. Much of China's day-to-day business still relies heavily on personal connections and relationships, even if the importance of *guanxixue* has eroded as businesses focus more on finding and working with effective and competitive partners.[7] Relationships with Chinese partners offer a wide range of benefits to foreign businesses. In broad terms, they enable key transactions, such as procurement, delivery and placement of orders. They offer a means of protecting the business and also of acquiring local knowledge. Relationships also lead to new opportunities through introductions to new contacts.

Relationships are especially important to entrepreneurs in China, particularly those running smaller businesses. For entrepreneurs, relationships address the resource and reputational deficits that are a feature of being a smaller business. For example, relationships are a way to build loyalty with key customers and suppliers. They also offer access to information and to the networks of individuals with whom they have good *guanxi*. Good relationships build trust with individuals in other businesses, allowing access that otherwise might be difficult to secure. In China, trust is focused on the family and closely held networks based on kinship ties, community, place and in some cases, ethnicity. Relationships reinforce these close networks and so are an important means of both enabling exchange within these groups and governing it.

Relationships outside the family, kinship group or local community allow entrepreneurs to extend their networks and build social capital with individuals with whom no socio-cultural linkages exist (or are available). This is especially important when businesses seek to expand to other parts of China and build wider market share. Developing relationships with non-Chinese businesses and business people represents both an opportunity and a risk for Chinese entrepreneurs. On the one hand, they extend an entrepreneur's networks and so lead to new opportunities for the business. On the other, engagement with non-Chinese businesses requires learning and investment in the relationship to secure the possibility of accessing these opportunities.

For non-Chinese businesses, developing relationships with Chinese entrepreneurs is both a major challenge and the means to ensure success in the Chinese market. Finding the right partner and then starting to build a relationship with them can be challenging for several reasons. First, identifying the right partners in such a large market can be time consuming and problematic. Second, gaining access to the key decision maker in a private business is often not straightforward, especially for foreign business people. Gaining access to the right networking events and using other people to make introductions for you will be essential, but also is time consuming and relies on the quality of those people and their credibility with the entrepreneurs with whom you are looking to link up. Although essential, relationship building in China is not easy. The following aspects of relationship development are important when developing a presence in China

Invest in relationship building

Building effective relationships takes time and requires effort and resources. In return, strong relationships offer access to the Chinese market and access to the networks of the individuals with whom you build relationships. A key starting point for market entry is to develop key relationships with partners, and also with fixers (see the use of intermediaries below). Relationship building continues after initial market entry. Existing relationships will need to be serviced and nurtured to maintain them and get the most out of them. It is advisable to build multiple relationships, both with businesses with which you are working closely, and other businesses and stakeholders. You will need some links with government, depending on the sector in which you are operating and the licensing and compliance arrangements that apply to your business. You may also want to develop links with universities and schools, as well as employment bureaux, if you want to recruit staff.

Focus on building long-term relationships

Chinese culture emphasises the development of trust and social capital through the formation of close relationships. This takes time, but signifies your commitment to these relationships. Recognising that you are in it for the long term when you develop important relationships will pay dividends as your Chinese partners realise that you are committed to them. Conversely, networking for quick or short-term gains is not considered an important part of *guanxi*; instead it would be more associated with *guanxixue*, and so has negative or at least dubious connotations. Chinese entrepreneurs are much more likely to be suspicious of networking for quick gain, unless the returns for them from doing so are high.

Recognise that business relationships will also become social relationships

Chinese entrepreneurs tend to do business over dinner and through social interaction as well as through formal meetings and negotiations. Whereas government officials and staff from SOEs are now limited in the price and range of food they can order at banquets, private entrepreneurs are not officially constrained by these guidelines. Although most will prudently choose not to obviously exceed these public guidelines, they have the flexibility to spend on a wider range of entertaining than do public officials. As a consequence, developing relationships with private entrepreneurs will involve social events and engagement as well as business meetings and activities. In general, the stronger the relationship the more likely socialising will be. In addition, if a relationship is considered important to the entrepreneur, they are more likely to spend more in terms of money and effort on that relationship. If you are important, or become important, to a Chinese entrepreneur, expect to spend time out of working hours and outside the office with that person. This time need not be in formal banquets, with lots of drinking and toasting, although these dinners will most likely be common in the early stages of relationship development. Over time, as you develop the relationship, you can explore and suggest other forms of social engagement, provided you show a commitment to the relationship and an interest in getting to know the entrepreneur better.

Use intermediaries

China has many intermediaries who provide an important bridge to the entrepreneurs with whom you are seeking to develop relationships. In the early stages of exploring the Chinese market, these intermediaries will be essential sources of information as well as introducing you to key contacts and potential partners. Through the reform period, there has been a growing group of 'fixers' who offer their services and networks to businesses and individuals who are looking to develop relationships and *guanxi*. In the earlier days of economic reform, a Chinese fixer was both necessary and, if effective, of tangible benefit to foreign businesses looking to establish a presence in China. Without a well-connected and capable fixer, entry into the Chinese market is very challenging. As with finding the right partner, having the right fixer or intermediary will be hugely important.

Referrals from other international businesses that have successfully entered the Chinese market are a useful first step in finding an intermediary. Representative organisations such as chambers of commerce and other business associations can also identify and recommend intermediaries. Fixers in particular and intermediaries more broadly will expect compensation and reward for representing you and finding suitable partners. Not surprisingly, the better the fixer the higher the fee. However, the converse is not always the case: the desire to enter the Chinese market means that Chinese individuals are more than willing to charge international businesses high fees even if they do not have the networks and expertise of good intermediaries. Seek references and double check those once you have received them, preferably by talking directly with an individual who has used the intermediary you are considering employing.

Developing a successful presence in China

There are many case studies of businesses that have successfully entered the Chinese market. Two of those cited regularly are KFC – through the China division of its parent company Yum Foods – and Starbucks. Both entered the market relatively early and were able to localise their offerings while retaining Western aspects of their brand that were attractive to mainland Chinese consumers; in particular good customer service, cleanliness and food security. In both KFC and Starbucks, customers can buy local dishes as well as standard offerings of fried chicken and coffee. This theme runs through many of the cases of successful market entry into consumer markets – non-Chinese brands retained their core essence in ways that were attractive to customers in China, but localised the business model to respond to China-specific expectations and requirements. They became hybrid businesses, offering non-Chinese, typically Western, products and experiences alongside a range of Chinese products that have become increasingly popular.

A large and growing number of non-Chinese businesses have established manufacturing facilities or sourcing arrangements in China. In many cases, these companies have out-sourced some or all of their manufacturing capacity to China. In the early years of reform, foreign businesses sourced these products from Chinese manufacturers because there was no legislation to allow them to set up their own facilities. Legislation was introduced to allow joint ventures, but control was retained by the Chinese partner initially. As wholly owned foreign enterprises were allowed in the 1990s, more foreign businesses set up their own production facilities in China.

More recently, and particularly since WTO accession in the early 2000s, small and medium-sized businesses have begun to offshore their production, through either sourcing or establishing a manufacturing venture in-country. Export-driven manufacturing has stimulated high levels of growth and prosperity around the Pearl River Delta, in particular, as local and Hong Kong entrepreneurs have set up manufacturing businesses that now sit alongside the factories of some of the world's largest companies.

However, manufacturing in China has moved from this 'made in China' exporting model to also becoming a platform for selling in China itself. One example of this is Nike, the sports shoe manufacturer, which established procurement facilities in southern China during the early years of reform, mainly to benefit from lower labour and hence production costs. China has now become the company's fastest-growing market and the future profitability and share value of Nike is driven by its sales in China.[8] For many businesses that began engaging with China to benefit from low labour costs, China has become a key market and key driver of sale growth. These businesses are manufacturing in China to export to other markets and also to sell in-country to an increasingly wealthy population.

The following four aspects of entering the Chinese market and building a durable and successful presence have been derived from the experiences of many of these businesses. Each offers a means of increasing the prospects of succeeding in the China market.

Do your homework first, in depth and in person

China is a country where desktop research does not really give you a sense of the nature of the market and the opportunities it offers. The market research industry is underdeveloped in China and there is only a weak tradition of consumer feedback and survey research. When surveyed, individuals often do not wish to participate in market research and respond to questions that they may see as overly intrusive. There is some nervousness about how data will be used and who will have access, and individuals can still be reluctant to record personal views in ways that can be reviewed by others. Trying to interview business leaders and entrepreneurs in China is notoriously difficult, and has become more so as anti-corruption investigations have extended to senior executives of large private enterprises. Moreover, desk and market research in China is often quickly outdated, given the pace of change. Finally, the scale of China constrains the ability to generalise from most surveys. Undertaking representative national surveys would require a scale that makes them very expensive undertakings.

Data are improving, however, and China's national statistics are increasingly considered an accurate reflection of actual economic conditions. This is in contrast with the recent past, when statistics often reflected the desires of local officials to report in glowing terms about the economic growth in their areas. Most recent academic analysis concludes that China's national statistics are no longer subject to these concerns and are converging with international practice.[9] This suspicion about the data lingers, both in the international press and also among Chinese leaders, who claim that they use different forms of energy consumption as their means of assessing economic growth. Even though overall national statistics have improved in accuracy, industry-specific data continue to be very limited, and lack the depth to provide real insight into specific sectors.

Therefore, second-hand data about China are limited, and although it is important to do the analysis, and where necessary appoint consultants and researchers, this should be complemented by direct experience of the country. Spending time in China and seeing how your industry or market actually works will be invaluable experience as you enter and build a market presence. It will also help you to start building a China network. Seeing China first hand should not be limited to the major cities. Second and third tier cities, and also larger townships, should be visited, as this is where the majority of Chinese people live. Although more people have lived in urban areas than in the countryside since 2012, rural areas should also be visited as more than half a billion Chinese people still live there. It is also worthwhile to visit different kinds of economic entities and sectors. Across China, there are industrial plants and estates, as well as rural markets and urban supermarkets. Each gives a sense of how the Chinese economy functions. You should also engage with your chamber of commerce or trade organisation, and should visit the Chinese trade or industry body for your market or sector. You may also want to meet with entrepreneurs' associations and other business networks. Experiencing China and gaining first-hand experience of how it operates will be invaluable when making decisions about the development of a presence in that country.

Have a clear entry strategy and stick to it

There are many options for entering the Chinese market. There are also many different views about the best strategy and approach. Based on the research you have undertaken and the contacts you have made, you should develop an entry strategy that works for your business. Entry strategies vary considerably by sector and also depend on which part of China is being targeted. For example, if the focus is the big cities, be aware that competition is intense and many other non-Chinese businesses are targeting these locations. The examples of KFC and Starbucks mentioned earlier in this chapter reinforce the importance of developing an entry strategy that is specific to your business and that is based on a clear and long-term approach underpinned by research. It is possible that other businesses and some China experts will not agree with your approach. However, they are likely to have less direct knowledge of the market opportunities and how your business can exploit them than you do, as long as you have done in-depth research and tested your approach with key contacts and partners. There is merit in sticking to the agreed strategy, even though there may be temptations to move to exploit opportunities that you see as they arise. In the short term, this may generate profits, but over time the business will become dependent on finding and then harvesting the next opportunity to sustain income and profit. Sooner or later, an opportunity will not be spotted or will not come along at the right time.

Develop a long-term presence and nurture it

The foreign businesses that have been successful in China have built businesses based on long-term commitment to the market. They have developed organisational capabilities, networks, and production and distribution facilities that enable this, and that also position the business to take advantage of China's growth. Setting up this kind of presence takes time, effort and investment. The payback may also take time, which means it is likely to need to be substantial to cover the upfront investment. Seeking to establish a long-term presence is recognised and appreciated by Chinese customers and partners. Partners will be more ready to develop relationships, and enable your venture to succeed, if they are convinced you are in it for the long term. Similarly, consumers will appreciate a commitment to China if demonstrated, and business customers will come to rely on you as a key supplier. As has been mentioned, appearing to be in it for quick gain over the short term does not generate the reputation that makes businesses successful in China over the long term.

Constantly test your strategy and its suitability

China is a dynamic and uncertain economy with rapidly developing markets and changing macroeconomic conditions. As such, your strategy will need updating and refining to ensure it stays fit for purpose in such a volatile environment. Regularly testing your strategy against changes to competition, market structure and customer demand is recommended. There is a fine line between adjusting to changing conditions and sticking with your strategy. Making judgements on whether to change approach will be demanding at times, and often it will be difficult to determine whether your decision was a sound one until some time after you have made it. In general, adjusting a strategy that was developed based on careful analysis and thinking, alongside extensive preparation and planning is advisable when significant shifts in external market conditions occur, but not necessarily in response to short-term shocks or opportunities.

Dealing with the environment around you

China's dynamism means that the environment within which you are operating is vulnerable to frequent and often unexpected changes. Many of these changes cannot be planned or anticipated, placing an emphasis on being able to adapt and being flexible.

Be ready for uncertainty and volatility – they are a given

By entering the Chinese market and establishing a presence, businesses are accepting, either consciously or implicitly, that the environment within which they operate is uncertain and volatile. Uncertainty comes from other new entrants, changes in patterns of competition, and from responses by customers to rapid economic growth and its effects and side effects. Volatility is amplified by intense competition between businesses, and also by a still-developing regulatory and governance framework that continues to be unclear on how aspects of the market operate and should be enforced. For businesses active in China, this is the norm, rather than an exceptional state of affairs. Preparation is challenging, not least because the nature of change is difficult to anticipate, and also because the change may be rapid. This environment rewards an organisation's ability to adapt and react, and to do so without sufficient data or knowledge to be fully confident that any decisions that are made are the most appropriate or effective. Decision making with limited or insufficient information is the norm in this environment.

Be ready for state intervention and changes of national and local policy

Although the state has withdrawn from direct control and management of production and trade, it is still highly influential and can choose to intervene in specific markets and companies without warning. Sometimes these interventions can be planned – for example, to support a struggling SOE, or to investigate or punish corruption – however, at other times intervention is not planned and there is no warning that it may happen. For example, government may impose extra *ad hoc* taxes on entrepreneurs running successful businesses, in response to increases in costs or a need to finance a new project. Some private enterprises have suffered from the 'fat pig policy', which means that they are acquired by the state and nationalised once they have reached a certain size and degree of success.[10] Even though China has a national property law that recognises private ownership, this is often ignored, especially by government if it feels there is a need or benefit from intervening. The scale of intervention is decreasing, however, and in recent years impromptu interventions have become much rarer than in the 1980s and 1990s.

National policy may also change quickly, especially when a new administration comes to power. The period after a change of power is the most likely time when new policies and policy directions will be announced. Other policy developments are typically broadcast through each five-year plan, which identifies national development priorities for the plan period and so gives notice of where government investment and regulation is most likely to be focused.

Be ready for contracts and laws to not be upheld

As has been mentioned, China passed a property law in 2007 that recognised private ownership of property and the right to retain profits and assets. This marked a significant development in policy terms, because for the first time the Communist Party formally enshrined private ownership in its laws, even though the party's constitution recognises state ownership only. However, the property law, as with other legislation, has not been uniformly or consistently upheld. These issues relate to other laws including, for example, those upholding personal rights, consumer rights and media expression. Although there is extensive legislation on the books, it is not necessarily upheld or complied with.

Some companies take a similar view of contracts, which many foreign businesses see as legally binding. However, not all Chinese businesses take the same view of the power of contractual agreement. Although adherence to contracts is improving, and there is a growing body of case law to refer to should a partner not honour a contract, there continue to be many instances where a contract is not seen as binding. Even where Chinese partners work within the parameters of a contract that has been mutually negotiated and agreed, its interpretation can be open to debate, and sometimes dispute. Do not assume that a contract is cast iron, in other words, but monitor it carefully and see it as a 'guide' to how a partnership will operate. Adherence to this guide will vary from partner to partner.

A final, brief caution

All of the comments and recommendations above apply to China most of the time. However, China is a huge, complex and rapidly changing country, with significant variation from place to place, and from market to market. As such, this chapter should be read as a set of generalised suggestions on how to operate in China. In practice, these suggestions approximate what actually goes on in China and even though they are broadly accurate, they will be regularly challenged by contradictory behaviours and practices. As with any advice, take it with caution and develop your own understanding of China and how business is done there. Experiential learning is the most effective way of learning, and is a must in China because the rules of the game are fluid and constantly changing.

Notes

1 Clissold, T 2010, *Mr. China*, Constable & Robinson, London, UK.
2 Yan, R 1994, 'To reach China's consumers, adapt to Guo Qing', *Harvard Business Review*, September–October, pp. 66–75.
3 Feuling, B 2010, 'Developing China sales and distribution capabilities', *China Business Review*, July.
4 Guthrie, D 1999, *Dragon in a three-piece suit. The emergence of capitalism in China*, Princeton University Press, Princeton, NJ.
5 Guthrie, D 1998, 'The declining significance of guanxi in China's economic transition', *China Quarterly*, vol. 154, pp. 254–282.
6 Atherton, A 2008, 'From "fat pigs" and "red hats" to a "new social stratum": the changing face of enterprise development policy in China', *Journal of Small Business and Enterprise Development*, vol. 15, no. 4, pp. 640–655.
7 Atherton, A & Newman, A 2016, 'The emergence of the private entrepreneur in reform era China: re-birth of an earlier tradition, or a more recent product of development and change?', *Business History*, vol. 58, no. 3, pp. 319–344.

8 'How China could be the key driver of Nike's future revenues' 2016, *Forbes Magazine*, 13 January.
9 Holz, C 2013, *Chinese statistics: classification systems and data sources*, SOSC Working Papers, Hong Kong University of Science and Technology, Hong Kong, http://repository.ust.hk/dspace/handle/1783.1/7710 (viewed 3 June 2017)
10 Atherton, A 2008.

10

THE FUTURE OF ENTREPRENEURSHIP IN CHINA

Introduction

It has been four decades since China began its journey on the path of economic transformation from a country where the state controlled almost all facets of the economy into one in which the private sector accounts for the overwhelming majority of economic output, and entrepreneurship has flourished. In this book, we have not only examined the process by which entrepreneurship in China has evolved and emerged, but also asked who are China's entrepreneurs; analysed the main models of entrepreneurship in China; and examined how Chinese enterprises are financed and the nature of domestic competition and international expansion of China's private sector. We have also considered the influence of Chinese culture on entrepreneurship and the role the government plays in both encouraging and constraining the emergence of private entrepreneurs. In the last chapter, we applied much of this insight to develop a series of recommendations and an overall framework for building a successful presence in China.

In this final chapter, we examine what the future holds for entrepreneurship in China. In doing so, we highlight some key challenges that may constrain the continued development of entrepreneurship in the future, and highlight key growth sectors for private enterprises in China.

Key challenges facing private entrepreneurship

Economic development has slowed down in recent years as China makes the transition to the 'new normal', an era where rates of economic growth are significantly lower than they were in the early stages of opening up and reform. Policy responses to the new normal of lower growth propose a further restructuring of the Chinese economy towards a greater role for services and a stronger consumer economy. Within this context of continuing structural change, Chinese enterprises are facing multiple challenges, including increased domestic and global competition, demographic changes as the population ages, environmental degradation, an education system that was not designed to support entrepreneurship, and an ever-uncertain institutional environment.

Domestic competition

Recent business surveys highlight growing domestic competition as one of the major concerns of entrepreneurs operating in China today.[1] This has resulted in lower profit margins and higher rates of bankruptcy than in the past. More traditional sectors of the economy such as manufacturing and construction, which profited significantly from decades of rapid growth, have been especially hard hit by domestic competition. In many of these sectors there is overcapacity, and private enterprises face increasing costs as a result of rising employee wages and the need to comply with stricter labour and environmental standards. As a result, China is witnessing a shift away from more traditional forms of network-based entrepreneurship focusing on the production of low-cost labour and intensive production, to higher-value-added, innovation-based forms of entrepreneurship.

Global competition

Increasing global competition is also putting significant pressure on businesses operated by Chinese entrepreneurs, especially those in traditional industries such as manufacturing, where labour costs continue to rise. As the Chinese economy has developed, labour costs have increased markedly, making it more expensive to manufacture in China. Since China entered the World Trade Organization in 2001, labour costs have risen by around 11 per cent per year.[2] However, productivity levels have not increased at the same rate, so the costs of production are increasing year on year.[3] This has led multinational enterprises to seek suppliers in other emerging economies such as Vietnam, Indonesia, Cambodia, Laos and Myanmar, where labour costs are much cheaper. For example, large multinationals such as Foxconn that mainly manufacture in China have recently begun to open plants in neighbouring countries such as Vietnam and in other emerging markets such as Indonesia and Brazil.[4] Investing in such locations allows multinationals to benefit from lower wage costs and provides access to growth markets elsewhere in the world. Global competition has also led Chinese enterprises to consider moving overseas to compete with their global rivals on price.

Demographic changes

Many scholars agree that China's demographic policies over the last 40 years, especially the one-child policy introduced in 1979, have had a significant impact on the Chinese economy. As a result of the one-child policy, birth rates have fallen significantly from around 5.8 children per woman in the 1960s to around 1.6 today, and the median age of citizens has increased. At present, around 9 per cent of the Chinese population is more than 65 years of age; a figure predicted to jump to around 30 per cent by 2050.[5] Although policy changes led to the abandonment of the one-child policy in 2015, a recent report suggests the population will continue to age, making China the world's most aged society by 2030.[6] The median age of people is predicted to increase from around 30 years today to 46 in 2040, and the ratio of retired people to employed people is predicted to drop from 1:5 to less than 1:1.6.[7]

China's ageing population presents significant challenges for entrepreneurship in China. The existence of a large and relatively youthful labour force was an important factor in China's rapid economic growth in the early stages of opening up and reform. As a result of the demographic changes outlined earlier, China's working population has begun to decline over the last decade, and economists have predicted that the labour force could shrink to a point where the number of wage earners is not sufficient to cover the welfare costs to care for the elderly.[8] The availability of a huge supply of low-cost labour was a major factor behind the success of private enterprises as low-cost surplus labour enabled them to generate profits and use these surpluses for investment. As the pool of labour dries up, it is becoming increasingly difficult for entrepreneurs to recruit enough skilled workers, especially highly skilled workers with the requisite skills to work in more innovative knowledge-based industries. As a result, wage rates in China are increasing at a faster rate than productivity growth. This is making Chinese enterprises less competitive than enterprises in other countries in the region, and is encouraging manufacturing to move overseas.[9] An ageing society also presents huge policy challenges for government due to the burden it places on the welfare state, which may lead the government to tax business and individuals at a higher rate. High tax rates are likely to discourage entrepreneurs from establishing businesses in China and to look to alternative markets.

Although the ageing population brings many challenges for entrepreneurship in China, we must also be cognisant of the opportunities it brings for entrepreneurs. As we highlight in the second half of this chapter, opportunities exist in developing products and services specifically targeted towards retired people. A recent government report suggested that the percentage of domestic consumption accounted for by retired people is likely to rise from around 8 per cent today to around 33 per cent by 2050.[10] As is seen in mature Western economies, growth in this 'grey economy' will bring new innovations and market opportunities for entrepreneurs focused on this market segment.

Environmental degradation

Environmental degradation is one of the most serious consequences of China's rapid industrialisation and related economic growth over recent decades. Although China's GDP has increased rapidly and citizens' living standards have improved, this has come at the expense of the environment and public health. China is now the world's largest producer of carbon emissions, and neither water nor air quality meet international health standards in many areas of the country. In 2014, the Organisation for Economic Co-operation and Development (OECD) estimated the annual costs of air pollution at more than USD1 trillion and found that over 90 per cent of all Chinese cities had polluted groundwater.[11] China's largest cities regularly have levels of air pollution that are many times greater than the United Nations Environment Programme (UNEP) maximum guidelines. This has led to increasing health expenditure and decreasing life expectancy rates in the most polluted parts of the country.

The costs of doing business for entrepreneurs have increased as they have to deal with increasing compliance requirements that have arisen from the introduction of environmental regulations by the Chinese government. These regulations are particularly focused on reducing air pollution and dumping of toxic waste in China's water systems and on land. Given the scale and public impact of excessive pollution, enforcement of these regulations looks to be more actively implemented than historically, when local governments in particular were lax in their approach to environmental protection.

Although environmental degradation has a negative effect on economic growth through its effects on the environment and public health, it has also brought opportunities for entrepreneurs as the government looks to reduce carbon emissions and invest in infrastructure to combat environmental degradation. For example, as highlighted in the second half of this chapter, opportunities exist for entrepreneurs as the Chinese government introduces policies to support the growing renewable energy sector. Pollution control and management equipment and systems represent opportunities for entrepreneurs, as does the emergence of new 'eco-cities' across the country. The design requirements, control systems and environmental technologies required for these eco-cities offer major new entrepreneurial opportunities in China.

Education system

Commentators have argued that a key constraint on entrepreneurship in China is the lack of an entrepreneurial mindset among young people.[12] The quite traditional Chinese education system has delivered high levels of performance in international Programme for International Student Assessment (PISA) scores, especially for mathematics. However, at primary and secondary levels in particular, the Chinese system promotes rote learning over creative thinking, risk taking and challenging the status quo, all of which are necessary components of entrepreneurial thinking.[13] To support the growth of entrepreneurship in China, the Chinese government has recognised the need for reform to create a different style of education system that encourages more independent learning and thinking, which in turn enables innovation-driven entrepreneurship. The government has begun to make small but meaningful reforms to the college entrance examination and admission systems that allow students a greater choice of subjects on which to be examined, and students are now allowed to suspend university study to pursue entrepreneurship.[14] More autonomous secondary schools in the major cities such as Shanghai and Beijing have begun to introduce styles of learning that require students to think more creatively by getting them to work on applied projects and to tackle 'real-world' issues such as community-based problems.[15] The government has also introduced guidelines that limit the amount of homework and exams that primary schools set for students, and is encouraging schools to support students to undertake activities in the local community. These recent initiatives should make Chinese education more encouraging of entrepreneurship. However, they will be resisted by the traditionally held approaches to education that still hold sway in many schools, colleges and universities.

Institutional (political and legal) environment

Entrepreneurs continue to face a turbulent and uncertain institutional environment as the Communist Party seeks to maintain one-party rule. As successful entrepreneurs amass resources and become publicly known, the party is becoming increasingly wary of private individuals who gain too much power and influence in society. Recent investigations and detentions of entrepreneurs in mainland China and in Hong Kong demonstrate the increased levels of state scrutiny that successful entrepreneurs are experiencing. It is still unclear as to whether the party under Xi Jinping's leadership is fully committed to the continued development of the private sector when this entails greater competition between state-owned and private enterprises, or intends to strengthen state control over the economy. Xi Jinping has stressed that he will continue to support the growth of the private sector through lowering taxes and providing wider market access to private enterprises.[16] However, the anti-corruption drive that he launched after coming to power in 2012, which focuses on eliminating collusion between corrupt officials and private entrepreneurs, seems to be having a negative effect on the Chinese economy. Local officials are increasingly hesitant to pursue projects with private entrepreneurs that may lead to scrutiny from government authorities, even where there is no corruption.[17] This nervousness by officials to engage with entrepreneurs has led to delays for many private enterprises in obtaining approvals and signing contracts.

Beyond the current government crackdown on corruption, the lack of a fully developed institutional environment inhibits entrepreneurship in China.[18] Key aspects of an institutional framework that enable private enterprise in other countries are missing in China; just as importantly, legislation such as the Property Law 2007 that gives legal rights to private ownership often are not implemented or respected.[19] Scholars point out that meaningful progress in developing the market institutions that will enable future private sector development cannot be made without greater government transparency, an independent judiciary and freedom of the press.[20] In parts of the country, government connections rather than market forces still determine the success of private enterprises, although this is much less so in the more developed and open coastal economies where China's economic prosperity is concentrated.[21] Many private entrepreneurs still find doing business extremely difficult as rules and regulations are not always transparent or consistently applied, contracts are sometimes difficult to enforce and intellectual property rights violations are widespread. China still has considerable work to do to develop an institutional environment that enables and effectively protects entrepreneurship.

Key sectors for growth of private entrepreneurship

In the previous sections we highlighted some of the key challenges facing entrepreneurs in China. In particular, we highlighted how growing competition – both domestically and globally – combined with lower levels of economic growth in China present challenges for entrepreneurs who are now generating lower profits, especially in traditional sectors of the economy. We highlighted how an ageing population, the current education system and institutional uncertainty all create broader conditions that adversely affect entrepreneurship in China. In light of the challenges that have arisen from China's transition to an economy with lower rates of growth and profitability, entrepreneurs have had to rethink their business models, improve efficiency, invest in research and development, and enter new markets.

As well as dealing with the challenges that result from changing economic conditions, entrepreneurs should not underestimate the opportunities that arise due to such conditions. In particular, the economic transition has led to new opportunities in sectors as diverse as renewable energy, healthcare, aged care, e-commerce and agriculture.

Renewable energy

In recent years the Chinese government has introduced stricter environmental regulations with the aim of reducing its reliance on fossil fuels and improving air quality. In addition, as part of the United Nations Framework Convention on Climate Change, the Chinese authorities agreed to increase the share of renewable energy to around 20 per cent of total energy consumption by 2030.[22] As well as limiting further environmental degradation, such developments will increase opportunities for entrepreneurs to invest in the development of renewable energies such as solar and wind power, as China moves away from reliance on fossil fuels such as coal and gas. Through government encouragement, a domestic solar energy sector has emerged that is now competing internationally as well as domestically.

Healthcare and aged care

As highlighted earlier, the ageing population in China will lead to increasing opportunities for entrepreneurs over the coming years as a result of increased demand for healthcare services, technology and products.[23] China is presently one of the world's largest markets for medical equipment, and healthcare spending is expected to constitute around 7 per cent of the country's gross domestic product by 2020.[24] Demand for healthcare should increase as a result of the government's stated intention to provide all citizens with access to basic healthcare by 2020. Although current funding mechanisms may not be sufficient to provide for universal healthcare in the face of China's rapidly ageing population, the market for healthcare will grow significantly as incomes continue to rise and individuals place greater importance on their health.

The government has begun to promote the use of technology in the healthcare sector, including the use of internet-based health information and consultation, and maintaining electronic health records. This presents opportunities for entrepreneurs with expertise in technology to provide solutions for the growing healthcare market. In recent years we have witnessed growing innovation in the healthcare industry. Entrepreneurs have created app-based technologies to allow patients to verify the authenticity of their drugs, be monitored remotely, receive medical consultations online through telemedicine and obtain prescriptions online.[25] These developments are likely to revolutionise healthcare in China, enhancing the quality and lowering the cost of healthcare provision.

Demand is also expected to increase exponentially over the coming years for aged care services, as richer Chinese families outsource the provision of care for elderly family members. Although Chinese traditional culture dictated that sending parents to a nursing or aged care facility would not be filial, and most families cared for their elderly at home, aversion to using professional aged care facilities has begun to change.[26] In most families both parents work, making it increasingly difficult for them to look after both their children and elderly parents. As a result of such changes, there are likely to be opportunities for entrepreneurs to invest in the aged care industry over the coming years.[27]

E-commerce

As highlighted in Chapter 4, innovation-based forms of entrepreneurship have flourished in China as entrepreneurs have made use of internet-based technologies to undertake business. E-commerce is one form of entrepreneurship that has grown rapidly in recent years as China makes its transition towards a consumption-based economy, and away from an export-oriented economy dominated by manufacturing. In 2015, the sales of goods and services online increased by more than 37 per cent and reached 3.8 trillion RMB.[28] Given the increasing urbanisation that is being witnessed in China and continued increase in average incomes, e-commerce sales will continue to increase as retailers shun bricks-and-mortar stores for more direct online business with an increasingly digitally connected consumer market. As distribution networks improve, the pace of growth of e-commerce will accelerate.[29] Regulatory changes introduced in 2015 that placed restrictions on foreign ownership in the e-commerce sector are likely to see a wave of foreign investment, which will also encourage Chinese entrepreneurs to enter into or expand in this sector. Over the last few years we have witnessed a wave of activity by foreign organisations in the e-commerce sector. For example, Wal-Mart acquired the leading online retailer Yihaodian, and other large multinationals such as Zara, Unilever and Timberland have signed deals with e-commerce retailers to sell and distribute their products in China.

Agriculture

There are growing opportunities for entrepreneurs in the Chinese agricultural sector as demand for high-quality products increases as a result of changing dietary preferences, an increase in living standards and demographic changes resulting from the removal of the one-child policy. Food security has become a very important consideration for many families in China, with concerns about the contents of foodstuffs, their origin and their safety as well as quality. Successive prosecutions of businesses that supply unsafe and unhealthy foods have compounded this concern with food security. For example, over the last few years we have witnessed a growth in demand for organic produce and baby products such as infant formula in the wake of arrests of executives whose businesses supplied toxic products that have injured or in some cases killed babies.

There is also a general increase in the quantity, range and nature of foodstuffs that is associated with rising household incomes. This has increased demand for food nationally. To increase productivity and crop yields domestically, entrepreneurs will continue to innovate and invest in new technologies. In addition, Chinese entrepreneurs are likely to increase their foreign direct investment overseas to gain access to supplies of agricultural products, food processing capabilities and advanced technologies that can be used domestically including genetically modified seeds and advanced irrigation technologies. Recent acquisitions of land in sub-Saharan Africa and Eastern Europe provide some Chinese businesses with greater capacity to grow and ship food to China, as well as to other countries.

Impact of the 'One Belt One Road' initiative

The One Belt One Road foreign policy initiative was introduced in 2013 by Xi Jinping's government to foster closer links between China and more than 60 emerging market countries and developing countries in Asia, Europe and East Africa.[30] It forms an important part of China's 13th five-year plan that lasts from 2016 to 2020.[31] Under this initiative the Chinese government will direct significant investment through the establishment of the Asian Infrastructure Investment Bank (AIIB) to improve connectivity and cooperation between China and countries in these regions.[32] Key components of these initiatives include directing financing to upgrade existing infrastructure and build new infrastructure such as railways, airports, ports, highways and electronic communication networks in China and overseas. This infrastructure will substantially improve travel and trade links between China and the *One belt one road* partner countries – spreading China's influence across central Asia into Eastern Europe, Asia Minor and, by sea, Eastern Africa.

As part of the initiative, China has also begun to discuss with its partners the opening up of new 'free trade zones' and 'trade cooperation zones'. Through promoting the efficient transportation of goods and people between China and its neighbours, the initiative is expected to enhance cross-border trade. Extending the Go West policy, in which the Chinese government encouraged investment in the lesser-developed western regions of the country, the One Belt One Road initiative is expected to spur economic growth and entrepreneurship in the west and south of the country, as entrepreneurs take advantage of new opportunities to do business in these regions and work on state-sponsored infrastructure projects overseas.[33] The 'new silk roads' that will be created by the One Belt One Road initiative will open up these parts of China to new opportunities for growth that will be increasingly interconnected with countries sitting along these 21st-century trade routes.

The future of entrepreneurship in China

The growth to date of reform-era China has been driven by the emergence of a private sector that has replaced the state-owned sector to become China's most important driver of economic development. Through much of the reform era, the state has been both supportive of private sector development and relatively *laissez faire* in its regulation of entrepreneurs. This has allowed the private sector to fend for itself rather than relying on government support and subsidies. However, state support has tended to focus on small-scale and micro enterprise, and on absorbing surplus labour to reduce unemployment, especially during the first two decades of reform. As private businesses have grown – in some sectors to become the largest businesses with dominant market share – these successful enterprises increasingly come into competition with the remaining state-owned enterprises (SOEs) that the government actively promotes. At this point, the state clearly prefers these SOEs; thus, in cases of competition or conflict with private enterprises, it will come down on the side of the SOE. In addition, there continue to be examples of state intervention – both informal and official – to investigate highly successful entrepreneurs and to extract resources or place burdens on private businesses.

However, these impediments to future private sector development are specific to individual businesses, and so cannot be seen as standard government policy. Instead, policy has tended to be *laissez faire*, leaving the private sector to look after itself. Moreover, the government is now focusing on improving macroeconomic conditions in China, which will be good for private enterprises, and is also seeking to address market failures, in particular under-provision of finance by state banks to private businesses. The state, in other words, is not getting in the way of entrepreneurs who want to grow their businesses, even though in specific instances government actions can be hostile to individual private businesses.

Wider macroeconomic conditions suggest that the future of entrepreneurship in China is promising. Although commentators lament the fall in GDP growth, current rates are well ahead of the OECD countries and most other major global economies. Convergence to global growth rates is likely to take time, as the shift to a more services and a consumer-focused economy takes place over the next decade or so. As indicated in this chapter, this restructuring is creating new entrepreneurial opportunities, particularly (but not only) in sectors that will become more important as the changes take hold. Positive attitudes towards entrepreneurship as a future career opportunity are strong among younger Chinese people. These views are gaining greater traction because role models, of which Jack Ma has been one of the most prominent, have demonstrated the attractions and benefits of setting up and running one's own business.[34]

The greatest potential impediments to future growth in entrepreneurship in China are the institutions and laws that still are not sufficiently developed or applied to fully enable and protect private enterprise development. These institutions – in particular, an independent legal system with strong enforcement powers of its own – and laws protecting private enterprise will need to emerge in China for the private sector to continue to grow. These institutional and legal developments represent a challenge to the power of the party in particular, and so are likely to be resisted. Nonetheless, they may still occur as the economic power of the private sector influences the party more and gives entrepreneurs greater public and social influence. The private sector has already emerged as the dominant force in China's economy even though the requisite institutions and laws were not in place, or applied, through much of this period of emergence. There is no reason why this should not continue, pushing society and the state to further adapt to private enterprise.

Conclusion

In this final chapter we examined the future for entrepreneurship in China, with a specific focus on the main challenges faced by entrepreneurs in China today and the sectors of the economy that hold the greatest promise for entrepreneurship. We concluded that although entrepreneurs face a myriad of challenges, ranging from increasing domestic and global competition to a turbulent and uncertain institutional environment, they will also be able to benefit from a range of opportunities for future growth, including newer developing industrial sectors and areas of China.

Notes

1 KPMG 2016, *China outlook 2016*, KPMG, Beijing, China.
2 *The Economist* 2015, 'The future of factory Asia: a tightening grip', *The Economist*, 14 March.
3 Yan, S 2016, '"Made in China" labor is not actually that cheap', *CNN Money*, 17 March.
4 Jennings, R 2015, 'Vietnam growing more attractive to foreign investment, including tech', *Los Angeles Times*, 8 October; Byrne, B 2013, 'China's manufacturing metropolises: inside Foxconn's sprawling city', *CKGSB Knowledge*, 23 January.
5 Winsor, M 2015, 'China's one-child policy change will take decades to relieve economic pressures of aging population, experts say', *International Business Times*, 29 October.
6 Winsor, M 2015.

7   French, HW 2016, 'China's twilight years', *The Atlantic*, June.
8   Denyer, S 2015, 'One is enough: Chinese families lukewarm over easing of one-child policy', *Washington Post*, 27 January.
9   Das, M & N'Diaye, P 2013, *The end of cheap labor*, International Monetary Fund, Washington, DC.
10 Bradshaw, D 2015, 'Ageing population in China creates business opportunities', *Financial Times*, 29 March.
11 Organisation for Economic Co-operation and Development (OECD) 2014, *The cost of air pollution: health impacts of road transport*, OECD Publishing, Paris; Mullany, G 2013, 'Concerns grow about "severely polluted" water in China's cities', *New York Times*, 20 February.
12 Abrami, RM, Kirby, WC & McFarlan, FW 2014, 'Why China can't innovate', *Harvard Business Review*, vol. 92, no. 3, pp. 107–111.
13 Jackson, A 2015, 'Here's the one big problem with China's supposedly amazing schools', *Business Insider Australia*, 9 May; Little, A 2014, 'Fixing the best schools in the world', *Bloomberg Businessweek*, 25 September.
14 Wu, B 2015, 'Why reforms to China's college entrance exam are so revolutionary', *The Conversation*, 16 January.
15 Fuller, B 2015, 'A shifting education model in China', *The Atlantic*, 14 December.
16 Wu, J 2016, 'Xi promises wider access to private firms', *China Daily Asia*, 5 March.
17 Wang, X 2016, 'Leftists die hard, but Xi Jinping's blessing for China's private sector has positive message for economy', *South China Morning Post*, 6 March.
18 Du, J, Guariglia, A & Newman, A 2015, 'Do social capital building strategies influence the financing behavior of Chinese private small and medium-sized enterprises?', *Entrepreneurship, Theory & Practice*, vol. 39, no. 3, pp. 601–631.
19 Atherton, A & Newman A 2016, 'The emergence of the private entrepreneur in reform era China: re-birth of an earlier tradition, or a more recent product of development and change?', *Business History*, vol. 58, no. 3, pp. 319–344.
20 Li, C 2013, 'Top-level reform or bottom-up revolution?', *Journal of Democracy*, vol. 24, no. 1, pp. 41–48.
21 Zhu, J & Zhang, D 2016, 'Does corruption hinder private businesses? Leadership stability and predictable corruption in China', *Governance*, doi:10.1111/gove.12220.
22 *Xinhua News* 2015, 'Enhanced actions on climate change: China's intended nationally determined contributions', *Xinhua News*, 30 June.
23 Chandran, N 2016, 'China's health care system needs to be more people-oriented, says World Bank', *CNBC*, 22 July.
24 KPMG, 2016.
25 Shobert, B 2015, 'China's telemedicine industry gets ready to roar', *Forbes Asia*, 3 March.
26 Birtlies, B 2015, 'Australian aged care companies chasing China's "silver-hair" gold rush', *ABC Online*, 1 December.
27 Nelson, C 2012, 'Senior care in China: challenges and opportunities', *China Business Review*, 1 April.
28 iResearch 2016, *2015 China E-commerce & O2O Summary Report*, http://www.iresearchchina.com/content/details8_19531.html (viewed 3 June 2017).
29 *Xinhua News* 2016, 'E-Commerce in China heading in new direction', *Xinhua News*, 11 November.
30 Wu, J 2015, 'China to play a bigger role as a world contributor', *China Daily*, 20 April.
31 Kennedy, S & Parker, DA 2015, *Building China's 'One belt, one road'*, Center for Strategic and International Studies, Washington, DC.
32 *The Economist* 2016, 'Our bulldozers, our rules', *The Economist*, 2 July.
33 Ferdinand, P 2016, 'Westward ho – the China dream and "One belt, one road": Chinese foreign policy under Xi Jinping', *International Affairs*, vol. 92, no. 4, pp. 941–957.
34 Atherton, A 2015, 'China's move to entrepreneurship – will the private sector continue to grow?', China Policy Research Institute, Nottingham University.

INDEX

Locators in *italics* refer to figures.

achievement, cultural context 106
age *see* generational context
aged care 157–8
agriculture: future of entrepreneurship 159; Wanxiang Group 19; reform era 27, 35; rural employment 119
air pollution 7, 155
Alibaba: business context 33, 45; local knowledge 71–2; peer-to-peer lending 91–2; as source of financial support 46–7
ambiguity, uncertainty avoidance 104–5
angel investment 89
ascription, cultural context 106
authoritarian leadership 104

Baidu 46–7, 90
bank lending 85, 92–4
Beijing: Bohai Basin 65; high-technology zone 2, 42–4; infrastructure 64, 65; pollution 6–7
Bohai Basin economic area 65
British Council 49, 51
business culture *see* culture
business practice recommendations 130; culture 136–42; diversity 150; environmental context 148–50; *guanxi* networks 133–6; local knowledge 130–3; relationship building 142–5; successful presence 145–8
business registrations 33, 122

'Cantonment' 20
Canyou Group 51
central government 115–16, 117; *see also* state
central planning *see* planned economy
centralisation 117
China National Offshore Oil Company 68
China National Petrochemical Company 68
China Petrochemical 68
Chinese Panel Study of Entrepreneurial Dynamics (CPSED) 9–10
ChiNext 90
Chongqing–Chengdu growth corridor 66
civil non-enterprise institutions 50
clothing sector: 'follow the leader' 74; Metersbonwe 40; successful presence 146
clustering 27; 37; 42–43; 69–70
coast; coastal areas 2; 15; 21–22; 27–29; 63
Collectives 27, 33, 116
collectivism 103–4
commissions, government system 115, 123–4
communism: emergence 23–4; enterprise policy 123; entrepreneur relations 126–8; influence on culture 101; *see also* Mao era
Communist Party: access to financial support for members 93–4; factions and debates 117–18; party system 113–14
competition: future of entrepreneurship 153; innovation-based entrepreneurship 48–9; market dynamics 68–75
conflict avoidance 138–9

Confucianism: early 20th-century China 23–4; Imperial China 19; influence on culture 100; innovation-based entrepreneurship 47; philosophical context 98–100
consumer markets: Chinese context 3; financial crisis (2008) 6; innovation-based entrepreneurship 48; market dynamics 57–8; regional context 62–5
contracts, business practice recommendations 149–50
copycatting: innovation-based entrepreneurship 47–8; market dynamics 69–71
corporate culture *see* culture
corruption, state 126–8, 156
credit *see* financial support
credit associations 83
crowdfunding 91–2
Ctrip 77
Cultural Revolution 25–6, 28
culture: business practice recommendations 136–42; geographical and generational diversity 108–10; holistic approaches to study 108; innovation-based entrepreneurship 47; key dimensions 102–8; local knowledge 130–3; philosophical and ideological influences 98–102; *see also guanxi* networks

Daoism, influence on culture 100–1
data, market research industry 146–7
debt financing *see* financial support
debt levels, local government 116–17
decision-making, business culture 139–41
de-collectivisation 116
demographics *see* generational context
Deng Xiaoping 4–5, 26, 114; *see also* reform era
Didi Chuxing 43–4
diffuse, cultural context 107
distribution: local knowledge 132–3; regional context 66
diversity of Chinese culture 108–9, 150; *see also* regional context
DJI Technology 45
domestic competition 153
drinking, social rituals 138
dynasties, Imperial China 19–22

earthmoving equipment manufacturing 73
eating, social rituals 137–8
eco-cities 155
e-commerce 158–9; *see also* technology sector

economic growth: enterprise policy 122–3; financial crisis (2008) 31–2; future of entrepreneurship 152–3, 160–1; historical context 20–9; market dynamics 57–8, 71–2; means of encouraging growth 33–4; private sector emergence 30; regional context 62–5; social entrepreneurship 49
economy *see* evolution of entrepreneurship; financial crisis (2008); global context; market economy; planned economy
education: entrepreneur demographics 10; future of entrepreneurship 155–6; globalisation 102; human capital 25, 52; innovation-based entrepreneurship 47; Mao era 25; R&D 125
elderly care 157–8
emergence *see* evolution of entrepreneurship
emotional/neutral 106
emperors, Imperial China 19–22
energy sources 157
enterprise policy 119–23
entrepreneurs: comparison with non-entrepreneurs 12–13; demographics 9–10; generational cohorts 10–12; industrial breakdown 13–15; political roles and significance of 128–9; regional disparities 15–16; relations with state officials 126, 134, 135; winners and losers 6–7; *see also* business practice recommendations
entry strategies 61, 147–8; *see also* international expansion
environmental context, business practice recommendations 148–50
environmental degradation 7, 154–5
Europe, historical context 21, 22; *see also* Western influence
evolution of entrepreneurship 18; dynasties, order and the emperor 19–22; early 20th-century China 23–4; financial crisis (2008) 31–3; late Imperial China 22; Mao era 24–6; reform era 26–31
exchange, social rituals 137–8
exports, reform era 5–6; *see also* trade
external direction/internal direction, cultural context 107

face 106–7
fake goods 70–1
family: collectivism 103–4; interpersonal financing 82–3
Fang, Tony 108
fashion industry, Metersbonwe 40
fat pig policy 127, 149
femininity, cultural context 105
financial crisis (2008) 5–6, 31–3

financial support 79–80; external sources 92–4; formal sources 85–90; informal sources 80–2; innovation-based entrepreneurship 46–7; mechanisms 80–4; microfinance 90–2; social entrepreneurship 51–2
five-year plans 118–19, 159
fixers (intermediaries) 144–5
food: future demand 159; reform era 27; social rituals 137–8
foreign businesses *see* business practice recommendations
foreign direct investment (FDI): early 2000s 30; financial crisis (2008) 31; reform era 27, 28–9; regional context 61–2; venture capital 86–9
Foundation for Youth Social Entrepreneurship 50
foundations (legal form) 50
Foxconn 45, 76–7
free trade zones 160
friends, interpersonal financing 82–3; *see also guanxi* networks
future of entrepreneurship 152–61; key challenges 152–7; key sectors 157–60

generational context: culture 108–9; entrepreneurs 9–12; future of entrepreneurship 153–4; *One Child Policy* 48, 109, 153–4
geographic context *see* regional context
getihu 13–16, *14*, *15*, 38
gift giving 137–8
Gini coefficient 62
global context: competition 153; financial crisis (2008) 31–3; international expansion 61–2, 75–7, 145–8
global supply chains 132–3
globalisation, influence on culture 101–2
'Go West' policy 16, 160
Golden Wings 52
government *see* state
graduates, entrepreneur demographics 10
Great Leap Forward 25
Gross Domestic Product (GDP) 5
Growth Enterprise Board 90
Guangdong: income 62; infrastructure 64; innovation-based entrepreneurship 41–2
Guangzhou: Imperial China 20; infrastructure 64; 'local' markets 65
guanxi networks: business practice recommendations 133–6; models of entrepreneurship 38, *39*, 41; officials and entrepreneurs 39, 127–8; particularism 106; relationship building 142–5

guanxixue 134, 137–8, 142, 144
guarantee agencies 86

Haier 73, 76
Hall's high/low-context dimension 102–3
Hangzhou: high-technology zones 44–5; infrastructure 65
HAX 45
healthcare: demographics 157–8; Mao era 25
hierarchy: authoritarian leadership 104; cultural context 140–1; Imperial China 19–22
high/low-context dimension 102–3
high-technology zones 42–9; *see also* technology sector
historical context 1; dynasties, order and the emperor 19–22; early 20th-century China 23–4; financial crisis (2008) 31–3; late Imperial China 22; Mao era 24–6; reform era 26–31
Hofstede's cultural dimensions 103–5, 108
Hong Kong: comparison to mainland Chinese 141–2; infrastructure 64; local knowledge 132
household enterprises 28, 119–23
Hu Jintao 100, 118, 124
Huawei 70, 76–7
human capital: Mao era 25; social entrepreneurship 52; *see also* social capital

ideological context, Chinese culture 98–102
Imperial China 19–22
income inequalities, regional 62–5
individualism 103–4
industry *see* manufacturing sector
inequality, regional 62–5
inflation, financial crisis (2008) 32; *see also* economic growth
infrastructure: economic growth 34; high-technology zones 42–9; local knowledge 132–3; *One belt one road* initiative 159–60; regional context 63–7; state influence 123–4
in-groups 103–4
Innovate 99 51–2
innovation-based entrepreneurship: challenges 47–9; high-technology zones 42–7; market dynamics 74–5; state influence 124–6
InnoWay, Beijing 43
institutional environment 156, 161; *see also* state
intellectual property 88; *see also* copycatting
intermediaries 144–5

internal direction/external direction, cultural context 107
international expansion: entry strategies 61, 147–8; market dynamics 75–7; regional context 61–2; successful presence 145–8; *see also* business practice recommendations
internet: business registrations 33; e-commerce 158–9; entrepreneur generational cohorts 11; local knowledge 71–2; stock exchange 90
interpersonal financing 82–3; *see also* peer-to-peer lending
interpersonal relationships *seeguanxi* networks
investment *see* financial support; foreign direct investment (FDI); R&D investment
iSoftstone 77

Japan, state-owned and controlled enterprises 58–9
JD.com 92
Jiang Zemin 118
Jiangsu: high-technology zones 44–5; Southern Jiangsu (Sunan) model 40–1

KFC 145
knowledge, local 71–2
Korea, state-owned and controlled enterprises 58–9

labour costs: Guangdong (Pearl River Delta) model 42; moving up the value chain 72–3; Wenzhou (Zhejiang) model 39–40
land redistribution 24–5
language: local knowledge 131–2; market dynamics 71–2
leadership 104
legal environment 156
legislation: business practice recommendations 149–50; business registrations 33, 122; Confucianism 99–100; corruption 127; early 2000s 31; enterprise policy 119–23; future of entrepreneurship 156, 159–60, 161; microfinance 90–1; *One belt one road* initiative 159–60; social entrepreneurship 52
Lenovo 76, 77
liberalisation, market dynamics 67–8
local government 115–17, 126–7
local knowledge: business practice recommendations 130–3; market dynamics 56–7, 61, 71–2
'local' markets 64–7

logistics sector: local knowledge 132–3; regional context 66
long/short-term orientation 105
long-term presence 148
Lu Guanqiu 10, 11–12

macroeconomics 123–4
mainland Chinese culture 141–2
Makeblock 45
manufacturing sector: copycatting 47–8, 69–71; entrepreneur generational cohorts 10–11; 'follow the leader' 73–4; future of entrepreneurship 157–60; Imperial China 21; market dynamics 60; moving up the value chain 72–3; private sector 13–15, 15; successful presence 145–6
Mao era: Communist Party factions 118; economy 3–4; evolution of entrepreneurship 24–6; influence on culture 101
market dynamics 56–7; competition 68–75; economic growth 57–8; international expansion 75–7; liberalisation and state control 67–8; private sector 59–61; spatial nature of domestic markets 61–7; state-owned and controlled enterprises 58–9
market economy: innovation-based entrepreneurship 48; models of entrepreneurship 37; social entrepreneurship 49; *see also* evolution of entrepreneurship
market research industry 146–7
masculinity, cultural context 105
Metersbonwe 40
microfinance 90–2
mimicry, fake goods 70–1
Ming Dynasty 19
ministries, government system 114–15
models of entrepreneurship 36; innovation-based 42–9; network-based 36–42; others 53; social 49–53
money houses 83
motorcycle manufacturing 73

NASDAQ stock exchange 90
national culture *see* culture
National Development and Reform Commission (NDRC) 115, 123–4
National People's Congress (NPC) 114
negotiations, business culture 139–40
Nest 49
network-based entrepreneurship 36–42; *see also guanxi* networks
neutral/emotional 106

Nike 146
Ningbo 39
non-government organisations (NGOs): Positive Planet China 92; social entrepreneurship 49
Non-profit Incubator (NPI) 49, 50, 52
non-verbal communication 102, 140

officials: corruption 126–8, 156; relations with entrepreneurs 126, 134, 135
oil sector 68
One belt one road initiative 159–60
One Child Policy: future of entrepreneurship 153–4; generational context 109; innovation-based entrepreneurship 48
opening-up and reform period *see* reform era
Oppo 74, 75
opportunity seizers 75
original equipment manufacturers (OEMs) 66, 77
out-groups 103–4

parallel entities, government system 115
particularism 106
party system, government 113–14, 117–18
paternalistic leadership 104
pawnbroking 83
Pearl River Delta: copycatting 69; income 62; infrastructure 64; innovation-based entrepreneurship 41–2; local knowledge 132, 133
peer-to-peer lending 91–2; *see also* interpersonal financing
People's Liberation Army (PLA) 114
personal relationships *see guanxi* networks
personal savings, as source of financing 82–3
philanthropic foundations 51–2
philosophical context, Chinese culture 98–102
'phoenix' firms 2
planned economy: financial support 81; five-year plans 118–19; Mao era 18, 26; network-based entrepreneurship 36–7; social entrepreneurship 49
political capital: access to financial support 93–4; role of entrepreneurs 128–9
political environment 156; *see also* state
pollution 7, 154–5
Positive Planet China 92
poverty, reform era 27
power distance 104
practicing business in China *see* business practice recommendations

private enterprises: classification by legal form 13; industrial breakdown 13–15
private equity, innovation-based entrepreneurship 46–7
private sector: early 2000s 30–1; enterprise policy 120–3; future of entrepreneurship 152–3, 160–1; historical context 1, 3, 5; informal sources of financing 80–2; Mao era 24–5; market dynamics 59–61; *see also* models of entrepreneurship
privatisation 5–6, 29, 41
Programme for International Student Assessment (PISA) scores 155–6
property law 48, 149–50
provincial government 115–17
Pudong, infrastructure 65

Qing Dynasty 19–22

R&D investment 125
rationing 27
rebellions, Imperial China 22
reform era 1–5; bank lending 85; Communist Party 117–18; Communist Party factions 117–18; enterprise policy 119–23; entrepreneur generational cohorts 10–11; evolution of entrepreneurship 26–31; financial support 79, 80; six-day week 11; Wanxiang Group 11–12
regional context: business practice recommendations 150; culture 108–9; innovation-based entrepreneurship 42–7; local knowledge 131–3; market dynamics 61–7; *see also* rural areas; urban areas
registration system 33, 122
relationship building, business practice recommendations 142–5; *see also* culture; *guanxi* networks
Ren Zhengfei 10–11
renewable energy 157
retail, Western influence 2–3
reverse engineering 70, 72
risk-taking, innovation-based entrepreneurship 47–8
rule by law principle 99–100, 106
rule by man principle 99–100, 106
rural areas: consumption 6; de-collectivisation 116; entrepreneurship 2; Mao era 25; microfinance 90–1; private sector 15; reform era 27–8; regional context 62; regional disparities 15–16
'rust belt' 2

science-based innovation 125
sectors, future of entrepreneurship 157–60; *see also* manufacturing sector; private sector; service sector
sequential, cultural context 107
service sector 11, 13
Shanghai: high-technology zone 44; infrastructure 65; 'local' markets 65; social entrepreneurship 49; stock exchange 89
Shanzhai economy 70–1
Shenzhen: Canyou Group 51; high-technology zones 45–6; stock exchange 89–90
short/long-term orientation 105
siying qiye 13–16, *14–15*
skills *see* human capital
small and medium enterprises (SMEs): early 2000s 31; external financing 92–3; financial crisis (2008) 31; financial support 79, 80, 85–6, 91; labour costs 39–40; venture capital 88–9
smartphone sector 70, 74–5
smartphone use, Chinese culture 140
social capital, access to financial support 93–4
social entrepreneurship 49–50; challenges 52; financial support 51–2; future of 53; models of 50–1
social hierarchy *see* hierarchy
social organisations 50–1
social relationships 144; *see also guanxi* networks
social rituals 137–8
Sohu 71–2
solar industry 69
Southern Jiangsu (Sunan) model 40–1
spatial context *see* regional context
Special Economic Zones 27
specific, cultural context 107
Starbucks 145
stasis 22
state: business practice recommendations 149; conditions for entrepreneurship 123–4; control by 67–8, 113; corruption 126–8, 156; enterprise policy 119–23; entrepreneur roles 128–9; five-year plans 118–19; nature of 113–18; relations with entrepreneurs 126, 134, 135; technology sector 124–6
State Council 114
state-owned and controlled enterprises (SOCEs) 58–9, 60
state-owned enterprises (SOEs): early 2000s 30, 31; enterprise policy 121, 122; financial support 80–1, 86; historical context 3; market governance 33–4; network-based entrepreneurship 38, 39; oil sector 68; reform era 28, 29
stock market 89–90
Sunan model 40–1
Supreme Court 114
Suzhou: Industrial Park (SIP) 44–5; infrastructure 65; Southern Jiangsu (Sunan) model 40–1
synchronous, cultural context 107

Taiping rebellion 22
Tang Dynasty 19
Taoism 100–1
taxi company app 43–4
technology sector: e-commerce 158–9; financial support 87, 88; 'follow the leader' 73–4; healthcare 158; high-technology zones 42–9; innovation 42–9, 74–5; international expansion 75–7; Metersbonwe 40; moving up the value chain 72–3; opportunity seizers 75; smartphones 70, 74–5; state influence 124–6; *see also* internet
Tencent 33, 46–7, 71–2
textiles *see* clothing sector
Torch programme 125
township and village enterprises (TVEs): early 2000s 30; enterprise policy 121; Guangdong (Pearl River Delta) model 41–2; historical context 2; reform era 27–8, 29; Southern Jiangsu (Sunan) model 40–1
trade: evolution of entrepreneurship 32; *guanxi* networks 134; Imperial China 19, 20–1; Mao era 4; market dynamics 61, 64; One Belt One Road initiative 159–60
trade cooperation zones 160
trade credit 83–4
transport, regional context 63–7
Trompenaars' cultural dimensions 105–8
20th-century China, evolution of entrepreneurship 23–4

Uber 43–4
uncertainty, business practice recommendations 148–9
uncertainty avoidance 104–5
underground financing 83
United States: global brands 71, 74; Imperial China 22; NASDAQ stock exchange 90
universalism 106

urban areas: eco-cities 155; pollution 7, 155; private sector 15; regional context 62; regional disparities 15–16

value chains, manufacturing sector 72–3
values, comparison of entrepreneurs and non-entrepreneurs 12–13; *see also* culture
venture capital: innovation-based entrepreneurship 46–7; start-ups 86–9
Vivo 74
volatility, business practice recommendations 148–9

Wal-Mart 133
Wanxiang Group 11–12
war, early 20th-century China 23
water pollution 155
Wen Jiabao 124
Wenzhou (Zhejiang): informal financing 84; as model of entrepreneurship 37–40
Western entrepreneurs *see* business practice recommendations
Western influence: brands 2–3, 71, 74; globalisation 101–2; Hall's high/low-context dimension 103; Imperial China 22

women, social entrepreneurship 50
Women's Development Association 52
World Trade Organization (WTO): early 2000s 30; logistics 133; reform era 29

Xi Jinping 114, 118, 129, 156
Xiaomi 33, 70, 74–5
Xiaoping *see* Deng Xiaoping; reform era
Xixiang, Women's Development Association 52
Xu Xiaoping 89

Youchange 50
Yu Venture Philanthropy 52

Zhang Ruimin 10
Zhangjiang Hi-Technology Park 44
Zhejiang: external financing 92–3; high-technology zones 44–5; informal financing 84; as model of entrepreneurship 37–40
ZhenFund 89
Zhongguancun, Beijing 42–3
Zhou Chengjian 40

Taylor & Francis eBooks

Helping you to choose the right eBooks for your Library

Add Routledge titles to your library's digital collection today. Taylor and Francis ebooks contains over 50,000 titles in the Humanities, Social Sciences, Behavioural Sciences, Built Environment and Law.

Choose from a range of subject packages or create your own!

Benefits for you
- Free MARC records
- COUNTER-compliant usage statistics
- Flexible purchase and pricing options
- All titles DRM-free.

Benefits for your user
- Off-site, anytime access via Athens or referring URL
- Print or copy pages or chapters
- Full content search
- Bookmark, highlight and annotate text
- Access to thousands of pages of quality research at the click of a button.

REQUEST YOUR FREE INSTITUTIONAL TRIAL TODAY

Free Trials Available
We offer free trials to qualifying academic, corporate and government customers.

eCollections – Choose from over 30 subject eCollections, including:

Archaeology	Language Learning
Architecture	Law
Asian Studies	Literature
Business & Management	Media & Communication
Classical Studies	Middle East Studies
Construction	Music
Creative & Media Arts	Philosophy
Criminology & Criminal Justice	Planning
Economics	Politics
Education	Psychology & Mental Health
Energy	Religion
Engineering	Security
English Language & Linguistics	Social Work
Environment & Sustainability	Sociology
Geography	Sport
Health Studies	Theatre & Performance
History	Tourism, Hospitality & Events

For more information, pricing enquiries or to order a free trial, please contact your local sales team:
www.tandfebooks.com/page/sales

 Routledge
Taylor & Francis Group

The home of Routledge books

www.tandfebooks.com